Losing the New China

A Story of American Commerce, Desire and Betrayal

ETHAN GUTMANN

ENCOUNTER BOOKS
SAN FRANCISCO

Published by Encounter Books, an activity of Encounter for Culture and Education, Inc., a nonprofit tax exempt corporation.

Encounter Books website address: www.encounterbooks.com

Manufactured in the United States and printed on acid-free paper.

The paper used in this publication meets the minimum requirements of ANSI/NISO Z39.48-1992 (R 1997)(*Permanence of Paper*).

FIRST EDITION

Library of Congress Cataloging-in-Publication Data

Gutmann, Ethan.
    Losing the new China : a story of American commerce, desire and betrayal / Ethan Gutmann.
        p. cm.
    Includes bibliographical references and index.
    ISBN 1-893554-83-X
    1. Technology transfer—China.   2. Technology transfer—United States.   3. Americans—China—Social life and customs.   4. Corporations, American—China.   5. Corporate culture—United States.
6. Corporate culture—China.   7. United States—Foreign economic relations—China.   8. China—Foreign economic relations—United States.   9. United States—Commerce—China.   10. China—Commerce—United States.   11. United States—Commercial policy.
12. China—Commercial policy.   13. China—Economic conditions—1976–2000.   I. Title.
HF1456.5.C6 G88 2004
337.73051—dc21

                                                                2003070175

10 9 8 7 6 5 4 3 2 1

For my wife

Contents

PREFACE

Thanksgiving, 1998: A wind is howling off the Atlantic, but inside the beach house in Southampton, it's shimmering, warm and bright. I am with the extended family of my friend Terry Halsey, and the Classic Moment has arrived: A large turkey is placed on the table, Terry's mother looks on, and boys in white shirts and rep ties jostle for position. All around the table, the grownup faces have a martini glow. Later that evening we'll hold a blind wine-tasting party; and as a de facto kindly uncle, I'll organize a Gatorade-tasting party for the kids. While we savor the rich scene, Terry beckons me to lower my head so he can whisper to me.

"Think about this twenty years from now, Ethan—no, make that thirty-five, when the kids are grown up and they have their kids, and they are living in what would seem to us to be just *unimaginable luxury*. And security, don't forget that. And they will propose a toast: to us, Uncle Ethan and Uncle Terry. The visionaries! The ones who could see the light, who knew even back then that China was it. That it was *the Gold Mountain*."

We smiled at each other knowingly, but I didn't say anything because I knew that what lay ahead wouldn't be so easy. Terry had probably seen a CNN report and noticed that the Chinese weren't wearing Mao suits anymore. Perhaps he had some trace memory of antique titles such as *Four Hundred Million Customers* and *Oil for the Lamps of China*. But he was actually riffing off a contact high from my own China bug. What he didn't understand is that I was more motivated by the idea of changing China than by the prospect of making a profit. Not that these were incompatible; I believed in the power of free enterprise to transform societies. I wanted to see the capitalist miracle that had occurred in so many countries finally coming about in China—and perhaps to be a part of it.

Maybe Terry didn't know China, but he knew me. Somewhere in my subconscious, he had glimpsed some embers glowing and he wanted to stir them. He was sharing in the adventure ahead. Even his whisper was carefully staged to show the table his special friendship—with me, the visionary who would shortly be leaving for a new life on the Gold Mountain!

I had not caught the China bug by watching *Kung Fu* as an adolescent or by doing spreadsheets in business school, but by working as a correspondent for a television documentary series. Like every other journalist in Washington, I had followed the surreptitious Chinese campaign contributions to the Clinton administration through the 1990s. But I became weary of the cast of characters from Arkansas. At the same time, I was increasingly interested in the mysterious offspring of China's top leadership, the so-called "Princelings" who seemed to be scattered throughout the upper ranks of Chinese political, economic and military enterprises—and in their relationship to "red chips," the Chinese state-owned enterprise shares that were quietly being sold to American institutional investors such as CalPERS. It all had the look of a trans-Pacific Tammany Hall. Yet somewhere along the line, as I interviewed Wall Street reps who promoted red chip sales—their eyes glowing as they described a "tidal wave" of Chinese companies about to hit the market—my investigative zeal had melted into simple awe at the sheer size of the figures involved and the prodigious rate of China's economic growth.

Even here, though, my Gold Mountain fantasies were grounded by my wife's academic background. As a scholar of Chinese history, she had extensive firsthand experience of China's corruption and (like most China scholars) a longstanding love/hate relationship with the place. She was already in Beijing setting up her research, supported by a grant for the coming year.

We would be together very soon. I had left my television network, and now, with the name card of a Beijing producer

carefully stored in my wallet, I planned to live on my wife's mea-
ger grant until I could get the financing to make some kind of documentary on the Chinese economic miracle. I would begin with
the topic of small American businesses starting up in China, and
eventually move on to something more controversial, like the
unique power of the Princelings.

I was headed for China expecting to find a vibrant entrepreneurial culture clawing its way through the crust of an authoritarian state. I knew that the way the current situation was being
framed was inadequate. On the one hand, China optimists pointed
to the incremental evolution of the ruling Communist Party as if
this justified unrestrained engagement. On the other hand, the
exiled Chinese dissidents held that the system was near collapse
and needed a good, hard shove, not economic props. Like the
quiet American, I was predisposed to look for a group that could
act as a "third force," a class with an interest in democratic reform
and a level capitalist playing ground—some path of development
that did not involve the agony of another revolution.

The great unknown was the emerging Chinese middle class.
From what I had heard, Chinese entrepreneurs seemed to embody
all the promise contained in the country's explosive growth. I
sensed that this class, having emerged in an environment of political extremes, would be composed of thick-skinned, canny, practical types, but perhaps they could find common cause with the
West. Wouldn't economic necessity dictate that they would eventually become interested in wielding political power? As capitalism resculpted the Chinese landscape, I wondered if the "China
issues" that Americans saw in their tunnel vision—corruption and
human rights abuses—could be just the growing pains of a transition that remained largely invisible to Western eyes.

American business could be the facilitators of the Third Force,
the vanguard in creating the New China. As Americans, wouldn't
we naturally carry a smattering of democratic values, culture and
respect with us to China? We didn't bribe government officials,
as the French did. The Europeans and the Japanese merely went
through the motions of controlling dual-use technology transfer;
American and British companies had to take it seriously. Europeans and Japanese protected their markets; we didn't. And then

there was the size of the American investment: all of the Fortune 500 were present and accounted for in the China market, each with at least a small office in the shining new towers of Beijing, Shanghai and Guangzhou. Scattered outposts along the New Silk Road, perhaps, but wasn't it inevitable that they should become beacons of political change at some point down the road? There would be friction, but so what? Rub the lamp hard enough and the China you wished for might appear.

The optimistic belief in capitalism as China's savior is centuries old and has always been curiously bipartisan. In the 1980s, President Reagan confidently referred to China as a "so-called" Communist country. In the early nineties, the Clinton administration applauded China's double-digit GDP growth and even awarded China the title of "strategic partner." China was one of the fastest-growing economies, estimated to be approximately the seventh-largest in the world; but if one used the indefensible-but-fun measure of purchasing power parity, China was almost ready to surpass Japan as the world's second-largest economy, nipping at the heels of the United States. American China hands claimed that American business interests stood in a good position to exploit this growth, because stunning economic advances had arguably been paralleled by equally strong cultural changes. The consensus was that China was becoming a modern state dominated by individuals who were free not only to wear designer clothes and eat cheeseburgers, but to fail or succeed by their own entrepreneurial efforts. And that whatever else they were (or weren't), the contemporary Chinese were no longer automatons programmed to act out every perverse twist of the government line. The tortured phrase "socialism with Chinese characteristics" was widely seen as a laughable attempt at continuity with a fading Communist past. Mao's portrait still overlooked Tiananmen Square because he was the father of the country, not because he retained any political authority. (The proof was in the Mao-pop T-shirts my wife always brought back from China.) As long as reformers such as Premier Zhu Rongji were at the helm, China's future looked bright. The leadership might speak of "the New China" to represent Communist triumph, but in truth, they were powerless to stop the momentum of the new capitalism.

These were not just academic or journalistic fantasies on my part as I packed my bags. Similar views were shared by the big boys of international capital as well. Before leaving, I interviewed top China consultants at Deloitte & Touche, the American Chamber of Commerce in Washington, and representatives of the Bank of China in New York. There was remarkable unanimity: in spite of the Asian economic downturn in 1998, they were maximum bullish on China's future. We would all benefit.

On Christmas Eve, 1998, I flew to Beijing. As I felt the plane lift above the snowstorm and saw the lights of Manhattan spinning away, neither Christmas nor sleep seemed to matter anymore.

Finally we were across the Pacific, and even from eight miles high, China looked truly strange, organic, not fully planned—or if planned, only partially executed. Villages were built in a basic grid pattern, but the skewed angles gave the appearance of a spider's web constructed under the influence of narcotics. Blighted fish farms resembled windows half-buried in snow. This was the Old China. But as I approached the New China—Beijing—order appeared: highways, massive mixmasters, and fantastic skyscrapers piercing through layers of yellow smoke.

My wife had borrowed a little Beijing hideaway from a friend, not far from the Forbidden City. Off a tiny alleyway there was a passage so small that two people could barely pass each other, littered with heaps of coal, bricks, bicycles and bundles of leeks. At the end stood a red gate, and behind it, a tiny courtyard and two rooms complete with a Chinese cat, a coal stove, intermittent water pressure and remarkably thin walls. It was enough.

Later that day, as I stepped out of our little courtyard into the streets, my pulse raced as if I were embarking on a moonwalk. But a song from my childhood (slightly corrupted) floated into my mind:

So how can you tell me you're lonely?
And say for you that the sun don't shine?
Let me take you by the hand and lead you through the streets of
    Beijing.
I'll show you something to make you change your mind.

Between the monster complexes and buildings of Beijing lie the *hutongs,* the old neighborhoods—gray, single-story, medieval, broken-down. Roads become alleys that narrow into passages that turn into blank walls or doorways that you shouldn't enter. Sometimes the *hutongs* are mysterious and alien. Even if you pretend you know where you're going, eventually you'll find yourself running into a dead end. In the southern half of Beijing, the old Chinese city, the *hutongs* are like animal tracks in a meadow, with curved, irregular, eccentric patterns. In the northern half, the Manchu city, the imperial grid is interrupted by pathways of desire and blind alleys wearing the detritus of history, ranging from Qing architectural flourishes on the doorways to painted slogans left over from the Cultural Revolution. The claustrophobic effect is oddly intensified by the one-story buildings, remnants of the days when only the emperor and his instruments of state power were allowed to build any higher.

Today, the *hutongs* lie next to outsize intersections as big as Times Square. There are shopping centers in lurid purples and vast office buildings, some unadorned socialist gray, some bright pink and red, sporting garish gold Chinese characters and Chinglish labels: "Jiang Hypermarket," "China Tobacco Building," "Beijing Chain City." On the streets, an endless game of chicken is played out among cabs and big-shot Audis, Jeeps and Benzes, and long electric trams that squawk recorded threats and admonitions at pedestrians. Although trucks are everywhere, many of the goods are still pulled by humans on industrial bicycles, with large pallets of coal, vegetables, or human waste.

Step back inside the *hutongs* and they seem comforting and intimate. People are washing, tending to their pet birds, gossiping, exercising. Young girls hang out in pajamas, not caring who sees them. Men stroll down the alleys to the ubiquitous open-air toilets. On a main road, people will try to sell you a bootlegged CD, or look away if you catch their eyes fixed on you. In a *hutong,* people still stare at a white man.

Actually, it was reciprocal. Like an adolescent boy, I suddenly felt an awkward wonder (along with a pointless lust) for the plainest Chinese girl as she cycled by on a battered Flying Pigeon. Never mind the Chinese language; there was a whole new body language to discover. I convinced myself that the warmest passions burned beneath the tightly controlled Chinese exterior. All those walls only increased the potency of the intimacy that was harboring within.

From my arrival on that frigid Christmas day, I fell in love with the duality, the cacophonous New China and the dead end: the smell of the coal burners, the tiny dumpling shops with their cracked Plexiglas windows obscured by steam, the warmth of that first Chinese smile as I tried to make myself understood. The first time I walked through the neighborhood and saw Cyrillic, it shocked me—but after all, the Russians were much closer than we were. I could hear the Central Asian cadences, the Muslim songs on the street. They were all coming to Beijing. And I sensed China's power as well. In the brilliantly lit streets at night, with the vast Communist Party headquarters floodlit in blood red and pearl white, I felt the strength of the emerging Chinese empire: open-eyed, confident, ruthless in its security as it went about creating the New Imperial City.

You never forget that moment when you "discover" something that has been there for years—a place so immense and startling that for a while it feels as if you can leave the old, jaded self behind and step into a wonder-mode where everything seems endlessly rich and young, and even the walls seem to tremble with a latent energy.

Such euphoria has many half-lives; it's never completely gone. But a few months later, I was forced to recognize that China was moving in a strikingly different direction from what I had initially imagined. A decade earlier, in May 1989, the "Goddess of Democracy," a Chinese student rebel's homage to the Statue of Liberty, was rapturously rolled into Tiananmen Square. Now, in the days following the Belgrade embassy bombing of May 1999, cardboard mock-ups of a diminished yet menacing statue brandishing missiles and sporting swastikas were marched past the U.S. embassy. The chant in '89 was for Li Peng (head of the State Council at the time) to come out. The chant in '99 was for the U.S. ambassador to come out. Both calls were spontaneous. Yet in '99, I found myself

speechless, unable to process the New China—to reconcile the
rapidly modernizing state that was preparing to join the family
of nations, with the peculiar combination of victim-ecstasy, belligerent racial pride, obsession with territorial claims, flashes of
sadomasochistic pleasure in submitting to authority, cynical contempt for democracy and raw xenophobia that I saw on the streets.
I couldn't neatly label it either: *Chinese hypernationalism? Fascism
with Chinese characteristics?* China was too corrupt to compare to
Nazi Germany, and too inefficient to compare to Imperial Japan.
Yet the movement that I was glimpsing was occurring in a country much bigger and with far more economic potential than the
Axis combined.

   This was the dark basement of the collective Chinese psyche.
If on the first day of the U.S. embassy riots in Beijing I had seen
the sudden opening of a furnace door, revealing something incan-
descent, voracious and frightening—*so this is what powers your country,* I thought—well, the American captains of industry, consultants
and lobbyists saw it too. Perhaps they had even indirectly fuelled
it. On the east coast of China you won't find anybody who is not
directly or indirectly tied to U.S. trade. If the Chinese government
had successfully turned a generation of students into anti-American, anti-democracy agitators, they could not have done it without the prosperity and legitimacy that had flowed into the New
China from American investment. And indeed, while the Chinese
state would continue a drumbeat of belligerent Chinese nationalism, increasingly it became the job of the expat American businessmen—my job, too—to keep visitors out of the basement, in
exchange for further normalization of trade.

   To a great extent, the American business and diplomatic community was successful. It took a year for the Chinese government
to agree to restart discussions on human rights, and American
naval ships were forbidden to dock in Hong Kong for a bit longer,
but the business relationship—reflected in the rate of U.S. investment in China—barely reacted to the cooling of bilateral relations. Instead, it followed the inexorable go-go trend established
in the early 1990s. With more investment and higher stakes came
a more dominant role for U.S. business, and the views of the China-
business lobby prevailed in virtually every area of contention in

U.S. policy toward China. Instead of holding the Chinese government accountable for the threats to Taiwan, the crackdown on the Chinese press and a truly brutal sweep of Falun Gong practitioners, it was seen as a higher therapeutic good to reinforce the brittle Chinese self-esteem. Instead of human rights, the *rule of law* became the new catchphrase. China stopped receiving annual condemnations from the U.N. Human Rights Council and ascended into the WTO regime, while Beijing won the right to host the 2008 Olympics. The Chinese leadership's internal and external position was bolstered by the rapid construction of the world's greatest Big Brother Internet, acquisition of "fourth-generation" military technology, and for the first time, the emergence of an indigenous— and globally competitive—research and development capability.

Thus, under the Communist Party's careful direction, China is headed back to the future by building a society dominated by a goal that has not appreciably changed since the nineteenth-century "revive the nation" movement: to become a "rich country with a big army." This goal resonates in China exactly where it shouldn't—that is, in the Third Force I imagined I'd see there: in the universities, dot.coms, entrepreneurial centers, even the country's avant-garde, who hide behind an anticommercial, antiforeign pose.

This book considers what went wrong in the New China and how the American presence contributed to this ambiguous outcome; it also hints at what we can do about it now. As Americans, we have a thing for China, and in truth, they have a thing for us, too. Yet I suspect that in the future we, as Americans, will face a complicated situation: a potential enemy that we respect and trade with, a potential enemy that we, on balance, love.

The following chapters look at the lovers, and at the financial and political compromises flowing out of that relationship. This book isn't exclusively about technology transfer or the potential China threat, which is why it isn't titled *Losing the War with the New China*. It's about business, but more specifically about the *tribal culture* of business in Beijing, and that's why it isn't called *Losing Money in the New China*, either.

I have tried to understand the subtleties of the marriage of convenience between the New China and American business, along with the petty squabbles, financial arrangements, emotional corruption, and occasional sublime joys. The allure of the Chinese market has drawn some truly remarkable Americans into its orbit. They vary from outright criminals to some of the most honest and sincere people I have ever known. Whatever their personal morality, they tend to be pioneers—canny, game, ready to improvise—and they share one defining characteristic: the capacity to live and even thrive in contradiction, a state of being that can have a deeply corrosive effect over time. Although many are lone wolves by nature, they band together when threatened, which is much of the time, and that leads to a surprising level of groupthink up and down caste levels and across the professional boundaries of journalism, business and diplomacy.

I rarely use the actual names of the participants or even the companies involved. There are two reasons for this. First, there are a few businessmen and diplomats who want to reveal the truth, but—understandably—also want to preserve their confidentiality. That's true on Wall Street, and it's doubly true in Beijing, where they are subject to surveillance not only by their own community, but by the Chinese State Security apparatus. Protecting my sources is not just a matter of journalistic tradecraft, but of avoiding potentially serious consequences for individuals and businesses.

The second reason is that I threw myself into the life of a business expat in Beijing and held back little. In return, many individuals in the Chinese and American business communities of Beijing placed a fair degree of trust in me. They also showed personal camaraderie and even friendship of an intensity that I am not sure I will experience again. They did this in spite of the fact that I wrote several rather critical articles about American business and the Chinese media during my time in Beijing (my own way of handling the state of contradiction). Even after I had—by their standards—transgressed, they let me back into their meetings, their luncheons and their happy hours.

I don't want to be mawkish about it, but there is no denying the fact that Beijing was potentially a terribly lonely place for all of us. I won't forget the singular warmth of the former head of Dow Jones, after one of my more caustic essays was published, motioning me over with a kind of indulgent shrug to share a bourbon with the other American Chamber reps and captains of industry at the towering Capital Club, and to rejoin the tribe, as the sunset faded over the city's dark squalor below.

For the reasons that I've explained, they will not find their names in the acknowledgments. But I could not have written this book without their contributions. And to them I say with true affection: thanks for the times.

1.
The Happening

I really wasn't in the mood to go to the "happening," as they were calling this contemporary art show, but my wife insisted. So we began pedaling to a gallery that she said was located in a hidden courtyard just west of the Forbidden City. As we rode side by side, I asked, without irony, "Are we having fun yet?" Her eyes smiled and she said yes, and the spring air seemed to fill with the satisfaction of two foreigners making it in a strange culture.

It was May 8, 1999, and we weren't living the most glamorous life, it was true. As I have said, I had arrived in Beijing on Christmas Day, 1998, to make my own television documentary, a piece on smalltime American businessmen trying to start capitalist ventures in the wild, wild East. After making the rounds of the American business community, I saw that many liked the idea, but not enough to fund it. Rather than admitting failure and leaving Beijing, I had been treading water by creating feel-good talk shows for Chinese-style wages as the only Westerner at an independent but exclusively Chinese television production company. Now, in a relatively short time, we had met new friends, identified favorite restaurants, joined Frisbee teams, explored the city, and settled into the expat life of Beijing. Meanwhile, my wife was pursuing her scholarly career the Asian way: poring through the moldering historical archives of the Qing emperors, slumming with the poor academics who had made it through the Cultural Revolution to emerge as slightly less poor academics in the New China.

The day before the art show, I had been named executive producer of a new television show, a Chinese attempt to place themselves in the American market. And even better, a top state-run TV network, Beijing Television, had signed on. That meant, down the road, 100 million-plus viewers! 150 million! More if Shanghai picked it up! True, I could only do shows about divorce and pollution and other "nonsensitive" topics that didn't offend the prickly censors. But still, I was at the top of the masthead, working with enlightened Chinese producers to help build the New China. My wife, too, was methodically building her *guanxi,* her contacts and connections. Evidence of her success was clear: the occasional lavish banquet at Deng Xiaoping's favorite Sichuan restaurant, the growing trust between her and her masters, the cultural exchanges that seemed more intimate every day. What's more, high art, the kind my wife studied, was becoming a corner-stone of legitimacy for the New China, as it drugged the populace with large doses of nostalgia for imperial China's tokens of power, culture and authority.

The contemporary Chinese art scene was really just a sideshow for the two of us, but the invites kept coming. Politeness had become warmth, and then something close to actual friendship. And I had basked in that reflected warmth! We were turning down invitations, we were a happening couple . . . these were my heady thoughts as we parked our bicycles at the art show near the For-bidden City.

We were greeted by the kind of eager, young, lithe beauty that you come to expect at this kind of event. Always wearing a black bodysuit, the universal symbol for sophisticated, interna-tional, avant-garde culture. Always, "Please sign the book, please!" Always the shy and expectant smile.

We grabbed glasses of wine off a makeshift table and quickly toured the exhibits: huge, carefully posed photographs of a thin Chinese man and a blonde girl with dark roots wearing little see-through raincoats; battery-operated dildos undulating in raw chunks of meat; an imperial robe constructed of lime-green plas-tic; and plastic models of various Chinese state buildings filled with birds, goldfish and crickets. The guests were piling in: half of them Chinese artist types with bohemian hair configs; and half expats, white girls with more black bodysuits and short haircuts, white men with textured checked shirts and skinny Chinese girl-friends, everyone talking excitedly, pleased to be at the Very Center of the New China on a brilliant Saturday afternoon.

A recent acquaintance caught my eye, a jocund Chinese art broker from Fort Worth, Texas. He hailed me from across the garden and I joined him under a finely painted Chinese canopy. He beamed at me. I beamed back and, after a short interlude of small talk—I couldn't wait!—I mentioned my new television show.

He began to nod knowingly, very good, very good, Beijing TV, eh? "You hear the news?" he asked.

I shook my head.

"I just heard about it on the way over—a bomb hit the Chinese embassy in Belgrade last night. Just a little damage, I guess, but they say eighteen people were hurt. There's bound to be some trouble."

I was surprised—God, another stupid accident!—but I was relieved as well. No deaths, that was the main thing. I flashed back to the previous weeks: lunching with my Chinese co-workers as they occasionally tried to rake me over the coals for air strikes in Kosovo. They hadn't seen the lines of refugees, only shots of bombed-out buildings. "NATO atrocities" played monotonously on Chinese state-controlled television. I always asked them the same things: "Do you know how long this war has been going on? Do you know what it's about? You keep talking about the Opium Wars—but that had an economic element. Do you think that America is trying to make money in Kosovo?" Once, a girl with Trotsky glasses who ran my television production company's accounting department closed the meal by shouting something translated roughly as "America is the worst country!" But in general, my co-workers were a thoughtful and likeable bunch; they tended to give my position, to the degree they understood it, a kind of compartmentalized respect.

No deaths—that was the main thing I took away from this first report of the embassy bombing. Could have been caused by a leaky gas stove. Anyway, no deaths, I repeated to myself as a small, nearly naked Chinese man locked himself in a plastic bubble, painted himself green, stuck a hose inside, and began to fill the bubble with water as the cameras rolled. The "happening," however, seemed to be slowing down, freezing up. Rumors about casualties were spreading. There were deaths. First it was one, along with twenty-three injured. Then two dead. One of the organizers of the happening, Li Zhenhua, shot through the crowd on his way to an urgent phone call, acknowledging me with a nod and a sort of twisted smile. Finally a Yugoslav journalist acquaintance informed me rather definitively (he had seen CNN): three missiles and three deaths, including a female journalist from the Xinhua news agency—top of the state heap.

It dawned on me that we should do something, and I urged my wife to kiss cheeks and exchange cards. Then we set out, bicycling east with the Yugoslav, thinking about heading straight for the American embassy. We waved to a Chinese friend, Tang Di, who was on her way to a massage. In what now seems like a particularly surreal moment, we almost chose to go to a book fair instead, but then the Yugoslav's cell phone tinkled, and he was informed that, indeed, something was going on near the embassy.

On Jianguomen Avenue, as my wife and I approached Beijing's closely guarded embassy district, we passed our first rapidly marching squadron of police, the commander barking orders as he rode a sleek, black bicycle alongside them. Turning the corner at the Citic Building, the police began to increase in density: one every ten yards, then one in five, then one in three. As we turned the corner down Embassy Row, we heard a roar in the distance, the sound that calls a man as surely as bagpipes.

My heart was racing now. We pedaled fast until suddenly we came upon a police barricade, with about fifty Chinese onlookers peering down the block toward the embassy. My wife and I simply walked past the police cordon, making a big show of nonchalantly chaining our bikes to a consulate fence. The police would not stop people like us from entering, because foreigners could still do what they wanted in Beijing.

The roar we'd heard came from the first battalion of young student protesters from some obscure university as they advanced down the block. It was textbook: long red banners with Chinese characters splashed on in black paint; little fists waving mechanically; freshmen and sophomores mostly. The hipper Chinese students had torn scarves wrapped around their heads, while the majority were clean-cut. We ran past them toward the embassy and found ourselves a cramped space just in front of the gate.

Beyond the gate, all was normal. Spreading trees turned the area into a kind of large grotto, dappled with gentle sunlight, although the wind was picking up. The U.S. embassy was well kept, as always, and its facade showed no signs of life; why would it on a golfer's Saturday? Surrounding it were the cameramen, mainly foreign, although a few were from China's official state television station, CCTV (China Central Television). About fifteen policemen in green uniforms lined the gate, appearing relaxed, smiling, almost in a holiday mood. (As my wife pointed out, any break in the monotony of life in an authoritarian state is so lovely! They were finally being given something to do.)

About five hundred student demonstrators stood in front, with long red-and-gold banners and hand-painted signs: USA GO TO HELL, FUCK USA, US KILLER, FUCK NATO, NATO = NAZI. My wife translated the chants: Plead Guilty! U.S. Killer! Go Home! Murderers! U.S. Pigs Go Home! Ambassador Come Out! Come Out, Come Out or We'll Go In! People's Republic of China—*Wan sui!* (literally, ten thousand years). This was all very loud and high-pitched, over and over, led by a man with a megaphone. The screaming would change pitch and pace every minute, and when it did, the faces relaxed. Were they having fun yet? Their eyes smiled yes. Then the megaphone organizer would start pumping his arms, and the mouths would open again, and the hands would begin to thrust spasmodically, in precision drill, highly responsive to orders, as if the protesters were reacting to mild electric shocks. Still, the holiday atmosphere prevailed; after all, such is the kind of pure, angry, righteousness-defining moment that college students the world over dream of. In China, for ten long years since Tiananmen, there was nothing—and now this!

No one touched us, no one shoved. Behind the fence, inside the courtyard was a flag—mine—and a little plot of safe land. Yet I felt heady and faint just for being here, in the capital of the next century's Superpower, with its youth chanting Borg-like in unified loathing of our flag and our little piece of their soil.

After a while, when the chanting lost its steam, the megaphone leader would strike up a short sing-along of the national anthem. This was the signal for the protesters to shuffle on and give the next university its chance to demonstrate.

As new waves of students arrived, several British journalists discussed the numbers with me. They felt it was low, about three thousand. In a kind of Chinese scarf trick, the same student groups were being led around the block so the same faces reappeared after an hour or so. One of the students, when isolated and interviewed by one of the journalists, was naïvely forthcoming; in broken English, he earnestly explained that the university authorities had awakened them early, told them to make banners, and arranged for the buses to bring them here.

So the whole demonstration was canned, and yet fresh chanters were arriving from Peking University. Coming from the intellectual center that had a major part in Tiananmen, they had a legacy to uphold. Their demonstration went through its cycles; the patriotic song drifted off, time to leave, but suddenly someone sat down. Immediately, fifty more sat, and then the rest, while the organizer yelled impotently. From the moment of my arrival in Beijing, I had always sensed the weird political static electricity that seemed to hang over Chinese crowds, capable of causing a split-second breakdown of the rules or an unpredictable flipping of aggression.

As the Peking University students sat down, we wondered, were we present at the birth of a new Tiananmen? Just as quickly, it became clear that they were the wrong cast: too young, too clean, too neophyte. Excited by their own petty audacity, the sitters stayed put for a minute and then allowed themselves to be herded off. The cops doubled in front of the embassy and locked arms. I implored my wife to conserve our film.

Next up, Qinghai University, "the MIT of China," was back, along with a few of the Peking University students. The chanting reached a fever pitch, and then a lull ... something flew out of the crowd and crashed against the embassy, close to my face. A moment of silence, then a roar of joy. Then another flying object, and another, the collisions sounding like bugs smacking on a windshield. Now we could see the hands releasing the chunks of concrete. The lamps topping the fence were quickly destroyed, then the windows, while the cops stood by impassively.

The day was over, but a night of sport and destruction at the embassy was just beginning. Groggily, I began to apprehend that my new TV show was probably gone, and maybe my job too. After ten years the state was showing its fist to the world again, not just to a few China watchers and China hands.

Yet in all my feverish imaginings over the next few hours, I failed to predict what would follow: The nonstop xenophobic exhortations on TV, with the weeping father in Belgrade holding his daughter's bloody clothes to his chest. The total blackout of American statements of explanation, apology, regret. The cancellation of all American movies and music. The burning of the Chengdu consulate. The Serbian war films in the afternoon. The beating of American journalists. The sanctioned racist catcalls on the streets. The condescending "tolerance" at work. Most of all, the feeling that something had shifted under my feet.

I really didn't understand it all until years later, when I was on my way out of China. That's when I met Wang, a diminutive Peking University student with wire-rimmed glasses, a Muslim background, and a soft, almost whispery voice that I strained to hear as he told me his story, tentatively and piecemeal.

Throughout late winter and into the early spring of 1999, Wang had felt a tension growing on his campus. The Tiananmen massacre had happened on June 4, 1989. With the ten-year anniversary looming, strange e-mails had been popping up regularly on computer screens throughout the city, but particularly in the university system. They were so-called "push e-mails"—messages sent from strange dissident groups, the servers located far from China. Unsolicited spam, perhaps, but with China's paltry bandwidth, the concept was still novel to the students. They tended to ridicule the e-mails, as Wang himself did. It was the safe and sophisticated thing to do. But Wang wondered: how had their addresses made it onto the dissident lists?

The messages gave uncensored news of China—arrests, corruption, leadership gossip and the like—but they also advocated certain ideas. This year, it was time for action on June 4: demonstrations, passive resistance, slowdowns, anything that would show that the masses, particularly the students, had not forgotten the blood sacrifices of their brothers and sisters ten years earlier. Using all available arguments, however tangential, the language of the e-mails was designed to fan the coals of anger against the government. For example, the regime had repeatedly blocked Chinese students from demonstrating against the Japanese failure to apologize "sincerely" for the occupation of China during the Second World War (a perennial student favorite). The e-mails asked: wasn't it the students' right to proclaim their pride in being Chinese and to redress this historical outrage?

The Chinese leadership read these messages too. Its concern over the upcoming anniversary of Tiananmen could be measured in the uptick of arrests and surveillance of anyone who had participated in the original demonstrations or had made contact with the underground China Democracy Party since that time. But the Chinese Communist Party's sense of vulnerability led to overreactions even by their own standards. In one story that made the expat rounds, drunken foreign students from the University of California system had dropped a few beer bottles off the top of a Beijing Normal University dorm during a typically rowdy beer night. It so happens that the Chinese term for "little bottle" is homophonous with Deng Xiaoping's name, and thus the university authorities assumed that this was the beginning of a major political demonstration and called for help from Chinese State Security.

To prevent Tiananmen itself from being used as a rallying point, a construction barrier was erected in late 1998 around the entire perimeter of the square, on the pretext of ongoing renovation. Grotesque and abnormally high, like a mini Berlin Wall, it created an evocative visual hole in the heart of Beijing, and remained unfinished well past June 1999—an unheard-of construction delay for the Chinese government. Some of the students read this Chinese ground zero as a physical manifestation of the regime's fear and guilt.

The irony was that the Chinese students of 1999—with money, access to the Internet, and Michael Jordan high-tops—considered themselves a world away from the Tiananmen generation. Almost all of them had bought into one or another revisionist history of the student movement anyway. Certainly Wang did: the Tiananmen students were naïve, they went too far, and the opportunistic ringleaders had left to make money in America. Yet some students in 1999 still carried a nagging sense of survivor's guilt, a feeling that they had been complacent, apolitical, and solely concerned with their own advancement.

Wang respected sincerity above all. An African exchange student had once tried to convert him to Christ. As a Muslim, he regarded conversion as unthinkable, but he listened to his friend's pitch for thirty days, fascinated by his ability to *believe*—so different from the narrow-eyed materialism of Han Chinese culture. (Wang loved that same quality in American life; whenever he could get hold of a copy of *Time* magazine, he would read it over and over.) Even if he was repulsed by the naïveté of the students in 1989, he knew too that many of them had believed passionately in what they did. Wang had made no plans to demonstrate (or to *"anti,"* as he liked to call it) on June 4, but he was haunted by a lingering unease about not doing so.

Now, on May 8, 1999, as the university bus parked along the tree-lined avenue next to Ritan Park, Wang felt his heart beating. *Maybe this time it will be different. Maybe they cannot stop us.*

Wang had known about the bombing since the early hours of Saturday morning. Sitting in his dorm, informed that U.S. missiles had been fired into the Belgrade embassy, he just felt shock. Then, for the first time in months, a sense of clarity began to emerge. He didn't like the Communist Party or its policies; and in all honesty, he felt little concern for the safety of the PRC's ambassador in Belgrade. But he didn't see the point of thinking about such things because the larger point was so obvious to him: We are not friends with the Americans. We are enemies. They are an arrogant enemy who has disgraced our people. The government won't do anything because it always plays the role of a coward, a dog to the foreigners. The only thing to do is to *anti*.

On his own, Wang began composing a big-character poster, the traditional Chinese form of protest. He drew up a message: *You cannot beat up the Chinese people. You cannot disgrace the Chinese nation.* Perhaps my poster is the first one in China, he thought. And with that, he signed his name to the bottom of the poster.

Then the anxiety hit: his act of open, nonsanctioned political activity could be the end of his academic and professional career. It could even bring torture, confession and prison. There was nothing hysterical about this line of thinking; when other students began to follow Wang's lead and create their own big-character posters, a professor saw Wang's composition. The professor was fond of Wang, so he nervously tried to cover the signature with a piece of paper. Wang appreciated the gesture, but felt that removing it now, especially after other students had seen it, would be cowardly. The signature stayed.

Now, on Saturday afternoon, Wang carried his signature openly, leading the demonstration for Peking University. Each time he passed in front of the embassy, he felt more excited. But even as he screamed out the slogans and shook his fist, he also felt naked. His daring and prominence made him a target; perhaps the Party would still crack down. In the middle of the demonstrations, he borrowed a cell phone, found a corner where the shouting was not quite so loud, and called his mother. He wanted to say goodbye; something might happen, he said, but never forget that he believed in what he was doing. Then he went back to *anti* as his fellow Peking University students threw the first stones.

Wang had ridden a wave, first of anger, then fear, then something that felt like heroism. He explained to me later on that in the embassy bombing, he had stumbled into the defining moment of his life.

The Chinese leaders typically take weeks of backroom negotiations to settle on even an obscure shift in policy. But in the early hours of May 8, faced with the political challenge of the NATO attack on the embassy, they had been decisive. The bombing could be a gift horse if only they could break it, ride it, and then get it back in the stable when the time came. If the students chattered that the government feared them because of the blood of Tiananmen, then here was an opportunity to show new confidence and strength. Substitute American culpability in '99 for Chinese culpability in '89 and channel the students' nationalism by letting them "take to the streets."

In '89, the students walked to Tiananmen. This time, they would be bused to the American embassy. In '89, Party informers were purged by the students. This time, informers would lead the demonstrations, dictate the content of the posters, take roll, and see that the students were back on campus in time for dinner. In '89, the Chinese media had been seduced by the dramatic antigovernment demonstrations. This time, the government would direct the action: deploy a massive police presence around the embassy district, get the national television cameras in place for the evening news, order colorful Tibetan monks to demonstrate when things got slow, stage photo-ops of the bodies being flown from Belgrade to Chinese soil, and lead memorial services with the eulogies given by Jiang Zemin and Zhu Rongji. Above all, the government would keep the message simple: the attack by U.S.-led NATO was deliberate, *yeman*—savage, brutal, barbaric—and a "blood debt" that had been incurred against the Chinese people. These slogans, chosen for their historical resonance with the Opium Wars and the Japanese invasion, were to be repeated all the way through the Tiananmen anniversary. (In case anyone missed the point, an "instant hit," a mushy ballad, was produced in honor of the three Chinese martyrs—featuring the chorus, *Ten more days! I will mourn you for ten more days!*—and was given massive airplay about a week before June 4.)

So as it turned out, Wang needn't have worried. On Sunday, May 9, a large picture of him and two fellow students from Peking University was featured above the fold in a leading Chinese newspaper. Shouting and carrying a big-character poster, they were the "it" boys, the ones who dared. Wang was not in trouble, he was a hero, a patriot who had empowered the students. (Now we can *anti* whenever we want, Wang thought after reading it.) He was back in the stable, happy and sweaty after his run. The Chinese leadership was happy too, but they had no intention of letting Wang *anti* outside the university again.

■

If Wang didn't know where he really stood with the Communist Party until that Sunday, the American businessmen of Beijing were suddenly starting to worry about their own standing, too. Saturday had seen something like 10,000 protesters; by nightfall the number had doubled. On Sunday, as a low-pressure system moved in, creating a flat, ominous light, the crowd was over 100,000. That evening, Vice Premier Hu Jintao appeared on CCTV, praising the students' patriotism but also telling them to cool down. American businesses throughout China rushed to prepare apologies, as well as e-mails expressing condolences to their Chinese employees. Others, like Ford and IBM, aired their "shock and regret" to the PLA News, declaring that they understood the reasons for the protests and gratefully acknowledging that foreigners' "lives and property had not been threatened." Given that the State Department had already released a travel warning for Americans in China, that protesters were stoning KFC outlets in several Chinese cities, that the Chongqing Holiday Inn had been briefly invaded by a mob who assaulted Western hotel guests, and that other, less visible industries had received threats, such statements had a whiff of the hostage's forced optimism. For corporations such as Motorola, with massive investments in China, regret was not enough. Motorola's vice president, Lai Bingrong, not only felt "grief" and "indignation" over the U.S. attack on the Chinese embassy, but also stated on record that "it is unforgivable" (just before he added that Motorola's president would come to visit China and that Sino-U.S. trade should be continued).

The American business community held the hopeful consensus that the embassy bombing would blow over. Many old hands pointed out that they had been through ugly crackdowns and anti-American campaigns: the clampdown following Tiananmen in 1989, and to a lesser extent, the Taiwan Strait crisis of 1996. But how long would it take to ratchet down, and with what losses to revenue streams?

So as the Chinese government petulantly rejected the American embassy's diplomatic attempts to begin a dialogue—Jiang Zemin had even refused to take President Clinton's phone call during the crisis—the local American business representatives of the American Chamber of Commerce in Beijing (AmCham) stepped in. First, they mollified the Chinese leadership as best they could. Then, for approximately three weeks they acted as the sole point of communication, passing messages between the two camps. By acting like a neutral force, they were able to get the two sides talking again. American business had reasserted itself as the quiet, but essential lubricant of the U.S.-Chinese relationship.

From the beginning, of all the business reps I met in Beijing, AmCham director Michael Furst was one of my favorites, partly because he was a tough bureaucratic infighter, and partly because he was among those who had come to the Gold Mountain not just for the money, but for the challenge of the climb. Michael welcomed crisis and was proud of AmCham's contortions—third-party communications, appeasement of the Chinese leadership—precisely because he didn't see these solely as self-serving acts to protect business interests. He would look into your eyes, smile and ask: How can Chinese anti-Americanism serve anyone? We are on a higher plane, negotiating, working and playing with the Chinese at a level of intimacy that the U.S. diplomatic corps can only dream of. I go out in the mountains and drink *Baijiu* (cheap Chinese liquor) with those guys. We understand what has to be done. (The implication: the State Department does not.)

In an informal meeting in his office, one prominent AmCham member identified the underlying problem: *Scratch a Chinaman— you'll find an inferiority complex.* So if the Chinese had a self-esteem problem, what was wrong with playing to their sensitivities? It didn't cost anything to be ambiguous and avoid parroting the U.S. embassy line.

Enter Ezra Vogel, the director of the Asia Center at Harvard University, a former senior intelligence official in the Clinton administration, and an influential voice for expanding U.S.-China trade, with extensive links to the American business community in Beijing. In a talk at the Hong Kong University of Science and Technology a month after the event, he claimed that there was an official cover-up of the U.S. embassy bombing. Vogel pointed to the fact that the "security side of the embassy was precisely hit." He then ventured that the PRC embassy, "like all major embassies, has a lot of electronic equipment," implying that it became a target primarily through its electronic signature rather than as a matter of mistaken location.

Vogel's remarks were dutifully reported by the *Hong Kong Standard,* a Beijing-leaning paper, and they buttressed a baroque version of events that was making the rounds in the Chinese Princeling cocktail circuit: all Serbian military communications and television signals were being routed through the Chinese embassy in Belgrade, central to Milosovic's war effort. The American military picked up the electronic signature, traced it to the Chinese embassy, and then exerted pressure on President Clinton to destroy it. In a scenario resembling the Cuban Missile Crisis, Clinton then made a secret call to Jiang Zemin, laying down a harsh ultimatum: Remove the communication assets from the Chinese embassy, or we will do it for you. But—and here was the money shot—unlike Khrushchev, Jiang stood firm. Thus Belgrade was only the backdrop for one act in a Superpower Beijing Opera.*

While Vogel later clarified his position—he had "only raised serious questions about the map explanation"—his statements had already been accepted as a gift from a fellow traveler, and from that point on he was continually cited in the Chinese state-controlled media.

In private, most AmCham members just shrugged and asked, what possible advantage could the United States have reaped from an attack on the Chinese embassy? Yet there were also a few who would lower their voices, look at you from the corner of their eye, and hint darkly that they had personal connections with unnamed intelligence officials who had informed them that the bombing was no accident. Most of these individuals had far better connections in China than they had in the States, but it isn't hard to imagine they were telling their Chinese business partners the same line. Even some congressmen and staffers who came over to China on short junkets were co-opted into the view that intimating that the Chinese were right (they would never come out and say so) would enhance their viability by playing to their host's sensitivities.

■

For a select group of Beijing's most prominent American business representatives visiting the United States, the moment of crisis on

---

*The bombing confirmed that the U.S. was a hegemon, confirmed that the Chinese had always been victimized, and confirmed China's construct of the "Middle Kingdom"—a China that had been dominant in the world for "five thousand years of history." So as U.S. explanations began to dribble belatedly into the Chinese press, the idea that the Chinese embassy was not a CIA target and not on any CIA database—simply not important!—was itself considered to be an insult to the Chinese people.

May 9 also happened to occur in the middle of the American Chamber of Commerce in Beijing's annual "doorknock" lobbying trip to Capitol Hill in Washington.

It had previously looked routine: meet with congressmen, promote loosening of restrictions on the Chinese market and other political impediments to China business. As the news of the embassy bombing and the Chinese reaction hit, the doorknockers initially sensed a spike in Capitol Hill's interest in anything to do with China, particularly on-the-ground assessments. AmCham representatives would have little trouble getting extended meetings with top senators and congressmen, where they could flesh out the business view, sketch out the stunning progress of the China market, and buttress critical relationships.

But the American business reps also found themselves facing a weird identity crisis. The objective was to avoid becoming the sacrificial lamb of deteriorating relations, and to stress the apolitical but constructive nature of the American business presence. Yet as the congressmen questioned them closely, searching for an understanding of the Chinese street and the motives of the top Chinese leadership, the doorknockers were tempted to give a short history lesson on Western bullying of China. As they explained the rational basis for Chinese sensitivities, the business reps kept catching each other sounding as if they had gone native, almost like de facto spokesmen for the Chinese leadership. The top AmCham reps regrouped and imposed a cadre system. No business representative would meet with a congressman alone; instead they would travel in groups of three to ensure that they stayed on message.

The first element of that message was not to downplay the Chinese reaction, but to explain it as an aberration, a circus for the Chinese masses. The Chinese leadership have their own polls (just like you, Mr. Congressman). The intense nationalism unfolding on the Beijing streets should not be construed as representative, or a guide to China's future trajectory. Rather, the Chinese reaction to the embassy bombing was a blip, a temporary setback, not a revelation of China's true character. (A similar spin, although far more discreet, was applied during the aftermath of the Tiananmen massacre by pro-China lobbyists in 1989.)

The second message the AmCham cadres would deliver was that the future of the U.S.-China relationship outweighed any bumps in the road (and thus it would be better if decision makers in Washington cooled their rhetoric). Robert Kapp, president of the U.S.-Chinese Business Council, portrayed the political discussion on both sides as an "ear-splitting exchange of media and political salvoes, some . . . in both countries—with gritty racial insinuation." Kapp promoted evenhanded blame, and used the word "racial"—a word with minor contextual impact in China, but the most effective term he could find to inhibit political discussion in America.

The third element of the message was oriented toward the Chinese audience: When there's media present, express as much sorrow as possible. As luck would have it, a crew from China Central Television (CCTV), the official mouthpiece of the Chinese state, was also present in Washington during AmCham's doorknock. It's not clear why, but the AmCham representatives agreed to a breakfast meeting at the Chinese embassy in Washington. When they arrived, the CCTV cameras were rolling. Someone—again, it's not clear who or exactly why—led the assembled business leaders in a prayer or a moment of silence before their meal.

Up until that point, all the footage that CCTV had from the United States was a few words of regret from an all-too-relaxed President Clinton, followed by more formal apologies from the secretary of state, the director of the CIA, and the head of NATO. All expressed deep sorrow, yet all added the yes-but caveat that the whole affair was simply a technical mistake. This sort of footage was useful for the Chinese government's handling of the middle stage of the riots at home, as a demonstration of China's international power and legitimacy. The perceived inadequacy of the apologies could effectively hold Chinese emotions at a high boil, thereby sustaining the Chinese government's perceived bargaining power and ability to keep the momentum going through the Tiananmen anniversary. But ultimately the caveats grated; nobody from the NATO command had been put before a firing squad, after all. How to ratchet down the Chinese public's emotions while enhancing the leadership's stature? A *real* apology was necessary.

Now CCTV finally had the shot that the leadership had wanted all along: the *kowtow!* Back in the Beijing studios, the footage from the breakfast meeting could be matched up with a Chinese voice-over solemnly intoning the sorrowful apologies of the American business community. The American captains of industry were bowing their heads low, not to the Lord, but to China! What valuable footage for CCTV, and what a good move for U.S. businesses in China—a win-win!

Tim Stratford, president of AmCham at the time (and head of GM in China), complained to me about the cynical way in which CCTV had used the breakfast meeting footage, saying that the Chinese embassy had given him assurances that the meeting would not be used for political propaganda, that they had tricked AmCham into the money shot. In my experience, Stratford was a model of contentious integrity, and certainly no patsy. Yet even if one discounts some selective memory, I still wondered why they were bowing their heads in the first place. (Throughout my time in officially atheist Beijing, I cannot recall ever having attended a single business meal function—breakfast, lunch, dinner or formal ball—that began with a prayer or the lowering of heads.) And even if this meeting was unprecedented, why were they bowing their heads in the presence of CCTV?

Shortly after the embassy bombing, the *People's Daily* called on the nation to accelerate the modernization of PLA weaponry to "safeguard national sovereignty and dignity." Army cadres spoke openly of resuming atmospheric nuclear testing to show their willingness to resist the U.S.-led NATO alliance. Beneath this bluster, a seismic shift had occurred. Chinese military interests and ambitions under Deng Xiaoping had been kept subordinate to policies that favored the wealth of the Chinese nation until some undefined future point when the Chinese economy had reached maturity. Jiang had continued the policy. The embassy bombing had acted like a blast of radiation, ripening the appearance of the economy (without really making it healthier), and strengthening "hardline" forces (crudely evidenced by steady double-digit percentage increases in the official Chinese defense budget in the years that followed). But reformers argued, correctly, that any hard-line plans depended on continued foreign investment.

American corporate behavior in the aftermath of the embassy bombing sent up a flare to the Chinese government that they would cooperate. American business interests were now welded not only to keeping the peace between the United States and China but also to assisting the Chinese leadership in creating what they considered a more equitable balance of power.

If this sounds like a contradiction, well, in Beijing we were all living one.

贪 2.

MTV for War

As Monday dawned, bright and lovely, my wife was weeping from the strain. The Beijing embassy riots had dominated our weekend, and a blood-for-blood feeling haunted every transaction we had with a Chinese person. My wife is normally the stoic one, but that day she begged me not to go to work. I tried to reassure her: I would ride my old Chinese bike so people could tell that I was a foreigner who worked in Beijing, rather than an American imperialist caught in the wrong place at the wrong time. I would wear dark glasses so people could not see my eyes dart nervously from side to side. I would be alert. She wrote down the characters for "deeply regret" and "accident" on cards for me to carry in my pocket as a final precaution.

As I retrieved my bicycle, I suddenly thought of Wei, the head of the Chinese television production company I was working for. She was in a hospital, probably far to the north of Beijing. The operation she had undergone was not especially serious, but I wondered what she knew. Had she seen the events on television? I suddenly realized what a bit part I had in this U.S.-China engagement thing. Few people in China had staked so much on a smooth Sino-U.S. relationship as Wei. How alone she must feel, I thought as I wheeled my bike out in the alley. Then the first Chinese pedestrian I saw, just a normal guy walking down the *hutong*, abruptly turned and gave me a hard, angry stare. I forgot about Wei.

The ride to work was an anticlimax. Perhaps I was expecting an Orientalist scene from the Boxer Rebellion—screeching old

19

ladies, slops being thrown out of windows, pigtailed crowds pursuing me with *numchucks* until I lost them in the Beijing alleyways. Instead, there were only a few incomprehensible catcalls,
all of them female, as I headed east on Ghost Street, the crowded
northern restaurant district. When I arrived at Fuhua Dasha, the
enormous neoclassical complex that housed Wei's production
company, the mood became more troubling. At the American Coffee Shop next to the entrance, the normally friendly employees
averted their eyes and the usual tape loop of "Hotel California"
had been replaced by something Chinese and funereal. As I walked
into the office, our receptionist (who had previously been my close
confidant, especially on Wei's shifting moods) would not acknowledge my existence. Nor would Wei's secretary. I made a beeline to
my office and threw myself into my imitation leather chair in disgust. Almost immediately the phone rang.

It was Wei, sounding weak, perhaps heavily medicated. Yet
before I could ascertain anything about her condition, she took
charge: How was I? How was my wife? We were not hurt? Any
trouble getting to work?

We were fine, I assured her, and started to rant about the dis-
tortions in the Chinese media.

"Listen," she said, her tone suggesting that I was being naïve,
"have you had any problems in the office?"

"No one is speaking to me," I said.

"Don't worry," she replied, "I'll fix everything."

Wei hung up. Fifteen minutes later, the receptionist escorted
me into the conference room. The entire staff was already seated,
waiting for me. As a way to relieve the tension, I put my fingers
up on both sides of my head, evoking the horns of the Devil. A
beat, two beats, and then the conference room erupted in laughter. (God bless the Chinese sense of humor!) Wei's office manager
(who was also rumored to double as our in-house Communist
Party rep) began a short speech. She told the employees that their
anger was justified, but that "Ethan is a friend of China" and "The
foreigner is not responsible for what his government does." This
last point brought friendly nods of agreement around the table,
as no savvy Chinese citizen takes any responsibility for his government's actions either.

Back to work, then. A television show on film festivals, one of the production company's standbys, was being edited that day. But when I peeked into the editing room, the show (a Tom Cruise retrospective, I think) had abruptly been dropped in favor of Serbian war film classics. Wei's secretary, who bravely accompanied me to lunch at our local Sichuan joint, was later admonished for her fraternization by the office manager. When we returned, the accounting office, led by a loud woman with Trotsky glasses, was staging a struggle session in the reception area to denounce American imperialism. Apparently the first demand was that my air conditioning—actually a simple exhaust fan—be turned off immediately.

Distracted by the Red Guards of accounting and wondering how to raise the money to buy plane tickets home, I was only dimly aware of what this turn of events meant for Wei and her company. The next day, she called me from the hospital and I took the call in the reception area. The conversation was a bit manic. She was determined to keep *Shared Street,* the joint U.S.-Chinese talk show we were collaborating on several weeks earlier, moving ahead. While we pumped up our enthusiasm about how the show was more-relevant-than-ever, I glanced over at the monitor in the reception area that was always tuned to China Central Television (CCTV) 1 or Beijing Television (BTV), the state-run news channels. Whatever had been showing faded, to be replaced by a slow pan of the gray skeleton of the Chinese embassy in Belgrade. Up volume on somber techno. Dissolve to slo-mo of a Chinese man, weeping convulsively, holding his daughter's bloody clothes to his chest. Cut to backlit silhouettes of looming U.S. soldiers' helmets. Cut to U.S. bombers offloading. Cut to tattered Serbian refugees. Dissolve to crying Chinese children. Bring up white screen with enormous graphic of swastika at 45-degree tilt. Slow zoom on swastika revealing that it's composed of high-contrast photographs of what appear to be burnt bodies and other U.S. atrocities from the Korean War to the present. Continued slow zoom to the center of swastika. Music crescendo. Tight on central image: President Clinton with a Hitler mustache.

This was not my first exposure to imagery of this kind. Over a month before, Wei's independent Chinese production company, oriented toward U.S.-Chinese cooperation and understanding, sat down with one of the BTV international news teams, along with tea and plenty of cigarettes, to see if we could work together. They gave us a private screening of their recently produced show. It opened as a news program, featuring a Chinese jock anchor (sporting aviator glasses a tad small for his face) presenting the subject: Clinton's episodic bombing of Iraq. After a short documentary introduction explaining the context of the Gulf War and its relationship to the ongoing U.S. imperialism in Kosovo and throughout the world, they got down to business. Two minutes of pure images followed, with the same somber music again: U.S. bombers, soldiers looming, terrified Iraqi children, crying Chinese children — that incongruous shot, perhaps the same one that CCTV used. They even had a special name for this sort of package, one that I have heard only in the Chinese television industry: "MTV for War."

How had I ended up, at least indirectly, doing MTV for War? Well, it had something to do with my understanding—or incomprehension—of China, and of Wei herself.

I had first met her a year earlier, on a windy Upper East Side corner. I knew only that she was an independent television producer from China who liked to work with Americans. But something about the setting of that first meeting seemed portentous—cinematically so—to me at the time: on my way to the subway, emerging from a screening of *Red Corner*, Richard Gere's nouveau–Cold War melodrama of an American television executive ensnared in the Chinese penal system.

Ironically, the screening was held at the Asia Society, a New York institution known for its genteel cheerleading for China. In a reassuring sign that it had not been taken over by Taiwanese financiers, a stylishly dressed Asia Society employee had appeared on the stage to make sure we understood how to think about what we were going to see. He patiently instructed the audience of perhaps twenty-five New York intellectuals to view *Red Corner* as anti-China kitsch, an artifact of the enemies of engagement (including the corrupt Buddhist disciple of the Dalai Lama, Richard Gere, it was implied).

Red Corner was Gere's labor of love, an attempt to produce mass-market entertainment that would bolster the Tibetan independence movement by vividly exposing the horrors of the Chinese state. Gere stars as a suave, globetrotting businessman seduced by a fiery Chinese sex bomb and then set up for her murder. It turns out that her charming Chinese Princeling boyfriend (a surprisingly accurate depiction) is actually pulling the strings. As a totalitarian courtroom drama, it also features Bai Ling playing Gere's ravishing state-appointed lawyer.

Gere overplays to type, with a lot of table-pounding and demanding his rights; but Ling's character was not scripted quite as one-dimensionally as our hosts at Asia Society had led us to believe. The lawyer so firmly believes in justice that she essentially takes on the whole of the rigid Chinese legal system, thereby wrecking her political and professional viability. But she also evinces a kind of stubborn Chinese pride. In one scene she plays an *erhu,* a Chinese stringed instrument (Hollywood shorthand for the glory of traditional Chinese culture). In another scene she angrily parries Gere's denunciation of China's police state by pointing to the horrendous crime rate in America. In the end, as the evil Princeling boyfriend is unmasked and Gere gains his freedom, he and Ling suddenly reveal their intense but unconsummated passion for each other at the airport. As a proto-Orientalist soundtrack swells, she bites back her tears, telling Gere that she loves him but she has no choice; she must stay in China to fight the good fight.

It's a touching conclusion, but a formulaic one. So when I ran into Wei en route to the subway, I was a little astonished to find tears streaming down her cheeks, a full five minutes after the closing credits. She was quite short, perhaps just over five feet tall, with a kind of pixie face: small luminous eyes, narrowly set, slightly pug-nosed, a little tight-lipped—perhaps not a stunningly beautiful face, but one that gave evidence of intelligence, canniness, and a kind of lively interest in the world.

"Are you okay? Did you like the movie?" I asked.

"Yes, I liked the movie very, very much" she answered with a clipped northern Chinese accent, smiling politely through her tears.

As we talked, I informed her that I would soon be traveling to China, and she gave me her business card. The early winter winds were howling around us, and she was accompanied by a kindly-looking older American producer type who seemed to have his own agenda, so we cut things short.

The meeting was not accidental; I had a tip that she would be at the Asia Society screening and I desperately needed to run into her. The fact is that I was in a corner myself, and it was red in the financial sense: the funding for my China documentary was in deep trouble, after months of pounding on doors. A top correspondent at ABC had turned me down with the words "too rich for our blood." PBS would soon follow. A CNN reporter, a former Beijing bureau guy, had simply looked me in the face and said, "I just don't think you can do it." Perhaps he was right, I thought: I had no assets, no platform, no clue as to how I would proceed. Even Richard Gere hadn't answered my letter.

Then I was saved—on a New York street corner. As a producer, Wei had the reputation of being simultaneously well connected in China, independent and America-friendly. I had been led to her by Danny Schechter, executive producer of Globalvision, a left-leaning production house. Schechter had talked me up, telling his old friend Wei that I was a major American documentary reporter and producer. Now, having been up-close with her, I was suddenly overwhelmed with excitement because I knew something else, and I knew it with certainty: Wei was a dissident.

I had met a few other Tiananmen Square leaders in exile at Columbia University. They had seemed cold, like beneficiaries of too much media attention too soon, arrogantly planning their triumphant return to their homeland like a long-forgotten royal family, dismissive of the problems of today's China, oblivious to China's exponential economic growth, which had left their paradigms in the dust. I instantly sensed that Wei was different: realistic, involved, in the heart of the struggle—yet weeping for the Chinese people in an unguarded moment on the street. And I would create television with her! (When I told my friend Terry about having met Wei, he drolly remarked that if I was lucky, we might even end up in the same prison cell.)

I never worked up the nerve to ask Wei why the movie had affected her so deeply. But after getting to know her, I realized that she was actually an interesting hybrid of the new China. It was not the anti-Chinese-government slant of *Red Corner* or the poor, oppressed Chinese people that moved her to tears, but the Chinese female lawyer. In this character she saw an idealized version of herself: fiercely proud, desirable and idealistic, fighting within the system for a better China, unsuccessful but independent, in a passionate clasp with America yet spurning it at the same time.

■

I went to work for Wei, and over time, as I became her friend, she revealed her past to me.* She was born in Nanjing in the early 1960s, the firstborn of a capitalist-landowner or "Black Class" family. Her grandmother came from a landowner family and her grandfather owned textile factories, warehouses and even two wives. Thus Wei was born with tangible social advantages, things that a child would notice; but when she was about age four, these advantages suddenly became grave liabilities with the onset of the Cultural Revolution. Wei's parents were forced to attend public struggle sessions, and Wei was sent to live with relatives.

As in the case of many other victims of the Cultural Revolution, Wei tried to overcome her outsider status by enthusiastically embracing communism and the Party. For example, she remembers proudly that at one point she was allowed to solo in "The East Is Red" for her school. Eventually, however, her Black Class background caught up with her and further education or advancement was blocked. In her early adolescence, she was sent to an

---

*Wei's story is one of a midlevel operator, but it's illustrative of the tragic dilemma of many in the modern Chinese intellectual/professional class. It's not dissimilar to many other memoirs of the Cultural Revolution, perhaps the most well-established genre of Chinese biographies for foreign audiences. At one point, Wei even asked me to discuss her life story with a potential U.S. investor that she was courting. The investor, it turned out, was completely uninterested in hearing it—he responded with a blasé "Boo hoo hoo"—yet Wei's story, and the Cultural Revolution genre in general, are actually quite relevant to any U.S. investor. If his potential Chinese partner is between 35 and 55 years of age, then chances are the Cultural Revolution directly disrupted his education, led to humiliating experiences, or made him do things that he is still ashamed of. Although these days the penalty is financial ruin, not prison, the same mechanisms that enforced the Cultural Revolution replay from time to time, haunting China in a flickering feedback loop.

out-of-the-way province, southern Shandong, to work among the peasants and be re-educated.

Wei overcame grim hardships by self-discipline, working hard in spite of her diminutive size, and by making people like her. In a sense, she absorbed the collective discipline of Maoist China and peasant life without giving up her personal ambitions. One recollection struck me as particularly ironic: as she was walking with a friend in 1976, the commune loudspeakers began to broadcast announcements of Mao's death; Wei fell to her knees and cried as if the world had come to an end. Yet her first real opportunities were opening up: as the Gang of Four's strict class codifications eased and the universities began to admit students again, she fought for acceptance, asserting her right to be judged on a level playing ground.

When she finally arrived at a university, Wei was excited to see her first American television show (*Seaworld*) on campus. There was also an American professor in residence and she began to visit him regularly. Like many who had been mistreated in the Cultural Revolution, she had become an idealist, and America seemed to embody freedom and fairness. At the same time, Wei had learned to work within the system. It's a short step from this practical stance to the belief that one can actually change the system by working within it, and Wei holds onto this belief even now.

Again, her story is not really unusual. Yet Chinese individuals drew different lessons out of similar experiences of the Cultural Revolution. Some learned to trust no established authority; they became revolutionaries and dissidents—or in most cases, just dropouts. Some constantly tried to make up for the privations, becoming materialists or even sexual hedonists. The survivors of the Cultural Revolution may have one thing in common: perennially insecure, they became a little addicted to the coping mechanisms they created. My sense is that Wei handled her situation adeptly, even showing great ambition, and learned one lesson very clearly: to succeed, she would always have to plan under conditions of great uncertainty. This meant constantly creating new options, replenishing her network like a squirrel gathering nuts, and creating a multitude of self-representations—like the guardian statues lined up along the entrance to an imperial tomb—to serve as defenses against struggle sessions, purges and humiliations to come.

After her first exposure to American culture, Wei clawed her way out of China, riding a bike through snowstorms to attend English lessons so that she could pass the Test of English as a Foreign Language (TOEFL), and traveling to Beijing, where she stood in the lines outside the U.S. embassy literally for days on end to get her student visa. When she finally arrived in the United States in the mid-eighties, instead of becoming an expert in an area of American studies or embracing some capitalist scheme, she established herself as a China expert in the rarified world of American television documentaries, first in the Pacific Northwest and then in New York City. Productions on China by definition usually handled only politically sensitive topics such as human rights and Tiananmen Square. Accordingly, Wei created a new persona, the one I first took her for after *Red Corner:* dissident. Wei won awards for her work in TV documentaries (particularly on the subject of the Tiananmen massacre) and established contacts with Chinese exiles and American academic and political China hands. But that was not enough. She was deeply ambitious, and was obsessed with the challenge of returning to China and creating an independent production company that would dominate Chinese television.

In 1994 she stepped off a plane in Beijing, checked into a hotel room, and began cold-calling Chinese television executives. She found a different Beijing from the one she had fled: a hothouse of entrepreneurial activity, and a media world that had made tremendous strides from a technical standpoint, aided by massive amounts of equipment donated by Sony and other corporations groping for a foothold in the China market. The product that actually appeared on the screen was another story: derivative and playing to the Party line, with all the sizzle of a stiffly animated red flag. Content was still a dangerous concept. Accordingly, Wei adjusted her persona again: she was no longer a dissident documentary film maker fearlessly exposing the truth, but an American producer of sophisticated entertainment.

At that time, independent production was not encouraged and foreign investment in media was forbidden, so Wei flew below the radar. A Princeling acquaintance with excellent connections but little business sense owned a moribund production company and an extremely unusual license allowing a foreigner to create

programming for Chinese television. Wei acquired the company
and the license. With the beginnings of a platform, she soon had
a contract from CCTV for several sports shows and a telemagazine
show that would cover Western movies and film festivals.

Wei's approach was to fly to film festivals all over Europe and
America with a crew of young Beijingers. On the ground, with the
camera running, she would aggressively latch on to an American
star and, instead of probing into their politics or their sex lives,
simply ask them how much money they were making, hounding
them for exact figures—precisely what the money-conscious Chinese audience craved. Chinese audiences loved Wei for her brash
American quality with Chinese characteristics. She was on her way
to becoming a role model for the next Chinese generation.

But Wei could always feel the undertow of the Cultural Revolution. In the summer of 1996, a rumor that she was actually an
American/Taiwanese spy blacklisted her from Chinese state television, the only real outlet in China for a television production
company, other than advertising or industry films. According to
Wei, this was a false charge, although it was no secret that she had
been in sympathy with the reformers during the struggle over
Tiananmen. Among Chinese expats at the time, who wasn't? Yet
there had been a kind of generalized amnesty both in China and
abroad, as long as you played the game by the Party's rules in the
here and now. And at this point, Wei was very much playing by
the rules.

She told me this attack was based on personal jealousy at her
meteoric rise. As State Security began to investigate her past, Wei's
company of about fifty employees went into financial freefall, losing half a million dollars as well as about two million from accounts
receivable. Wei cooperated, even encouraged the investigation at
the time, but she also told me that this was the single greatest education about how the New China worked that she had ever received.

Although she held a U.S. green card, Wei brushed off friends'
suggestions that she return to America. Instead she consoled herself by thinking of Deng Xiaoping's ups and downs, and tirelessly
worked on her *guanxi*—her connections—wining and dining any
Chinese official she could. Finally, Wei invented yet another persona: Chinese patriot and friend of the Party.

In 1997, Jiang Zemin was preparing a state visit to the United States, by invitation of President Bill Clinton. Wei knew that she would probably be denied access to follow Jiang around in China, but America was a different story. Would Americans stop an independent Chinese producer from filming, particularly one who spoke better English than much of the official CCTV crew? Apparently the Americans did not, although the tape that emerged does not give one a sense of high-level access. Even inside major assembly halls, the footage is often hand-held, as if it were a bootleg of a rock concert. These clips are punctuated by sycophantic statements by American friends of China lavishing praise on the New China and on Jiang's visionary strategic partnership with President Clinton. The one exception is Jiang's visit to take tea with a pivotal figure in China's relations with Taiwan. At the shoot, Wei met her future husband.

CCTV chose not to air Wei's documentary of Jiang's historic visit to the United States—although this decision could have been based on industry politics rather than quality—and the film did not make a profit. Nonetheless, Wei claims that the documentary restored her political credit. This was due in part to the advertising; Wei's company created a poster that became ubiquitous in Beijing for a time. It's a peculiar kind of Chinese kitsch: Jiang and Bill, side by side, Jiang just a little ahead (compensating for his short stature, but also suggesting China's we-try-harder position in the superpower race); an enormous white dove awkwardly flapping its wings above the two leaders; smaller photos of smiling American students, businessmen and happy crowds, punctuated by the words in Chinese and English: "He is very cool!"*

The poster greeted me when I arrived at Wei's production office on my third day in Beijing, a few days after Christmas 1998. Both of her identities—Chinese patriot and American TV producer—were on display that afternoon. An American and a Chinese flag sat by the doorway (the Chinese one slightly higher). On the walls were posters for past shows and gritty art photographs

---

*The phrase, from one of Wei's interviews, actually meant that Jiang was capable of keeping his head and avoiding any outright blunders, not that Americans thought the Chinese president was a cool dude.

of modern China clearly taken by an expat photographer—something one would never see in most Chinese offices. Perhaps most telling was a photo of a young Andy Warhol on a film set, a symbol of artistic freedom.

Wei greeted me quite warmly, agreed to give me office space, and over the next couple of days explained what she was up to. With her political credit restored, she was now preparing the groundwork to leave for the States to film *Shared Street,* the first U.S.-Chinese talk show to be aired on national television. The concept was simple: get some American experts, get some Chinese experts, put them together on a set talking about some important issue before a live audience. Presumably they would find some areas of agreement. Wei sincerely believed that the communication would lead to understanding, perhaps even tangible improvement in the Sino-U.S. relationship. However, for the show to have any chance of airing in China, it couldn't be too controversial, while to have any chance of airing in America, it couldn't be too polite.

Wei had already thrown vast resources into the first four shows: filming them at a Virginia Beach studio, flying in experts, acquiring an American co-host. Strangely enough, the Americans tended to be the problem. For example, co-host Mark Salzman was the author of *Iron and Silk,* perhaps the most popular book ever written about Chinese life and martial arts. Because he had cut his teeth in an out-of-the-way university in China during the eighties, when U.S.-Chinese relations were still novel, his approach to Wei's program was to avoid any sort of conflicting statement and to smile beatifically throughout the discussions, no matter what was being said. (Even the Chinese producers found his demeanor too saccharine and he was dropped after the first rushes were viewed). The rest of the American experts had been selected because they were friends of China in some fashion, and they went out of their way to practice a puritanical moral equivalence—not to be caught judging China by Western standards or engaging in any confrontation whatsoever.

The show on politics featured two retired ambassadors basically going on about how much they respected each other. All for naught: the American ambassador indulged in a longwinded critique of American hypocrisy concerning human rights, yet in passing also mentioned worker unrest in China, a forbidden subject that made the show unusable by Chinese state television standards. In the show on the environment, the Chinese professor was quite forthcoming on China's environmental devastation—in fact, dangerously so for his career. Yet the American expert from the EPA gave a purely technocratic performance that ignored any mention of Chinese environmental degradation. The experts on the entertainment show agreed that Chinese and American films are different, but good. The education experts agreed that they liked children.

While the program was ostensibly set up as a discussion between equals, the American attitude came across as weirdly condescending. One wonders how much of this harmonious discussion could be traced to simple American embarrassment over China's perceived inferiority in many areas and how much was the Chinese style, which favors discussion leading not to further differences but to a conclusion, a summary statement of some kind. Therefore, when Wei closed the environmental show by saying they could talk about it all night and not reach a conclusion, by Chinese standards she was being quite daring.

When Wei and her team returned from Virginia Beach, I could see that no amount of editing would make the tape usable by American standards. Didn't Wei understand what it took to make great television? Where was the controversy? Where was the clash of civilizations and ideologies? (Actually, I was missing the point: as events would soon prove, from the Chinese perspective, Wei had already taken one chance too many.)

I began to get sucked into Wei's production company. Wei had customarily kept one American expat on her payroll at all times, if for no other reason than to write visa letters and make sure that the company's correspondence used standard English. The long-term American expat who had filled this role for her wasn't happy in his job, and my documentary on American small businesses in China was going nowhere. So I stepped in as chief foreigner, and in a short time, I made myself indispensable, scripting a snazzy promo tape for *Shared Street* and working closely with the Chinese staff. I also promoted new approaches to the show: more controversial, sexier topics with special news packages shot by Western and Chinese crews.

I remember this as a golden period in some ways. China was still new. My documentary had not worked out, but if one window had shut, another was wide open at Wei's company. I was working hard but dancing on the table at restaurants at night. Lunching with my fellow Chinese producers, I told them that someday I would write a book about them all, titled *In the Shadow of Fuhua Dasha*. So it was a pleasant surprise but not totally unexpected when on May 7, a Friday afternoon, I saw the masthead for *Shared Street* and found my name just below Wei's. She was having health troubles and had just left to check into the hospital for a couple of days, so I had no way of thanking her or cementing the deal with a handshake. But that was okay. I was on my way, and I was looking forward to my wife's expression when I told her. And then events took their fateful turn with the embassy bombing in Belgrade.

Now it was a week after the bombing; I had work to do, and I didn't want to let Wei down. On paper, I was still executive producer of *Shared Street*, and we had been given clearance to produce a "nonsensitive" topic that I had pushed: divorce, American vs. Chinese style. In Beijing the divorce rate had doubled to approximately 25 percent in less than five years (a predictable result of looser laws and a higher standard of living), but was not yet officially considered a problem. America's divorce rate was among the highest in the world, and everyone was willing to talk about where we had gone wrong. The Chinese could feel superior to the Americans, thus making the show politically acceptable, but the Americans had something to teach the Chinese about where they were headed. *Voilà*, a genuine cultural exchange.

The Beijing Television (BTV) network executives had initially accepted the topic and agreed to the plan—a package shot in the States, plus an American expert on the live set. But Wei soon came back from the hospital to tell me pointblank: in the aftermath of the embassy bombing, no Americans and no NATO countries. Orders from the top. We searched together for new countries to compare with China. Jiang Zemin had declared that the Swiss weren't friends anymore after a few dozen human rights demonstrators got too close to his entourage on a recent tour. Australia's security treaties were suspiciously NATO-like. The Philippines had fired on "innocent Chinese fishermen" in the Spratly Islands. Israel, though also a developing country, was too damn rich. And China just wasn't having any comparisons with a sinking Russia. That left us with ... Sweden!

After several weeks of my repeated warnings that we had no story, and with the air date looming, Wei finally received permission from the top of the BTV hierarchy to shoot in America again—on the condition that it was not identified as such. "Can't you just call it Canada?" Wei asked. We settled for "the West."

Any of my doubts were overcome by the chance to go to America with what I was told was the first Chinese crew since the embassy bombing. But the shoot was short of time and money; what was supposed to be a state-of-the-art debate on family values with Washington experts became Los Angeles, then Seattle, where one of our crews happened to have alighted. There was a further snag: the BTV jock anchor from MTV for War's bombing-Iraq show—I'll call him "Mao," as I sometimes thought of him as a stand-in—was selected as the correspondent. Just looking at those aviator glasses and his unsmiling, rigid demeanor, I could see that he was going to be trouble.

I flew into Seattle alone and immediately began working the phones: some generic divorce experts, the contribution of divorce to Kurt Cobain's suicide, hopefully some deeply troubled couples. Mao, my anchor companion, arrived a day later and immediately wanted to go to work. I had scheduled an interview that day with a former Marine who now ran a support group for divorced fathers out of a dingy office—in short, a solid guy doing the Lord's work.

Mao swept into the office with the crew and asked the first question: "Why is divorce so high in America compared with China?" Our Marine gave an intelligent answer about no-fault laws and tried to steer the conversation toward his own work, helping men stay close to their kids and ... but Mao cut in: "But the divorce has already taken place; what's the good of that?" Again, our Marine attempted to turn the discussion to encounter groups, problems in black America with fatherless sons, and again Mao interrupted as if he were doing a local I-Team report on used-car salesmen: "Do you know anything about China?" Our Marine admitted that he knew very little. Mao smiled and went for the kill: "Who is better, America or China?" Our Marine, in a desperate attempt to maintain a polite atmosphere, stammered that China had those nice Oriental values, family values, that kept families together. Mao grinned at the cameraman: "End of interview," he said in Chinese.

I said something about needing to use the bathroom and raced out of the building. Livid, I waited for the crew at the rental car, then drove them back to the hotel with my shades on, my head fixed. My silence was interpreted correctly, so the tension was acute.

When we emerged from the car, Mao stood at the curb, looked me in the eye and said evenly: "We should talk."

"Yes, we will talk tonight." I touched his arm and said, "It isn't personal."

Mao nodded slowly, turned and walked to the lobby.

Back in my hotel room, I slowly worked myself over. How had I allowed myself to get into this mess—setting up their dirty work, contributing to the filthy propaganda of the Chinese state, seduced by the possibility of 200 million Chinese viewers? Or was I being too self-important? After all, wasn't this just one little step of an insurmountable problem? All the paranoia of living and working in China seemed to sweep over the room like a dark storm. Walking off the set, ruining the show, leaving Wei's Chinese crew helpless and abandoned—this seemed to be my only option. Yet hadn't Wei called me every day after the bombing, worrying about my safety? Hadn't she foreseen this kind of trouble and implored me to maintain the peace on the shoot? Hadn't she listened patiently as I poured invectives upon Chinese intolerance? She was sincere in her desire for a better China, a China where independently produced TV and capitalism and freedom would simply overwhelm the rotting system. But Beijing Television ruled, and they wanted a Punch-and-Judy show that would expose American barbarism, selfishness and decadence. I rocked back and forth on my bed with my head in my hands. Mao was a tool, Wei was a tool, I was a tool.

Slowly, something began to surface. I was in control; none of the crew spoke English very well, and they couldn't drive in the United States, let alone find the nearest Chinese take-out. It followed that on their own, they would not find Tacoma's ghetto district or a battered wife hiding out in a trailer park. They could only see what I would allow them to see.

Such a Potemkin Village strategy ran against my professional ethics; but had I asked for this? I picked up the phone and called ... Orcas Island. I carried a bottle of bourbon upstairs to Mao's room. For form's sake, I drank for the next hour and relentlessly dragged him over the coals: Look at the position he was putting me in—an American journalist being asked to do a hit piece on his own country! I knew they were mad about the bombing, but enough is enough! Mao listened seriously, sadly. Slowly, in broken English, he said, "But I never meant to do this. I want to make good TV. I want to tell a real story."

Of course he would say that. Mao knew I could walk, and if I walked, he could lose his job and his salary—minuscule by our standards, but ten times what the average Chinese family man earns. He just sat there gently nodding, his eyes filled with concern, even sympathy behind the too-small aviator frames. It was weird, as if we had become friends after a fistfight. I told him that I had some average couples for him to interview, though we would have to travel a bit. He brightened up and we shook hands. That night, I slept surprisingly well.

Orcas Island is a kind of northwestern never-never land of young, appealing slackers and untouched forests. It went beautifully—the video proves it. My friend Gillian Smith, a rare beauty, had produced equally adorable children. Her husband, Randy, played the guitar and chopped wood for the barbecue. Gillian took assiduous notes while Mao whipped up a superb old-lady bean curd with Beijing noodles. A friend of the Smiths' showed up, accompanied by her eight-year-old child, whom Randy also had fathered.

Mao questioned her about it on camera with Gillian smiling placidly nearby. None of us let him in on the fact that Randy had fathered the child as a favor to the woman and her lesbian lover. But at this point, everyone had drunk plenty of beer, and the country jamboree was proceeding so swimmingly that the scene came off as nothing more than further evidence that this was indeed a house of peace and love.

In fact, Gillian had taken me aside fifteen minutes after my arrival to ask what the hell was going on in Beijing. She had heard something about riots but didn't have the full story. When I told her, Gillian—perhaps a hippie, perhaps not, but always an American—needed no further cues. She is an actress by training, and beyond her performance that night, she arranged for some divorced friends to come by the next day. During the interview, Mao eventually extracted a few tears from the ex-wife, but the couple was hardly what the average American would call dysfunctional, and they were awfully attractive. In Seattle that same day, a deranged divorcee had shot up Interstate 5 and blown a couple of people away, but my Chinese friends never even saw the headline. (I threw the paper in the trash and put coffee grounds on it for good measure.) As we packed up in the afternoon, Mao came to me, put his hand on my shoulder and told me that the shoot had been a great, great thing. He had seen the real America and he liked it.

Back in Beijing a couple of weeks later, we shared this footage in the actual show, with a discussion panel, before a live audience of both *laowai* (foreigners) and Chinese. It had all the trimmings: an American expert, Amy Holmes from the Independent Women's Forum, flown in from D.C.; respectful but heated arguments with the Chinese female talking head; Beijingers in the audience relating Oprah-like confessions of their own divorces. The charade was dropped, the expert was identified as American, the site was identified as Seattle.

When the time came for Mao to introduce his package, he sat in the audience and leaned back informally with the microphone, implicitly asking the studio cameras to follow him. He began slowly: "I went to America expecting to find a place where people didn't care about each other or about their families, but only about themselves. A place like the one we see in the Hollywood movies." I froze up as he said this, but Mao continued, seemingly speaking from the heart: "But I found something completely different on a place called Orcas Island. I found a place where people care for each other, where men and women are serious about marriage, where they want to build beautiful lives for each other and for their children. I found the real America; in these two couples, one happy, the other unhappy, so will you."

Then Gillian's serene face appeared on the screen; she was holding her child, surrounded by the lush green of the Pacific Northwest. I will never forget my mixed feelings: pride, elation, shame, most of all irony—to have come from the aftermath of the embassy bombing to what felt like a real opening in such a short time! The Chinese were trying to become journalists again. Like Mao, they wanted to tell a real story. They aimed to make good TV, and by Chinese standards they did—BTV's judges gave it the highest rating of any new international show—despite the involvement of a reactionary saboteur such as myself.

But someone at the top of BTV took careful notice. Ms. Holmes, the American expert, was "too beautiful." Someone had sabotaged the Chinese expert's make-up. Wei was suspect. With the changed political environment in China following the embassy bombing, Wei's political credit was clearly running on empty again. One morning a week after the show, she emerged from her office and, with tears of rage and humiliation running down her face, haltingly told me that the show had just been killed for its "anti-Chinese" content.

A few nights later, several burly BTV employees made their way to Fuhua Dasha and raided Wei's tape library, confiscating every tape related to *Shared Street*. BTV had made a decision to produce the show by themselves, with a minimal budget and no political content.

A year afterward, I ran into Mao and his wife near the Celine Dion shop at the China World Trade Center. Mao was now the host of *Shared Street*, but he seemed far from proud, referring to it as "that stupid show." Mao's wife said she thought this was just a temporary phenomenon, that the roadblocks to America and to independent Chinese production would be lifted after a period of time. Other producers whispered to me that the Chinese would never forget U.S.-led NATO's barbaric acts. Until then, it would be MTV for War.

Shortly after the BTV raid, Wei's office underwent a dramatic remodeling. First there was the downsizing: in a single day, the production staff was ordered to vacate her second office, forcing all the editing equipment and the tape library to be consolidated in a small space. Nonessential employees who had performed bureaucratic or cleaning functions for years were dismissed, painfully, messily, one at a time. My fellow producers, who had previously seemed like a band of brothers, now became listless sleepwalkers, as if they worked for a Chinese state-owned enterprise, showing up at odd hours to revise their résumés and moonlighting on the company's editing decks. Meanwhile, the political fengshui of the office was bolstered with huge grainy blow-ups of Wei gripping Zhu Rongji's arm—snapshots taken on one of her influence-gathering trips to the United States—like sandbags piled up against a flood. They peered out at you from the hallways as you approached her office, a testament to the desperation of Wei's political retrenchment.

Wei's personality seemed to morph as well—she suddenly became more stereotypically Beijing in manner. Bombastic talk and short-term thinking ruled. Every day seemed to bring a new plan. On one particularly desperate day it was a game show for Americans—who wants to be a millionaire?—but featuring questions only about China: What is the capital of China? How old is the PRC? The prize would be a trip to China.

Her schemes became increasingly grandiose. One afternoon, Wei invited me into her office and in her typical staccato style told me she wanted to create an entire Chinese entertainment channel on the web. At the time, our computers, loaded with counterfeit programs, were riddled with viruses and our Internet connection had slowed to a crawl. My attention shifted away from her for a moment as I looked out the window. Basking in the golden light outside of Fuhua Dasha, three massive skeletal structures dominated the horizon. I had noticed these hulks my first day in Beijing. Some developer had built the foundations, erected the steel girders, then promptly run out of money or *guanxi*. Nobody seemed to know the story. But now, exposed to Beijing's harsh and polluted climate, the structures were rusting, and some day they would be torn down. In the foreground, adjacent to Fuhua, stood a sizable military headquarters covered in brown ceramic. It was extremely well kept and carefully guarded, yet some remains of a *hutong* had been preserved from the bulldozers, and PLA troops dressed in camouflage were practicing hand-to-hand combat inside the wreckage.

Wei was carrying on about the rate of expansion of the Chinese Internet. The underlying assumption was that the Internet was a much freer place than Chinese television, and that its momentum would simply roll over the old media. In a few years, she said, it would be immaterial whether Chinese people watched old-fashioned television or watched television over the Web. Yet they would still need content, and she would provide it.

"Why not do something a bit smaller?" I asked. "I mean get a Web presence started before you approach investors with the idea of an entire channel with twenty-four-hour programming and so on."

Wei followed my gaze out the window. "Do you see that shack out there?" she asked. I peered out. The custodians of the parking lot had erected some kind of shanty out of plaster and old building materials to protect themselves from the weather (and presumably to take naps).

"Yes, I see it."

"It took work to build it. But why should I want to build that shack when I can build Fuhua Dasha?"

Fuhua was built on foreign money, though, and Wei, sounding more and more like a Chinese hustler, was heaping scorn on American businesses for being too cautious in their investments. Americans are fools, she said; all they have to do is bring gifts to government representatives like the Chinese do. Increasingly I felt as if I were listening to an adolescent telling me how to subvert daddy's stupid rules. Yet underneath the bluster, I knew, there was pain and humiliation. She had built something, smaller than Fuhua Dasha perhaps, but it had stood for a minute, even in Beijing's harsh climate. Now it was rusting, and she needed American investment, but did not relish the prospect of dealing with American accounting rules.

Yet another wrinkle in Wei's new calculus could actually be traced back a month before the bombing of the Chinese embassy in Belgrade, when her long-planned wedding to an American-Chinese man from a politically prominent family went subtly awry. Because her new father-in-law was a mentor and personal friend of Jiang Zemin, the ceremony had been designed as a sort of coronation for Wei and her New China success. She had booked the largest surviving Catholic church (state-controlled, of course) in Beijing. Surrounded by high walls, it was a lovely, albeit eclectic setting: a full-scale Western cathedral, but still carrying something indefinably Chinese in its proportions and ornamentation, like a Chinese dollhouse for expats. A wide spectrum of Chinese television stars and producers attended. Wei wore a traditional Western white wedding dress, with matching limo and cell phone, while her entire staff had been elegantly uniformed in Chinese red and gold brocade silks. Along with comedians and other entertainers, Wei had hired an "exotic" Tibetan singer for the reception at the Great Wall Sheraton ballroom. Even the Beijing sky was clear blue for the ceremony, with a brisk wind from the mountains. Yet the Chinese paparazzi, clearly intended to be lured by the extravaganza, were conspicuously absent.

As I stood in front of the church's guardian lions, basking in the sunshine with Xiaofu, a close friend and one of Wei's top producers, I wondered aloud why the press didn't show. In a low voice, she said, "I have heard today—in the early morning—many, many people come to Zhongnanhai."

I did a double-take when Xiaofu said this, because Zhongnanhai is the Chinese leadership's compound, just west of the Forbidden City. It has limited road access and tight, tight security.

"Why?" I asked, "Who are they? Students?"

"No," she replied, "not students. Perhaps they are from the country. No one knows why. Perhaps they are still there. Perhaps the photographers go to Zhongnanhai too."

The people who had congregated in front of Zhongnanhai were from Falun Gong (more commonly called Falun Dafa in mainland China). I tend to think of Falun Gong as a religion with Chinese cult characteristics. The practice was founded by Li Hongzhi, a former Chinese postal employee, who combined various Confucian and Western elements of religion and moral philosophy with qigong exercise practices to create a movement that has been said to have over a hundred million followers in the Chinese mainland alone. Yet I had only briefly seen them before—in the dead of winter, as my wife and I clambered around the frigid, wooded hills of Peking University, looking for some obscure museum. I was freezing, and in an effort to get her to pick up her irritatingly slow pace, I had been shouting like an army sergeant—*one, two, three, march!!*—when I ran into a group of fifty Chinese students and faculty, eyes closed, arms frozen above their heads in a classic Eastern meditative posture, wearing nothing but shirts, trousers and sneakers, as if they were standing in a warm living room. I stopped shouting and instantly felt a little foolish. The mysteries of the East, I concluded, and hurried on.

So the silent demonstration on Wei's wedding day, with its passive show of force, came as a shock. Over ten thousand Falun Gong followers quietly and efficiently surrounded Zhongnanhai, guided only by a few organizers with cell phones. It was the first high-profile demonstration to come out of the China box since Tiananmen in 1989. (Ostensibly it was in response to a government publication that had described Falun Gong as a religious cult).* My friend Jasper Becker, the Beijing bureau chief for the *South China Morning Post,* admitted to me that he and the other Beijing journalists were completely blindsided. So was the Chinese leadership, but according to several Western journalists with pipelines into the Party's rumor mill, the demonstration had particularly incensed (or terrified) Jiang Zemin. By the end of Wei's wedding day, a crackdown had begun.

But Falun Gong made an unconventional target. Most of the followers were impoverished old people from disparate areas of the countryside. State Security had watchfully videotaped the entire demonstration, and anyone seen with a cell phone—a

---

*Falun Gong bears some resemblance to a few Chinese religious movements of the past, such as the White Lotus Rebellion, which almost overthrew the Qing Dynasty. Yet to a Chinese peasant, left behind by much of the materialist advances of urban and coastal China, perhaps the Falun Gong spiritual practice simply fills an acute personal need. The claim that Falun Gong exercises can heal just about any ailment is also beguiling to an elderly population that has access to antibiotics but, partly as a result of China's reforms, has lost an organized health-care system, even the barefoot doctors of the Maoist period. The implicit political message may have an appeal too, but it's an ambiguous one: Li Hongzhi calls for forbearance, benevolence and, above all, telling the truth— the kinds of things that are obviously insulting to a corrupt Chinese bureaucracy.

so-called "ringleader"—could be brought in for "questioning." Yet Master Li Hongzhi was living in the boroughs of New York City. And unlike the demonstrations of 1989, where the students were a recognizable class (to use Marxist terminology) and concentrated in a relatively small area of northwest Beijing (or at Tiananmen Square itself), Falun Gong was ephemeral, spread by word of mouth, cell phone and the Internet (where one could download Li Hongzhi's entire book free of charge).

A few days later, new protests, smaller in scale but more daring, began in front of Zhongnanhai. The demonstrations were reported in the Western press, but largely blacked out in the Chinese media, which called the first demonstration a "gathering." I left the office late that afternoon, loading my bike basket with guidebooks, maps and Starbucks paraphernalia (items that would buttress my claim that I was simply a lost tourist if I was questioned by the Beijing police). I rode nonchalantly past the police barricades and turned toward the entrance to Zhongnanhai. I caught just the tail end of it all: perhaps twenty buses filled with old Chinese peasants, mainly women, were being driven off to an undisclosed location for an interrogation session, while hordes of Beijing police sat on the curbs eating box lunches that had gone cold. The area looked trashed but vaguely festive, as if it were the end of a temple fair during Chinese New Year. The police, clearly exhausted though also relieved that their job was done, were spitting bones into the street and laughing. There was no blood, no sign that the situation had spun out of control, yet I sensed that there would be more tomorrow. The Chinese leaders had learned from the mistakes of Tiananmen: before you use strong words, prepare to back them up with systematic, ruthless force.

On the afternoon of July 21, 1999, the official restraint ended. Several of Wei's employees ran into my office and said, "Ethan, they are talking about Falun Gong on television!" I hurried out to the reception area to watch what at first appeared to be a CCTV emergency broadcast. The news anchor, his eyes unnaturally wide and his voice raised several steps for emphasis, stated that Falun Gong was now illegal. Chinese citizens were forbidden to gather for exercise or to practice Falun Gong in their homes. As we watched the screen, we heard a kind of scratchy shouting from the window. Sound trucks were driving around Fuhua Dasha—and apparently all over Beijing—announcing that Falun Gong was now an illegal organization. A few of Wei's female producers began laughing nervously, burying their faces in their hands, muttering that they had not seen such a thing since the Cultural Revolution.

The CCTV anchor moved on to the next order of business: a special investigative program would expose the danger that Falun Gong posed to the Chinese nation. As the report flashed across the screen, it was clear we were watching a highly sophisticated indictment of the movement, rivaling *Inside Edition* in production values, cinematic tone and narrative structure. There was a series of storylines about "ordinary" Falun Gong practitioners' lives—how they became involved with Falun Gong, how they lost control of their lives and stopped caring for their families. And finally, the minutiae of self-immolation—how they destroyed themselves through medical neglect or, in several cases, outright suicide. The bereaved spouse would act as a kind of narrator, only to break down abruptly in bitter tears that capped off each segment. (Many older Chinese can shed tears when it is politically imperative for them to do so—another byproduct of the Cultural Revolution).

The stories were filled in with the wackier predictions of Li Hongzhi and the movement: flying saucers, Armageddon, apocalypse now. Back to the newsroom, this time with a female anchor: Falun Gong was neither moral—because they killed their followers—nor forbearing—because they did not tolerate questioning of their beliefs. Nor were they truthful—because their leader had a hidden agenda. The fact that he was based in America was deemed to be no accident, but part of a larger imperialist scheme. The female handed it back to the male news anchor and the cycle began again, word for word.

The presentation was a striking demonstration of the new sophistication of Chinese propaganda—brilliant use of selective quotation, graphic images of corpses and funerals, and the seamless splicing together of statements by Li Hongzhi and his overzealous followers to create a picture of a cult that had run amok. Yet the sound trucks outside suggested that a cruder security apparatus was being flexed again—perhaps only to keep its muscles from atrophying. In any case, the Chinese leadership had finally set the stage for a coordinated propaganda campaign, mass arrests and brutality.

I didn't know how Wei viewed Falun Gong. I only knew that she was floundering, looking for a project. A few weeks later, for personal reasons, both Wei and I flew into New York within days of each other. By chance, our mutual friend Danny Schechter of Globalvision had scored a media coup. Danny had done extensive reporting on human rights, and he had a close relationship with Gail Rachlin, a Falun Gong practitioner and the group's leading American spokesperson. Following the Chinese leadership's decision to ban Falun Gong, Danny was the only television producer in the world with access to Li Hongzhi. The Chinese government had asked for Li's extradition to China for a show trial and sentencing. Rumors of agents coming to New York could not be dismissed at the time, so Danny traveled with a minimal crew to the borough where Li Hongzhi had gone to the mattress. In his interview with Danny, Li asks the Chinese government for a dialogue and requests that his followers not be punished. The interview is short on drama, but it was the only one showing Li responding to the crisis in China—in other words, an extremely valuable document.

Arriving in New York, I went straight to Globalvision's offices at 49th and Broadway. In Danny's chaotic office, we began to hammer out the beginnings of a proposal for a documentary using interviews with Li Hongzhi as the centerpiece: funding, timing and so on. It was a given that PBS would be interested. A few days later, after Wei arrived, the three of us began to discuss the project. There was something reserved in Wei's manner. She had brought the CCTV investigative report on Falun Gong, which was of great interest to Danny and me, but she seemed to be distracted by Danny's interview with Li. She needed a copy of it to watch at home, she said. Danny firmly replied that she could only watch it in the studio.

I was concerned by Danny's approach; Wei was a proud woman, and it was my assumption that we could not shoot a real documentary that included the China side without her full involvement. When Wei and I were alone, I asked her how she felt about the Falun Gong project. She admitted that she had mixed feelings. The group was a bit alien to her, and she didn't see them as reformers because, for example, they lacked the intellectual underpinnings of the Tiananmen students. I found myself agreeing with her to some extent and hoping that her attitude would temper Danny's reflexive human rights approach with a more critical view. But she was in as long as some seed money came through, she said.

In the meantime, Danny set me up to do some preliminary shoots on Falun Gong practitioners in New York and D.C. This allowed me to get closer to some of the movement's leadership (including Rachlin, whom I interviewed in her home). While I was interviewing and shooting footage of Falun Gong adherents at their first Capitol Hill demonstration, I found myself becoming quite sympathetic. Perhaps it was the Beijing government's surveillance: middle-aged Chinese men, dressed in what mainland spies took to be "normal" American clothing, kept walking by the demonstration and attempting to blend in. Under these conditions, my interview style with the Falun Gong practitioners became increasingly friendly, to the point where they began to think of me almost as one of their own. Finally, a small group of well-dressed Falun Gong followers approached me. The demonstration was moving to the White House (where Jesse Jackson would march with them), but this small, handpicked group was going to enter the Capitol to lobby congressmen and senators. They had little experience in this area, however. I seemed like someone who might know something about Washington and politics; whom should they lobby?

"Well," I said, "have you thought about approaching Senator Ted Kennedy?"

"Why would we want to speak to him?"

"Because he's a powerful senator and he's Mr. Human Rights."

"OK, thank you, that's good. Who else?"

"Well, have you thought about talking to Senator Jesse Helms?"

"Who's he? Why would we want to see him?"

"He's chairman of Foreign Affairs and he's Mr. Religious Freedom," I replied. "He's tough on China and the Chinese leadership fears him. Just talking to him is like threatening all-out war."

They looked pleased: "Thank you very much!"

"Mind if I interview you before you go in?" I said to the apparent leader. He was a young, good-looking Chinese man, wearing a silk double-breasted suit with a crimson tie. He looked every inch the lobbyist and spoke English quite fluently. He had no objections.

The crew quickly affixed a wireless mike to his tie, and we headed off to the Capitol steps. I took some time setting up the shot, getting him exactly in position so the Capitol dome would loom over his shoulder, three-quarter angle, filling in the light and so on. "Rolling," I said. "Who are you going to talk to in there?"

He beamed at me: "I'm going to speak to Jessica Helms!"

I couldn't restrain a slight laugh. I said lightly: "I think you mean Jesse Helms; you guys don't know that much about politics, do you?"

The smile faded into a stricken look. Then he replied—slowly now, with a little shake in his voice: "No, we don't know much about politics. I don't know who I'm going to talk to in there, and if I can get anyone to listen to me at all. But I've got to try. I'm a computer programmer. I flew in from Toronto last night on my own, just to do what I can. I have no choice *because people are dying in Beijing.*"

He was not exaggerating. The news from Beijing was very bad: tens of thousands of Falun Gong followers, many of them sick and elderly, had been herded into the city stadiums. They had no shade against the mid-August sun and reportedly were being deprived of food and even water. The interrogations were becoming more brutal as the police and the Chinese leadership lost patience with this movement of martyrs.

I thanked the computer programmer profusely for the interview. He was angry at me because he felt that I made him look foolish. I tried to soothe him: "You spoke with conviction, but even more important, in Beijing they are saying that you are funded by the Americans, that you are a slick operation. But your interview—you couldn't make this stuff up. Falun Gong is poorly funded, naïve in the ways of politics. That's important; in a media world where every group jockeys for victim status, Falun Gong are true victims."

But few were listening. Congress sent off some statements. On the way back to New York, I even spoke to Senator Arlen Specter on an Amtrak train. He appeared concerned, but his mind was elsewhere.

So was Wei's. When I made it back to the Globalvision offices, it was clear that something was amiss. She had been in several times asking Danny again for the tape of the Li Hongzhi interview. Wei was barely keeping up appearances that she was interested in the Falun Gong documentary project; instead, she was interested in just getting the unedited tape and sending it to "some guys in Hong Kong." She offered several thousand dollars.

A day or so later, I cornered her. "Why do you want the Li Hongzhi tape?"

"It's just for some guys in Hong Kong."

"Why do they want it?"

"They're just interested," she said, smiling tightly and avoiding my eyes. "That's all."

I didn't press her. By now, I wanted to forget the Falun Gong project. Besides, Wei was my friend, and still my boss, at least for a day or two a week. We both knew she was in financial trouble. Wei was the only Chinese producer who had a practical chance to access Li Hongzhi's latest interview, and to get it she was trying to use friendship, a shared history of idealism with Schechter, and money. Perhaps she had no other options. She called herself an independent producer, but she still had to sell programs to "some guys in Hong Kong" (I couldn't help but suspect that this was a proxy for Chinese state-run television), or she was finished.

A week later, I flew back to Beijing. Unpacking my bags late at night in my little apartment in Ju'er Hutong, in a jet-lag haze, I discovered that along with my other papers I had somehow stuffed Falun Gong pamphlets, documentary proposal drafts and, worst of all, Master Li Hongzhi's book into my suitcase. I didn't have to think twice about what to do. These days, Chinese people exercising in the park were routinely being taken down to the station for questioning. Police had already stopped by our apartment from time to time—on complaints of noise or to make sure we had

registered with our local police department—and one never knew
for sure what one's neighbors might say or suspect of a foreigner.
My wife was still back in the States and I didn't have her Beijing
patois. If I met them at the door, the police would not hesitate to
search the apartment.

In my underwear, I carried the cheap pamphlets and notes
into the kitchen and threw them in the wok. I poured a little cooking oil over them, turned the ventilator on high, and lit the mess
on fire. I tore the book spine in half and began ripping the pages
out. Flames danced around the edges of the wok and the smell
was acrid, but I guessed that my neighbors would assume that the
foreigner was just cooking a bizarre stir-fry. It seemed to take forever. I felt dizzy—all those hopeless words, all that truth and justice and forbearance. Outside I heard someone playing an *erhu*, a
comforting, summery sound of Beijing. Eternal China, I thought.

As I sifted through the ashes with a metal spatula to make
sure there was nothing left, I reviewed my suspicions about what
Wei had done. A current interview with Li Hongzhi was invaluable to the Chinese government. They could splice it any way they
liked, make him say anything, morph him into a devil or a bleat-
ing sheep for the two-minute hate. CCTV and BTV were already
well into stage two of the propaganda campaign, television broad-
casts that would justify the deaths—by torture, exposure and neglect—of hundreds of somewhat obsessive but utterly innocent
Chinese individuals. It would end with mothers and children swal-
lowing gasoline and exploding into flames on Tiananmen Square,
photographed live by what seemed to be suspiciously prearranged
camera angles.

I thought back to Wei's tears on the street corner in New York,
when we had first met. She had identified with the lawyer in Gere's
Red Corner who was fighting within the system for a better China.
Then she had become something more akin to the television executive caught in the Chinese penal system. Now she was beginning
to resemble one of the state flunkies with a bit part. Like so many
others in Chinese professional society, Wei was boxed into her
own red corner. Her different identities flashed before my eyes:
Chinese patriot, engagement advocate, American producer, dissident. . . . All her temple guardians had served their purpose, all

were papier-mâché. Inside, I suspected, there was a paid accomplice in state terror—a collaborator, plain and simple.

And what had I become? I felt as if I had stumbled into an ugly family drama, one that I wish I had never seen, yet I had my own secrets. Sure, I didn't particularly like Falun Gong, but my distaste for investigating the story was based on something more elemental. I was afraid. Of being questioned, of being thrown out of the country, or possibly serving a few days in a Chinese jail. How could I judge Wei? Simply by avoiding the subject, I had become in some strange way complicit.

I ground the ashes of the books and pamphlets into a charred paste and left the wok sitting on the stove. As I walked away, I caught a glimpse of my reflection on my cheap little Chinese fridge. I was slouching, streaked with ashes and sweat. The elastic in my faded green Chinese army shorts was cracked and stretched, and hung loosely off my body. My eyes were hungry. It was time to become an American again.

贪 3.
Visiting Day

It's morning in the Beijing St. Regis. The sun shines directly onto an opulent banquet table set for twenty. While Chinese waiters discreetly appear with oversize fruit plates and overly glazed croissants, the guests file in: a handful of the top American business representatives in China—Boeing, Chase Manhattan, perhaps Ford—and a visiting congressional delegation.

They look a bit surly. Most business and congressional delegations tend to stay in Beijing three days on average. Their handlers have loaded their schedule with nonstop briefings, lunch meetings and "down time," which consists of whirlwind tours of the Forbidden City and the Great Wall. They're supremely jet-lagged. My guess, based on their rather clenched expressions, is that about half of them have been pacing their hotel rooms since 3:30 this morning.

They range from a young drop-dead blond female legislative assistant of a congressional Democrat from Washington State, to a gray-haired chief of staff for a Republican senator. Whatever their background, they share a common demeanor: sharp-eyed, fastidiously organized, polite but unsmiling.

Chris Murck, the director of Chase Manhattan, goes around the table shaking hands. He looks relaxed. I think he really is; almost everyone on our side is a veteran of the AmCham door-knocks, the annual D.C. lobbying trip of the American business community. So we have an all-purpose game plan. The "AmCham

China Washington D.C. Doorknock 2000 Spokesperson Training" clearly states the formula: Be "message-driven, NOT question-driven." Pay attention to the "Two C's": "Content + Control = Key to success." In plain English: take charge of the meeting.

For many American businesses in China, the impending visit of an American delegation is a critical moment, particularly if it's the CEO; but for the greater good of the expat corporate community, even political delegations have to be handled carefully. Our side has reasonably well-educated and savvy spokesmen, but it can always use a few more, and this goes a long way toward explaining how I became a senior counselor at a prominent American-run public affairs firm in Beijing.

I had burned Li Hongzhi's books in my wok on a hot August night. By October, I had made my way into the American community simply using the time-honored Chinese method of *guanxi*— meeting Americans, re-establishing relationships with the ones I'd already met, buttering them up by holding out the possibility of gigs on Chinese TV (my relationship with Wei was fading, but I still kept my finger in her production company as an adviser), maintaining a high profile, attending the right social events and clubs, and joining the correct sports teams. It didn't hurt that my wife was outgoing and universally liked, and we were told that we gave the best martini parties in town. So my sudden rise in status did not rest on any substantive achievement; it was almost too easy because business consultancy, public relations and public affairs support are among the most profitable foreign occupations in China. Companies like Burson-Marsteller, Ogilvy, Edelman and APCO are constantly hiring and expanding. Now, less than a year after being hired, I am enveloped in a warm cloak of corporate legitimacy, flanked by reps from Motorola, Prudential and Rockwell.

We know why the congressional delegation is here: they want to find out what is really going on in China, get some purchase on the issues, perhaps elicit a slip or a piece of information that their bosses can use. On the surface, the breakfast seems like just another event thrown into the schedule, but the delegation carries a lengthy checklist of concerns from Washington.

The Democrats want some sort of method to express their

displeasure over continuing Chinese human rights abuses against Tibetans, Falun Gong, the China Democracy Party and labor activists. They bring a healthy degree of concern over the ever-widening trade deficit and sweatshop labor subcontracted by American corporations operating in China, key whipping posts for their organized labor supporters. The Republicans are thinking about these issues too (their constituents are especially worried about forced abortion and about religious freedom for Chinese Christians), but their main focus is national security and they suffer occasional fits of anxiety over China's proliferation of ballistic missile technology to rogue states in the Middle East, particularly because no administration thus far (certainly not the Clintons, with their illusions about "strategic partnership") has been able to get beyond vague Chinese assurances that the transfers will stop. Some of the more hawkish Republicans would actually like to return to the now officially discredited policy of linkage—making American trade directly contingent on Chinese behavior—and so would some of the Democrats.

All of these competing imperatives will eventually boil down to the politicians casting a vote on Permanent Normal Trade Relations (PNTR) with China, the prerequisite for the Chinese ascension into the World Trade Organization. For us, the WTO regime is the next logical point in China's evolution and a vast opportunity to enter new areas of the Chinese market, such as banking, telecommunications, insurance and agriculture, on a much more level playing field. For Congress, it's the relinquishing of the annual vote on Normal Trade Relations (formerly called Most Favored Nation status, until the China lobby succeeded in changing the label).

We know that this delegation may not be the congressional leadership, the individuals who will actually make these decisions, but we aren't fools. Anything we give them can and will be used in China policy, and may be used against us. So our job is to make them feel okay about putting down the gun. Most of all, we don't want any probing investigative inquiries. In fact, we have anticipated their "Seven Deadly Questions" and have broken them into categories, such as:

- the false premise
  —*China really isn't serious about integrating with the world economy, is it?*
- the hypothetical
  —*What if China doesn't commit to enforcing WTO compliance? How can we force them to do so?*
- the absent third party
  —*Last week, Harry Hong said China continues to use prison labor for making export products. What do you think? Don't you agree?*

The breakfast proceeds. There's some probing by our side on their earlier meetings with Chinese government officials, really a way for us to showcase how well we know the principal actors. We offer up bits of gossip surrounding individual Chinese bureaucrats like little plates of dim sum. But we don't have to stress the point; we know the territory, they know we know it, and so the inquiries begin. The majority of their questions fall neatly under the Seven Deadly headings. In fact, almost all of them are intelligent variations on "the cast iron guarantee" trap: "how can you guarantee that the situation in Tibet . . . (or the military threat to Taiwan, or human rights, etc.) will improve when Permanent Normal Trade Relations has passed?"

It's a reasonable question. Other than corporate profits, what does America get in return if we let China into WTO? We know how difficult it is to get the Chinese government to cooperate simply in enforcing our most basic business concerns such as counterfeiting, let alone on an issue that the Communist Party really cares about, such as Taiwan. But we don't get into that now. Instead, we handle their questions by what's called "Flagging and Listing," using bridges to pass over to a different question entirely:

- Let's look at it from a broader perspective . . .
- There is another, more important concern and that is . . .
- You may be asking why _____ is true, but let me tell you this . . .
- That's a good point, but what is equally important is . . .
- To help everyone understand, let me give you some background information . . .

What we are trying to get them to do is focus on the *big picture*. Several on our side reminisce about the bad old days: China before economic reform, China without infrastructure, China with a separate currency for foreigners. "Look—just look at how much China has changed," one businessman on our side says, gesturing at the window behind him as a way of invoking the construction on Jianguomen Avenue and the looming China Trade Center. "I know you guys are under a tight schedule here, but it's too bad you can't get out and talk to the people, the small-business owners, the entrepreneurs—eat at a local restaurant, see the real China. . . ."

Invoking historical progress is always useful because it lowers the bar. (What could be worse than the Maoist economy during the Great Chinese Cultural Revolution?) It's also a good way to sidestep the new, and potentially catastrophic, questions about state-owned enterprise losses, the looming banking crisis and worker riots. Here, however, it's only partially successful. When one bright-eyed congressional aide begins to hammer on recent Chinese backpedaling on human rights issues, specifically the crackdown on Falun Gong and Christians (Deadly Question number 5: "The false choice—what's more important, profit or human rights?"), we nod, gravely acknowledge his concerns and then go into high bridging mode again:

- That's a good question, but even more important is . . .
- Let's not lose sight of the underlying problem . . .
- There's another challenge playing into this . . .

Following the doorknock directive to "Turn negatives into positives," we segue into the next message: American business is *the* long-term catalyst for better human rights in China. And we don't just rely on the simple-minded notion that capitalism will inevitably bring freedom. We list important areas of progress. We solemnly invoke the stated Chinese interest in rule of law, or just workable legal codes, and then suggest with a straight face that the growth of legal consciousness could be used for a regulatory end run around the Chinese leadership's totalitarian State Security apparatus. The groundwork for this entrapment is being laid through Western lawyers' exchanges with their Chinese counterparts. Why is this happening? It's an American business initiative, although we fret that we actually lag behind our European competitors in this regard.

Much more effective are the personal accounts. We talk about our own Chinese employees and their positive experiences working in an American corporate culture, trumpeting the socialization of democratic values—effectively heading off another Deadly Question: "So how many local staff do you have, what is their average wage, and how much less do you pay them than your American staff?"

These may not sound like devastating arguments, I grant you, but they have the virtue of being very hard for the congressional staffers to refute. They are only vaguely aware of the legal exchanges that we have been touting, although they sound important in an abstract way. Few of them have been to an American company office in Beijing, so it's hard to know if the Chinese employees have become agents of democracy—although the Chinese staff at the U.S. embassy seemed polite and well dressed. And, as our guy pointed out, these people are in China and they don't even have the time or the language expertise to eat at a *real* Chinese restaurant. So how are they to know?

We are moving now, starting to herd the questions toward the wide-open Chinese market, where we can really run free with the potential business opportunity for America. The doorknock tactic at this point is to "take the initiative." To make it seem natural, we use "hooking," a statement that by itself is basically meaningless, but is designed so that if you say it and then freeze as if the earth has suddenly stopped spinning, it "attracts the follow-up question you want." A hooking statement goes something like this:

- We just completed a survey about that . . .
- Passing PNTR helps us gain strategic advantage in China in four ways . . .
- We have short- and long-range plans . . .
- There are many forces at work in the China marketplace . . .

Now they ask, and we respond: about Chinese growth statistics, the exponential rate of Internet expansion, the largest mobile phone market in the world, and the opportunities for

American corporate expansion in agriculture, insurance and mobile technologies in a WTO China. At the end of our spiel, we even call for a show of hands to demonstrate our confidence in the expansion of the Chinese market over the next year and the next decade. Everyone's hands go way, way up.

This is not mere rhetorical posturing. The performance on our side is a remarkably effective statement of the business position, devastating in its insistence that Chinese convergence with America is a historic inevitability. Anyway, the proof is in the pudding, isn't it?

The congressional delegation, rising from the table, look stymied, and uncertain as to what they can do about it. Anyway, they are already being rushed to their next station of the cross, probably some event involving Chinese schoolchildren singing about environmentalism.

We shake hands all around and exchange cards. I head for the men's room. At the sink I run into one of the staffers, a slightly grouchy young man who works for a China-hawk congressman. We speak for a moment about his trip and, like two Bolsheviks in the washroom revealing their secret party membership to each other through a few code words, we subtly establish that neither of us fully buys into the China's-changing-for-the-better thesis. "What I want to know," he says, his voice registering a certain level of frustration at the Potemkin village tour, "is whether *this* is true." He pulls a *New York Times* article out of his pocket, something about Silicon Valley's spirit being alive and well in Beijing.

I study the article for a moment. Just a glance at the breathless, purple quality of the prose, which describes the pace of Chinese Internet innovation as surpassing the so-like-yesterday United States, tells me that another *Times* reporter has gone native. What my new washroom comrade is really asking is: If the Internet can save China, and you guys are building it, then can I let you guys off the hook? I glance under the stalls to see if there are any Johnston & Murphys belonging to someone from my side. "Not really," I admit. I'm about to launch into an analysis of the recent Internet crackdown in China, but I can tell he's impatient, so I suggest that he meet me for dinner. But the embassy has a tight schedule for the evening and he can't leave the group, so that's it for the transgressive portion of the tour. We shake hands and return to our places. I'm actually slightly relieved that he hasn't taken me up on my offer.

The system works. My fellow traveler is neutralized because ultimately a conversation in the washroom is not worth mentioning to his boss. As for the rest of the delegation, as canny and cynical as they are, they will take back at least a trace impression of a China that is changing and an American business community that is quietly making progress in transforming Chinese society through their employees, rule-of-law exchanges, and the Internet.

Staying on message with elected officials was even easier than dealing with their employees. Staffers are like teachers' assistants who take pleasure in grading exams harshly, and they tend to hit the briefing books hard before they come to China. Elected officials, on the other hand, concentrate on the interests at stake and improvise to get what they need.

In June 2002, Governor Jesse Ventura led 105 Minnesota businessmen to Beijing, the largest business delegation that the U.S. embassy had ever seen. I didn't get a chance to brief the governor or his entourage, but judging from the press, Ventura's interest in China trade didn't come out of the blue; Minnesota had a substantial amount of missionary activity in China at one time, and both Minnesota heavyweights, Hormel and 3M, had made efforts to set up a significant market presence in China during the nineties. But it seemed that something about China appealed directly to Ventura's expansive nature—his belief in the future, his belief in volume: "China has 20 percent of the world's population. In business, you don't want to exclude a fifth of the marketplace," the governor said. His aides took to calling this the mother of all trade missions.

Ventura had been the only governor to appear publicly before Congress and testify in favor of China's entrance to the WTO. So, shortly after his delegation's arrival in Beijing, he was rewarded with a high-profile banquet at the Great Hall of the People sponsored by the state-run China Council for the Promotion of International Trade. Yet in his testimony back in 2000, Ventura admitted to Congress that he didn't actually know very much about China. He still didn't when he made the trip two years later. Hanging out at Beijing's Grand Hyatt, he expressed his surprise at the city's modernity. "I expected to see them running around in Mao suits, everybody looking the same," he said. Instead, he found, "Everyone pretty much dresses as we do."

These observations, plus the excitement of facilitating deals for his business partners, and a few business community briefings like the one I've described (Ventura participated in at least three AmCham events in almost as many days) had a euphoric effect. "China coming into the WTO will be the biggest thing this century," he declared. In case anyone missed the point, in his keynote address for AmCham Beijing, Ventura thundered, "Opportunity isn't just knocking here in China, it's pounding. It's practically beating down the door. We'd be fools not to answer." Unconsciously echoing Lincoln Steffens' infamous pronouncement about the Soviet Union some eighty years earlier, Ventura declared: "I know when I've come face to face with the future." It followed that businessmen, and Americans in general, should not advise China on what to do commercially. We should "influence them as a friend, otherwise they won't listen." After all, Ventura said, "I think the Chinese are much more up on politics and policy than Americans." How to influence them softly? Ventura's response leapt right out of our playbooks: Chinese employees in foreign companies would be among the catalysts of change.

It's easy to dismiss Ventura as a naïf, but his lack of fight in Beijing and his lavish praise of his host country were awfully close to the norm. Others, such as a former congressman (whom I won't identify out of respect for our friendship) didn't even need cue cards. Freshly arrived in Beijing on a business trip, he gave a short speech at a private company dinner contemptuously referring to Falun Gong devotees "as a bunch of nuts"—precisely the Chinese Communist Party line of the day. (The death count of Falun Gong devotees in mental hospitals and rehabilitation camps was already into the hundreds.)

This kind of rhetoric was an ongoing tool of legitimacy for the Chinese government. You would see it every day in the papers. For example, the *People's Daily* would run a blaring headline stating that "U.S. Congress Members Call for Enhanced Understanding of China," with Rep. Simon Orvitz gushing that "China is growing by leaps and bounds and I have never seen an economy like China." When the World Wildlife Fund representatives visited China (by any measure, an environmental disaster zone for humans, let alone animals), the front page of the *China Daily*, Beijing's state-run English-language newspaper, featured the reps sitting in front of a pro–Beijing Olympics banner quite literally hugging pandas.*

Even in bad times, the messages seemed to stay positive; as the Severe Acute Respiratory Syndrome, or SARS crisis, reached its height, Bill Frist, the U.S. Senate majority leader, was heading an eight-member congressional delegation and fact-finding mission to South Korea, Japan, Taiwan and Beijing. Frist came at a point in the trajectory of the epidemic where no visiting American politician, especially one with medical training, could publicly duck the issue anymore. The Chinese leadership's cover-up of SARS was now over five months old and it had been a sloppy ride, even by Chinese standards: health officials in Guangzhou and Beijing military hospitals, SARS epicenters, had refused World Health Organization (WHO) requests to inspect the hospital wards (and lied

---

*There were exceptional politicians who did not succumb to Chinese pressure (and therefore didn't make the Chinese papers). For example, I spent several days escorting Rep. Tom Lantos around Beijing. Although representing a typically liberal Democrat district in southwest San Francisco, Lantos, born in Hungary and an anti-Nazi fighter in his teens, personifies a certain hard-edged integrity. Let loose in Beijing, however, he wasn't particularly dignified, just irrepressible. When my wife toured him through the Forbidden City, he insisted on dressing up in full Chinese imperial garb, and when I took him to the Great Wall of China, he engaged in an elaborate mock swordfight with ersatz Mongols. But while he was out to have a good time as much as the next congressman, when we talked about modern China as we drove through the countryside, it became obvious that he had little respect for the Chinese government and their friends. Nor was he interested in U.S. embassy arrangements. He had told embassy personnel to set up one high-level meeting with Chinese officials (where he harshly critiqued Chinese human rights abuses), but he largely waved off my attempts to get him to meet with top members of the American business community: "I don't need those people." With Lantos, the American expat system failed to get traction: Lantos fought long and hard against the passage of PNTR, and among Democratic congressmen he remains one of the most uncompromising critics of engagement with China.

about existing SARS cases); an expat businessman about to die on Chinese soil was indecorously rushed, dead on arrival, to a Hong Kong hospital; Beijing SARS patients were taken out of wards, loaded into vans and dropped off in quasi-abandoned hotels as if the WHO teams were UN weapons inspectors and the sick and dying were biological warheads. Such were the panicky Chinese government schemes to spin SARS as controllable and as simply an internal Chinese affair.

As Frist arrived, Hu Jintao, the new president of the PRC's Central Committee, made what several pundits called an amazing turnaround, acknowledging over three hundred patients to the WHO, promising to fight the SARS contagion with every available method, and firing both the minister of health and the mayor of Beijing. Up until that point, Frist had consistently charged that the Chinese leadership was ignoring the SARS threat and that the inadequate surveillance was part of a larger cover-up. Nonetheless, while he was in Beijing, Frist suddenly did an amazing turnaround himself, saying, "I give the president, President Hu, tremendous compliments—because he took bold action over the last forty-eight hours while we were here in China to boldly and courageously address this virus."

If Hu was "bold and courageous," what other options did the Chinese leadership have? They had tried to avoid a replay of what had already happened in Hong Kong: admitting the full extent of the disease's spread meant quarantine, restriction, loss of productivity, and investment flight. But it was too late. Rumors were sweeping Beijing and the Chinese Internet faster than the censors could wipe them out. Panic shopping, not only of herbal medicines but also of food staples, had already disrupted the distribution system. Productivity and consumer confidence were sinking. After growing at 9.9 percent for the first quarter, the Chinese GDP would show some retrenchment, according to Merrill Lynch estimates. Cell phone sales were down 40 percent in Guangzhou, and national tourism, normally about 6 percent of the GDP, had simply come to a halt. Expat government workers, NGO employees and Western investors were leaving en masse. (Motorola would eventually abandon its 18-story headquarters in Beijing for weeks.) The Women's World Cup soccer tournament and the women's ice

hockey tournament were pulled from China. A WHO official explicitly threatened Chinese officials with the prospect of an American boycott of the scheduled Beijing Olympics in 2008 unless they
changed the way they were handling SARS fundamentally and
quickly. Even the Chinese leadership's hidden estimates revealed
that SARS, unchecked, might well spread exponentially. As a retired
Chinese official told John Pomfret of the *Washington Post,* "Our
interaction with the outside world used to be based on one principle: fool the foreigners. But that doesn't work anymore. By fooling the foreigners, we just end up fooling ourselves."

■

Why do otherwise sensible politicians seem to lose their perspective when they arrive in Beijing? A former U.S. embassy officer
explained to me that standard embassy procedure for congressional delegations (or Codels, as they call them) is to keep most
senators and representatives who visit China close to the embassy,
starting with expedited full VIP treatment at Beijing's international
airport. Following the usual country briefing, a wrap-up of the current intelligence on China's economic and political situation, the
embassy then shifts into tour-guide mode, arranging cars for sight-
seeing, using the embassy's extensive resources, experience and
guanxi to make sure that the trip went perfectly:

> It was just, you know, congressmen off on a vacation. I believe that
> they would have a few senior meetings. It was just a junket—they
> were clearly on a personal visit for personal gain. There's a special
> detachment from the U.S. Army that do this shit. They fly around
> with the congressmen and take care of them. They are personal ser-
> vants at the taxpayer's expense. The military personnel are used to
> pour peanuts in a bowl.

Occasionally someone like Robert Rubin, secretary of the
treasury in the Clinton administration, could be "a pain in the
ass," recalled the former embassy officer. Rubin wanted Perrier
with ice and fresh limes available at all times, even when visiting
remote Guilin, in southwest China. Over time my confidant had
become disenchanted with the whole process; it seemed as if the
Codels were not engaged in official business but rather in picking

up business contacts or just indulging themselves as they toured beaten-path China at a relaxed tempo and collected counterfeit DVDs, pearls and other tchotchkes along the way. (I myself helped a former congressman acquire a substantial counterfeit DVD collection; it was implicitly part of my job.)

Codels were a critical element of the embassy's strategy. This was particularly because, as the former embassy officer complained, "We were always accused by D.C. of being sympathizers because ... we were always saying, well, the real situation is this: the Chinese really can't do this, the Chinese really can't agree to this provision, or this event. And D.C. would be like: you're just sympathizers, you're just too Chinese." So if the Codels were handled correctly, the embassy could win political support in Washington, not only on funding issues for staff, grounds and the like, but also by getting approval for military exchanges, fast-track visas for Chinese Codel equivalents who wanted similar junkets in the United States, and issues of critical importance to the Chinese leadership such as China's entry into WTO, technology transfer, and slowing weapons sales to Taiwan—items that enhanced the embassy's political currency with their Chinese counterparts.

The embassy's objectives and the business community's objectives tended to align nicely, but when a firm could not use the embassy's resources, it often turned to public affairs companies such as the one I worked for. We were in China to do the usual things—public relations campaigns, image-branding and industry analysis—but there were two particularly pressing requirements for American companies operating in the Chinese market.

The first was Chinese government relations. In the absence of real laws and in the presence of vast corruption, particularly in the Chinese civil service, American business simply did not have the option to ignore government in China. In fact, for any company to get licensed—simply to get in the game—government contacts had to be cultivated not just at the top, but at several lower levels of the hierarchy simultaneously, often including regional officials. This was an area where a well-run public affairs firm, which had attracted well-connected and reasonably high-ranking former Chinese government officials to its staff, could (in the popular jargon of our field) add value. Some companies, such

as Motorola, Cisco and Kodak, possessed robust government relations departments filled with well-connected in-house officials,
but they were the exceptions. Most corporations needed our connections to the Chinese bureaucracy and our strategic analysis.
We earned our retainers fairly.

Although it wasn't really in any of our brochures, the second requirement was home-office relations. When the CEO—or
even worse, the CFO—announced an imminent trip to Beijing,
many a chief representative would go into a controlled panic. To
avert the questions about profitability, the first line of defense was
massive verbiage. Thus, we could help generate extensive briefing
papers and PowerPoint presentations: well constructed, guardedly
optimistic, with vague projections of long-term market share opportunities, while still leaving wiggle room by acknowledging uncer-
tainties and stumbling blocks contingent on government relations.
The second line of defense was to hire mercenaries—that would
be us as well. Essentially, in internal company meetings we would
appear almost as if we were an independent auditor that, having
already gone through a process of rigorous examination, now
heartily approved of the chief representative's market plan. The
third line of defense was, above all, to keep the CEO or the CFO
occupied. Us again: we knew how to fill the schedule, not just
with entertainment, but also by setting up stagy meetings and
banquets with Chinese counterparts—events that would have a
constructive feel to them even if none of the details were actually
finalized (and in China, of course, the details can take a lifetime).

The Codels and the CEOs were kept in a constant shuttle
between hotels, banquet restaurants and embassy functions. Yet
almost universally the visitors returned to the States energized,
and in some cases with profoundly transformed opinions on China.
There *is* a new China; they had seen it.

How could we do this? Because beyond all the PR tricks and
luxury suites, we still preserved something of the charisma of the
pioneer; we had the fire of belief in our eyes, a belief made more
credible by the eternally American act of fearlessly pitching one's
tent on the farthest shore. And if you were to ask me why I went
along with this, even if I had my doubts about the thesis that
China was headed for political convergence with the United States,

my first reply would have been that I felt a sense of professional pride about simply doing my job for the American corporate community and doing it well. If that meant our interaction with the outside world was based on one main principle, fooling the foreigner—the pocket-protector congressional staffer or the vainglorious CEO—then yes, I wanted to fool them too. Inside the tent, there was warmth and friendship, oversize fruit plates and easy status. Like a stray dog, I had hung around until they let me in. Now I didn't want to be thrown out.

Inside, we could relax and be ourselves. Jimbo, a rather brilliant and physically imposing guy who headed up the rapidly expanding Beijing office of an American company, was a close friend of mine. One night, while we sat around his apartment with a couple of drinks, he dropped into a low, confessional voice and related a story to me about his CEO in Beijing on a quick business trip.

It had been going well and the CEO was pleased; Jimbo had aggressively pursued new business and the profitability of the China operation was beginning to rise. Most of the major business meetings were finished and there was an hour or two with nothing on the schedule, so Jimbo figured he would take the CEO on a quick spin around the Silk Market—several blocks of crowded and noisy outdoor stalls located in the embassy district where lower-class Chinese entrepreneurs aggressively try to sell foreigners counterfeit clothes and other goods. As they were strolling through, grooving on the Chineseness of it all, a little shoeshine boy approached Jimbo and, in an aggressive attempt to induce him to get his shoes shined, squirted a dab of polish on his shoe (a common and annoying ploy that the Chinese shoeshine boys tried on just about any white businessman). Jimbo had just coughed up well over $200 for the shoes on his annual trip to Washington. They were lustrously black, barely broken in; now one of them had the cheapest shoe polish in China clinging to the surface, like some sort of bloodsucking leech, Jimbo thought. Jimbo's face darkened as he looked down at the urchin smiling up idiotically at him. "Clean that off," he barked in perfect Beijing patois. The Chinese boy shook his head and pointed to a ratty chair, which the rep could presumably sit on while the boy went to work. "I said clean that off," louder this time. The boy shook his head and motioned again to the chair. Jimbo worked fast now: reaching down and grabbing the boy under the shoulders, he hoisted him into the air so that the boy's head faced him. Looking into the boy's eyes and balancing on one leg, Jimbo raised the shoe that had the dab of polish on it and wiped it back and forth, making sure to smear it equally on both of the boy's trouser legs. Then he dropped the shoeshine boy like a used Kleenex and strolled on. The CEO was clearly shocked by the incident, not acknowledging Jimbo's presence or saying a single word for a full twenty minutes.

After he told me this, Jimbo's eyes were searching for my reaction. I tried to look serious, but a smile kept breaking through, and I had to admit that I found the story amusing in a Dickensian way. It was obvious to both of us that Jimbo, in his tour-guide role, should have laughed off the shoe polish with a quick comment to the CEO—something to the effect that the Chinese were entrepreneurs from the moment they were born, especially now that we Americans had liberated them to do business again. Instead, Jimbo had morphed into the expat version of Mr. Hyde, the ugliest of Americans, a swaggering imperialist. The American CEO, who took pride in having a global operation run by people who were both *smart* and *nice,* must have been utterly at a loss as to what had just happened—a thought that brought endless, hysterical peals of laughter from me and Jimbo.

Why did we laugh? We knew far better than anyone in Washington that Chinese income differentials had reached a crisis point and that the countryside and the decrepit state-owned factories were creating a hundred million nasty little shoeshine boys. We knew what the real Chinese bureaucracy was like, the duplicity, the venal corruption, the pigheaded pride. We knew we were bending the American corporate rules and making questionable compromises for the privilege of having products stolen, copied, sold in the Silk Market and employed in the construction of the Chinese state. We knew that building the New China was a big gamble, that there might be hell to pay one day, and that we were culpable in some fashion. And we knew we had to keep up appearances on visiting day or the tent would collapse. For days and weeks at a time, we could live with the dizzying doublethink; normalcy and routine meant that doubts could be explained away, humored, liquored up or just ignored. But then, just when you were getting comfortable, something the Chinese leadership deemed wicked would come along—old people doing deep breathing exercises in the park, a democratic election in Taiwan, an American reconnaissance plane, the World Health Organization responding to a contagious respiratory illness—and our doubts would come back in fierce, violent waves, wearing us down, causing moral erosion. As individuals, we built seawalls of strikingly different construction. Some clung to the rock of the Chinese state; others relied on keeping an ironic, academic distance from the shore; some threatened children in the market; others adopted them; but the pressure remained. And it eased only slightly when the damn CEO was on an airplane home.

4.
El Dorado

It's easy to make friends in China. I met Ed on a cold winter's day in northwest Beijing.

It was January 1999 and my wife and I had been in town for only a couple of weeks, staying in other expats' apartments. Short on cash, my wife contacted an agent who specialized in gray-market Chinese housing for foreigners (still technically illegal at the time). A few days later, the agent called and said she had something inexpensive, reasonably central, close to the metro. And so, on a Saturday morning, we emerged from a metro entrance into the freezing wind and a classic Beijing transitory neighborhood— a crossroads defined by a series of post-Mao little shops and slightly upscale dumpling houses, nothing more than a couple of stories high, the neglect suggesting that all of it was slated for imminent destruction. The people, mainly working-class, were streaming by in bundled coats padded with thick cotton, stamping their feet on the ground to keep warm. We were expecting the female agent that my wife had spoken to, presumably a no-nonsense old crow. Instead, like a vision from another world, a middle-aged Chinese man appeared, dressed in the uniform of the Chinese nouveau riche: designer leather jacket, cashmere V-neck, the works. Urbane, speaking perfect English, he introduced himself as Ed and explained that he was actually from Vancouver. He was just showing the apartment as a favor to a friend. As we walked into a desolate construction area just outside the crossroads, he fell into step with me and casually asked what I was doing in China. I explained that

I was putting together funding for a documentary on American small businessmen trying to make it in China. He seemed interested, and we exchanged cards: he had something to do with a trade or development corporation that I had never heard of.

The apartment was located in a concrete block, and the furniture was covered with moldy red velour—something that a Chinese owner, having watched some American television shows from the eighties, might imagine would have foreigner appeal. I wondered about our privacy. A Swiss friend, an IT entrepreneur, had rented similar digs when he first came to China. Peering into his dimly lit kitchen airshaft one morning, he could see a microphone, the type used in Chinese press conferences, hanging in the gloom. My wife and I politely rejected the apartment and after a few more pleasantries with Ed, we hastened back to the metro.

A week later, Ed called. "I've been thinking about your documentary," he said. "Lunch at the Great Wall Sheraton?" I agreed, but Ed's conception of lunch turned out to be expensive: shark's fin soup and Chinese beauties playing the *pipa* next to an artificially babbling brook—an elaborate facsimile of South China on a summer day nestled within a ground zero complex of expat Beijing. At first, the conversation lagged. Ed looked sweaty, curiously tense, and I found myself trying to fight off a clammy feeling as well. I asked him about his background. He mumbled something about teaching business. Also something about Cuba for a couple of years as a representative of the Canadian government. Then he began to pepper me with questions: What backing did I have? Whom did I know in China? What was my view of the Chinese economy and political system? On instinct, I tried to convey a sort of enthusiastic neutrality, but Ed's pleasant though firm interest seemed boundless.

I didn't really like Ed, but he seemed to like me. A few weeks later he was complaining that I was difficult to reach. Where had I gone? Why? When I suggested that we meet at my favorite Sichuan hole-in-the-wall restaurant, he politely steered me back toward the Sheraton instead—pointing out that they did a very nice Western buffet. Something in his tone, the way he would subtly pause and wait for my invitation, implied that I was expected to pay from now on in what was to become a monthly event.

A pattern emerged. Ed would begin his free lunch by remarking brightly on the opportunities of the booming Chinese economy: "Well," he would say, "with Permanent Normal Trade Relations and WTO coming in, Americans are going to come to play! They cannot resist such an exciting market, yes?" Irritated and bored, I would throw out contrary economic figures and refer to the problems of counterfeiting and market restrictions. I even cited the surprisingly slow growth in the Chinese demand for energy, a figure suggesting that the Chinese GDP growth of 7 percent was just a case of the books being cooked. Ed would sadly shake his head. I would quickly reassure him that my intentions were, of course, to promote foreign investment in China—as long as it was sound and realistic.

The ostensible reason for these conversations was Ed's stated desire to help out with the documentary, yet the talk never turned specific. As the months wore on, I also explained to Ed that I had bigger fish to fry, and a prominent public affairs agency was hiring me to do investment work with top American corporations. So it came as a bit of a surprise when, after eight months of overopulent lunches, he wrote me an e-mail saying he had a potential investor for the documentary in Shanghai (unnamed, of course), and could I bring the proposal along to the Sheraton buffet?

It turned out to be our final lunch. Putting down his kiwi cream tart, Ed thumbed through my PowerPoint presentation for a moment or two and then flashed me a look that was simultaneously severe and beseeching. He was choosing his words carefully now: This proposal is not enough. The Shanghai investor needs me to write a signed letter explaining *exactly what I am doing in China*—how my documentary will help stimulate foreign investment, how my work is *good for China*.

Some nameless sense of dread told me to comply quickly. Back at the office, I wrote a letter on my self-made China Business Project stationery, a saccharine paean to U.S.-Chinese business understanding, and sent it off.

Ed never called again. I bumped into him a year later in front of the Kempinski Hotel, a mile from where we had first met, still wearing the buttery soft leather jacket. By now I guessed that Ed had done me a favor; he had used the letter to close my State Security file.

I called out his name. But Ed simply stared right through me, as if to say: Forget it, Gutmann, *it's Chinatown.*

■

There are a few Americans in every generation who want to look for a new El Dorado. It is not all rugged individualism and high adventure, however; there is an element of pack thinking involved in choosing a specific locale as a land of dreams. There was Hemingway's Paris, where the reward wasn't money but escape from dull, practical America to a bohemian utopia. In the sixties, the reward was spiritual enlightenment, so the location had to wear rags: India and Katmandu. For aspiring business gurus, Tokyo had a brief surge in the early eighties. By the nineties, retread bohemians came up with the Prague mini-break. But globalization had already done its ugly work; even bare-ass-cheap Eastern Europe was too easy, close and culturally familiar.

A real El Dorado needs a higher purpose, a power resident in the mysterious synergy between business opportunities, culture and struggle. The location should be far away and have linguistic and cultural barriers to discourage easy entry. There should be rewards available—financial, certainly, but also of the spirit—and these rewards should be attainable only after tests of character and endurance have been passed. Given all these strictures, it is no accident that the El Dorado of my generation was Beijing.

It didn't happen all at once. Even at the beginning of the People's Republic, there were Americans around, most notably Communist Party members such as Sidney Shapiro and Sidney Rittenberg, and friends of the Chinese leadership such as Edgar Snow. Their love for revolutionary China made them amenable to being used as propaganda mouthpieces by the Chinese Communist Party. Through a system of rewards, perks and unparalleled access to the leadership, they were also used as live exhibits to remind other expatriates—mainly academic and scientific types—that China would remember and reward its friends (or punish them: Rittenberg would spend sixteen years in a Chinese prison). China's revolutionary insularity and the intra-Party warfare of the Cultural Revolution discouraged a more comprehensive use of foreigners to serve Chinese interests until the late seventies, when Deng Xiaoping changed the status of individuals such as Shapiro from the exalted position of "international friends" to the disparaging position of "leftists"—essentially meaning that they had not followed the new party line closely enough. Being a friend of China now meant bringing in *money* (or at least technology or political credit). So there was a shift from rewarding foreigners based on their ideological loyalty to the Chinese Communist Party, to actively courting any foreigner who had business, government or military clout. The policy change, combined with the removal of many restrictions on travel to the People's Republic, encouraged a relatively large pool of Americans to rediscover China.*

A trickle became a flood during the eighties, as the first economic reforms and a generalized opening to the West took place. Figures who would play a prominent role in the development of China began to hang around Beijing (for example, Clark Randt, first secretary and commercial attaché at the U.S. embassy in the early eighties, now the U.S. ambassador to China). The mini Golden Age ended when the foreigners in China during that period— mainly dedicated China scholars, nongovernmental organization (NGO) staff, English teachers and a smattering of American entrepreneurs—chose to leave or were sent packing in the aftermath of the Tiananmen massacre.

The Chinese government blamed the Tiananmen movement in large part on foreign influences, so the Westerners who stayed were expected to exhibit a degree of ideological acquiescence or at

---

*Even in the eighties, many of the Americans attracted to China, particularly those from nonprofits and universities, were still driven by vestigial leftist ideals—not exactly what China was looking for. The American Left's idealization of China in the sixties and seventies is confirmed for me not only by the literature of the period, stressing the genius of acupuncture and the barefoot doctor, but also by my earliest China-related memory: While I was swatting flies in my home in Vermont, my aunt, an urban planning professor at M.I.T. and a leftist, was smiling and explaining to my mother that China had recently started a campaign to destroy pests, particularly flies, and apparently China was now fly-less. It was only much later that I was able to place my aunt's optimistic remarks in the context of the "eradicate the four pests" campaign that Mao signed off on during the Great Leap Forward—an attack not only on flies, but on human enemies of the state as well.

least a pretense of optimism about the Chinese future. The long-term goal—attracting foreigners who could make China powerful—would return, but so would the policy that foreigners would also have to prove that they were friends of China before they could reap the full rewards of friendship. Peter Batey, a former personal secretary to British prime minister Edward Heath and one of the wisest and most likable long-term expatriates in China today, sensed this and chose to apply for a Chinese business license a few days after the Tiananmen massacre. (The shell-shocked Chinese bureaucrats initially thought he was joking, but China remembers its friends; today Batey is the chairman of the European Union Chamber of Commerce and heads up APCO Asia, a top public affairs firm.)

By publicly confirming his confidence in China's long-term stability and growth, Batey was simply beating the rush. The potential of the Chinese market would not be apparent to most foreigners until 1992, following Deng Xiaoping's vaunted Southern Tour, when the political roadblocks to Western business investment were cleared. Gradually, in the early to mid-nineties, all of the elements of El Dorado fell into place: the possibility of huge money and wild-wild-East opportunities were mixing with the faded Marxist culture that the original China hands had brought with them, creating a hybrid ideology of born-again capitalism that cast aspersions on capitalism's Western companions (individualism, democracy and free speech) as unnecessary baggage for the New China.

The liberation from Marxism also meant the liberation of China as an aesthetic object, opening another avenue for foreigners to express their friendship. Even in the nineties, there was still true exoticism to be rediscovered: all that patina and castaway beauty of an older world, hidden and ravaged under Mao. It was unkempt, but still there, little pockets of Beijing glowing with Chinese cultural power, waiting to be rediscovered by art historians, NGO executives and Fortune 500 corporate philanthropy. "Five thousand years of history" wasn't just a phrase anymore, but an eternal flame burning bright now that the state was using Chinese heritage—Han heritage, the dominant ethnic group of China—for its own ends. American expats could feel the radiant warmth, and even acted as self-appointed arbiters of Chinese culture. There was a satirical art scene (mainly attacking American cultural materialism), a young generation who in many ways outdid their Western counterparts not only in the thinness of their hips, but also in irony and cynicism. For the first time, there was a bona-fide sexual revolution—made all the more sexy/illicit because Westerners were still somewhat forbidden fruit. As Chinese antiquity clashed in beautiful discord with jackhammers, cranes and other elements in the construction of a superpower, Chinese society appeared simultaneously more liberated and more confident in its newly invented Han-couture—particularly in the eyes of Western reporters, cultural historians and collectors.

The final wave of "cheap and cheerful foreigners" (as an old-time expat from the eighties called them) were flooding into a far more comfortable and urbane Beijing, fueled not just by traditional Chinese pork fat but by coffee beans, Marlboros, rudimentary mixed drinks and truckloads of sugar. Yet a few of the challenges that made it a quest for El Dorado were still there too: a horrendously large state apparatus, a carnivorous form of capitalism run without rules and without trust, a pigheaded manipulative form of negotiation that pervaded every transaction from trying to establish multimillion-dollar distribution systems for imported fruit to trying to establish the price of a single banana from a street vendor. Yet wasn't that the point? Now you could buy a banana in the middle of the Beijing winter, not just preserved cabbage. To complain, to criticize the New China—too much, anyway—indicated that you didn't really get it, that you weren't really a pioneer from the days when men were men and cabbage was cabbage.*

The new foreigners quickly grasped the idea that success in China meant government approval. This in turn meant you had

---

*Back in the eighties, it was the home office that was enthusiastically pushing its reps in Beijing to move ahead, while the reps, operating without basic creature comforts, professional working conditions, or legal recourse against Chinese bureaucratic corruption, urged caution and low expectations. But in the nineties, the situation was reversed. As China investment grew, it also became apparent that profits were difficult to achieve. Meanwhile, expat businessmen liked to remind us that China had changed—at least in terms of comfort and working conditions. Eighties-style conditions remained in distant western provinces, but shortly after my arrival, the State Department officially upgraded Beijing from its "hardship post" status (to the consternation

to be perceived as a friend of China. The Chinese leadership had established at least three ways that you could demonstrate your good will. The first way of friendship was pioneered by Shapiro and Rittenberg: follow the Communist Party line and work for the Party's objectives at any given time. Yet it wasn't as easy as just mouthing slogans anymore because over fifty years, the new Chinese leadership, while still relatively novice in the public relations game, had become quite adept at judging whether a spokesman had credibility in the West.

The second way of friendship was the way of all business in Asia: bring a gift (investment, political favors or technology). If Peter Batey could bring in investment and was willing to express confidence in the Chinese state at an hour when others were pulling out, he would be given access to the ministers he needed to run his public affairs shop for years to come.

The third way was the way of the academic and even the journalist: simple flattery, the praise and support of Chinese culture. Artfully, this latter approach could look like a sincere personal quest for the authentic China. Sometimes it actually was.

Every successful American expat used one or often two of these approaches. In my case, I had gone from helping to create state propaganda for Beijing TV (the way of Shapiro and Rittenberg) to bringing gifts by encouraging investment through my public affairs firm (the way of Batey). In addition, just by my choice of living arrangements, deep within the Beijing alleyways, I signaled that I admired traditional culture, that I was on a search for Chinese authenticity—a fact that never failed to impress my Chinese colleagues.

---

of many diplomatic employees). The State Department was right. My wife brought a suitcase full of tampons to China on the mistaken impression that her favorite brand was unavailable. I brought a case of contact lens cleaner only to find it in drugstores for a fraction of the U.S. price, with a free lens case conveniently attached. Trivial examples, but by the nineties it was possible for even a midlevel expat businessman to construct a Beijing life far more luxurious than in the U.S., with maids, drivers, ample and affordable child care, sophisticated social networks, high-status positions in AmCham, country club memberships, golf, outstanding dining, and the option of inexpensive and discreet sexual liaisons for those who wanted them. So while home offices developed boardroom fatigue with China, expat business reps were suddenly touting the importance of showing "staying power" in China.

It might be asked if all this perception control was really necessary. Did anyone really care whether I was a friend of China? Every expat has a different experience—although I believe that all of us had both positive and negative incentives to be friends of China. I won't try to speak for others' motivations, but I can relate my own gradual discovery of the facts. On one side, there was Ed—and on the other, certainly there were potential rewards to being a friend of China: status, financial gain, even a romantic lifestyle. These were all personified by an expat named Laurence Brahm, whom I met within a few months of my arrival in Beijing.

Michael Furst, the director of the American Chamber of Commerce in Beijing, told me about Brahm soon after I arrived in China. He was an American lawyer who had been in and out of China since the eighties, and a key player in Beijing society. Perhaps he would be interested in my documentary.

So on another frigid winter's day I set out for Brahm's office and home in Dongsi, located on a narrow east-west *hutong* near the center of Beijing. The sun shining through the Plexiglas of the taxi and the rocking of the worn springs conspired to put me into an almost drugged sort of sleep. Judging by the fare, the driver had taken a circuitous route around the entire city before I woke at the red wooden gates of Laurence's compound. I was now an hour late, cold, disoriented, and feeling reticent about ringing the bell. The decision was made for me by the sudden furious barking of a diminutive red-eyed Pekinese with attitude. (Like so many dogs in Beijing, Laurence's pooch suffered from conjunctivitis, an effect of the city's ever-present industrial haze). An assistant led me across the expansive courtyard toward Laurence's office. Peering through the miniature trees, I made out a huge home decorated with an almost stifling collection of revolutionary Communist art, figurines and imperial antiques, every detail consciously *über*-Chinese.

All this Eternal China stuff was impressive to my greenhorn eyes. There were few courtyard homes left in Beijing in 1999, most having been requisitioned during China's revolutionary period and turned into multiple dwellings. The neighborhoods they resided in were being leveled one by one as bulldozers stormed throughout the city. So to inhabit a mini-palace like Brahm's, exquisitely restored, you needed not only money but fluency— not only with the language but with the local Chinese bureaucracy.

Laurence was tall and well groomed, with the kind of sleek Caucasian appearance that must have seemed exotic to a native Beijinger: a long shock of silver hair, extremely steady blue eyes. Something about his face managed to convey both a flickering impatience and an existential acceptance at the same time. He had an office that a Chinese businessman would have considered passé, maybe even politically inappropriate: high-quality antique Ming furniture and wooden lattices punctuated by framed pictures of himself with various top officials and Princelings—an homage to his *guanxi,* his connections, both in the neighborhood and in the larger nation. In case you missed the point, the back of his name card featured a schematic map showing his office's proximity to the Foreign Ministry (and throwing in the Ministries of Justice and Culture for good measure).

The introductions were quick. Laurence told me that he had been in China and Hong Kong for twenty years, as well as consulting in Vietnam and Laos. As a consultant to the Chinese government during the nineties, he had used his training to assist various PLA-owned ventures in making the transformation into legally traded red chips on the Hong Kong stock exchange. He was the CEO of Naga Group, a boutique consulting firm that catered to Fortune 500 companies trying to make it in China. His wife was a Princeling from a high-ranking Chinese military-political family. He had directed the restoration of his courtyard home by artisans who had previously worked on the Forbidden City. Yes, as a lawyer he took a perverse amusement in the kind of absurdly drawn-out negotiation that accompanies real estate purchase and construction in Beijing. Most of all, he was an accomplished author with almost twenty books to his name (*China as Number 1: The New Superpower Takes Centre Stage; Zhu Ge Liang's Art of Crisis Management for China Joint Ventures; Negotiating in China—36 Strategies; When Yes Means No!* and so on). The majority of these books were published in Hong Kong and aimed directly at the wider Asian expat market. Laurence was fluent in both Mandarin and Cantonese, of course, and he had a black belt in karate.

Not once did I feel that he was bragging as he laid out his résumé; nonetheless, I was almost expecting him to mention casually how he was giving a solo piano recital at the Great Hall of the People or to start burning the palm of his hand with a Mao cigarette lighter. I was intimidated; he clearly wasn't going to fund any part of my documentary project, and although I'm not sure which negotiating strategy he used on me (Zhu Ge Liang? Sun Tzu?) I ended up forking over my wife's scarce cash for two of his recent books.

Back in my little one-room apartment in decrepit Chinese housing, I read both of them—wormholes into another way of thinking. *Red Capital*, written in 1997, was a glorification of China's growing capitalist clout and the Hong Kong handover. Hong Kong billionaire Li Ka-shing (a supporter of Beijing, whom I thought of as a crooked Asian version of Armand Hammer) was presented as a kind of *Übermensch* of Chinese leadership connections and dominant will; Brahm gives a gloating account of Li taking the wrecking ball to what had been the world's largest McDonald's to build the high-profile Oriental Plaza complex a shotgun blast away from Tiananmen Square. These vignettes were laid side by side with assertions that although the British had left metaphorical land mines—notably, a costly "white elephant" airport and a semblance of democracy—scattered around Hong Kong. Fortunately, the power of red capital and indomitable Chinese national will would inevitably overcome these obstacles.

Brahm's *Zhongnanhai*, titled after the Chinese leadership compound in Beijing, was, if anything, even more majestic, although parts of it read simply as a vanity book for the top Chinese leaders:

> Jiang Zemin looks out at the ancient gardens by the water. He recalls a speech by Abraham Lincoln on national unity that he once memorized, then a poem by Mao Zedong. Jiang reflects as he stares into the lakes of Zhongnanhai and asks himself how best to bring sometimes recalcitrant regions under the control of the Central government.

Reading *Zhongnanhai*, I recalled feeling that there was something curious about Laurence's accent during our conversation: it would rise and fall unpredictably, and words were subtly mispronounced as if he had little contact with his native tongue (or current

American culture—once when we were discussing a potential movie project, it became obvious that he had never heard of director Oliver Stone). Yet if there was something disquieting about Laurence the man, it was impossible to deny the occasionally brilliant analysis that was sprinkled throughout his writings. Brahm knew the dark structure of the Chinese side better than anyone, it seemed: corrupt Princelings, the real story behind the suicide of Beijing's vice mayor, and the power games between the different factions. The fact that he knew the leadership so well made his submission to the totems of Chinese authority all the more fascinating to me.

Laurence wanted to know about Washington; I wanted to know about Beijing. Naturally, we became friends—of an occasional sort, the kind of odd couple who are amazed by the fact that they can be in the same room together. When I would come by his *hutong* on some pretext or other, he used to surprise me with comments like: "I've been talking to the generals. They can invade Taiwan tomorrow; they've been practicing this thing for fifty years!" Laurence also liked to try out theories on me. He was especially fond of the notion that President Bill Clinton and Alan Greenspan had engineered the Asian economic flu of the late 1990s in an attempt to bring China to its knees. Yet we rarely argued; I knew that his currency in the expat business community—through organizations like AmCham and other forums—was strong not only because of his systematic knowledge and connections with Chinese officials, but because he articulated the independent political outlook of many long-term expats.* Instead, we were always looking for a joint project. (A TV show called *China Business Now!* was one concept: basically a bunch of Western businessmen sitting

---

*For several years, Brahm was one of the only expats with a regular column in the monthly AmCham magazine. It was titled "Black Cat, White Cat," a reference to Deng Xiaoping's pro-capitalist maxim that it doesn't matter if the cat is black or white as long as it can catch mice. The column was finally dropped when Brahm delivered a column accusing the Bush administration of purposely knocking a Chinese jet fighter out of the sky with an EP-3 reconnaissance plane. In the middle of an international crisis, that was too controversial a stance for the American business community (even for his friend Mike Furst, who said that there was no point in publishing the same crap that could be found in the *People's Daily*). Ultimately, however, Brahm went on to see his column find a new home in the far more influential *South China Morning Post*.

around a retro Chinese environment with steaming cups of jasmine tea. Mercifully, it never got off the ground.) Anyway, Laurence was constantly in motion, building his empire. Beyond Naga Group consulting, he created the Red Capital Club, a romantic *hutong* restaurant with an excellent menu, decorated in the same eclectic mix of imperial robes and Maoist memorabilia as his home. Red Capital Wines (again, his own label) were stored in the bomb shelter. When he opened the Red Capital Guest House (with Red Capital Cigars stored in yet another underground bomb shelter/barracks), Laurence gave me a private tour, and although it wasn't to my taste, how could you not admire the chutzpah of creating two "concubine suites" with an "Edgar Snow Room" in the middle? It was "Laurence unleashed," I remarked, and he took it, correctly, as a compliment.

I admired Laurence because he was not using one or two, but all three of the strategies of a friend of China. He not only toed the party line, he was a credible spokesman for it. He brought gifts: he had assisted major American corporations with market entry and relentlessly encouraged China investment. And he did not neglect flattery: the Red Capital empire, indeed, his entire lifestyle was a totemic expression of confidence in the once and future dominance of Chinese culture. One night, after too many drinks at the Red Capital Club, I asked what drove him. Was it, I asked quietly, the aesthetics of Chinese totalitarianism? Yes, he replied, smiling. Since I had a kind of voyeuristic fascination with Chinese fascist iconography myself, that made two of us, I thought. Except that Brahm was actually creating the stuff.

Was Laurence Brahm an aberration? If so, it was largely a question of his panache. Other American expats grew phototropically toward the center of Chinese power, but far less flamboyantly than he did.

The idea of such a center was more than a political concept. Tourists may perceive the Forbidden City purely as an attraction, a charming rundown museum; but what was formerly the largest imperial palace in the world is still the exact geographic center of the city and a transcendent symbol of Chinese culture and authority. Directly abutting the Forbidden City on the west is Zhongnanhai, the Chinese leadership compound, protected from Chinese and foreigner alike by high walls and layers of armed PLA guards. To the south of the Forbidden City's Gate of Heavenly Peace (with its famous Mao portrait that subtly changes from year to year) is Tiananmen Square. Flanked by the Hall of the People's Congress and the Museum of Revolutionary History, it serves as the ceremonial staging ground of Chinese nationalism.

When Beijing society is perfectly aligned by the state, as it was in 1999 for the fiftieth anniversary of the PRC, the leadership leaves Zhongnanhai and, standing on a gallery of the Forbidden City overlooking Tiananmen, waves as first the PLA guards and then selected citizens from the provinces parade through the square with floats and banners. The imperial echoes in the event, however historically inaccurate, are meant to summon up a sense of Chinese eternity. (For the Young Pioneers who act as terracotta stand-ins on Tiananmen Square, the ceremony just feels like an eternity; they are issued diapers to avoid any breaks in the ranks.)

Since the beginning of the city's history, everything in Beijing has been built around this imperial arena like circles around a bull's-eye. Where the city walls once stood, we now have the second ring road, the first of several massive highways that surround the city. Then a third ring road, a fourth, and now a fifth, completed well in time for the Beijing Olympics of 2008. These elaborate construction projects were not funded simply to keep traffic moving. They are also meant to demonstrate that Beijing is no longer an insecure fortress against marauding invaders, but an engine of explosive growth into the rest of China and the world. Yet the highways are also engineered to sustain the massive weight of PLA tanks and armored fighting vehicles should something go wrong.

Where expats chose to live in relation to the center of Beijing says something about who they are. Start at Beijing's airport in the northeast of Beijing, well beyond the fifth ring road. As you touch down, on the edges of the runways you see countryside: a patchwork of tree-lined lanes, poor villages with minute plots of farmland, light industry, decrepit factories and—although high walls prevent you from seeing in—ever-increasing swaths of expensive expat housing. These are the resting places for the American corporate reps. The majority of them are in China to advance their careers within their American corporate base, so although they might be viewed as winners of the expat lottery, most would prefer to be on a plane home. They cluster around the emptiness of the airport freeway, miles from the vibrant center of Beijing, in places like Dragon Villa:

> ... in the ravishing countryside of Shunyi County, close to prestigious Beijing Country Golf Club and Beijing Country Horse Racing Course. A total of 231 deluxe villas with 14 different distinctive designs are offered. The North American style architecture, large spaces and panoramic vies [*sic*], combined with a vast landscape reflect a flaw [*sic*] harmony, appealing to people, looking for perfection. The management team provides friendly and impeccable service to the residents.

These vast, rather sterile Western-style walled compounds feature closely cropped lawns, health clubs with heavily chlorinated swimming pools, grocery stores with a lot of canned Western goods, and extraordinary numbers of Chinese paramilitary guards. The residences and the foreign capital they represent support the rest of the expat pyramid and, to a great extent, China itself.

In theory, it would seem that the top corporate leaders would have no need to prove their friendship with China beyond the investment they represent. But in practice, most corporations had local Chinese partners who could cause difficulties, and even if they ran fully foreign-owned operations rather than joint ventures, government agencies and officials controlled (or just held up) licenses, approvals, import clearances, tariffs, the levying of taxes, real estate and construction. The only way to clear the inevitable roadblocks was to bring pressure further up the chain of command. Ultimately, you would have to approach someone on the ministerial level and do two favors, one for him and another for China (to cover the minister's ass)—for example, Xerox and GM's efforts to win the Olympics for Beijing; or James Murdoch, CEO of Star TV, calling Falun Gong a "dangerous" and "apocalyptic cult" in a public forum at the Milken Institute in Beverly Hills.

Constant maintenance was required as well. If you didn't make it to the "AmCham appreciation dinner," the annual banquet organized for American reps to show their gratitude to Chinese government officials, it could be hazardous to your corporate health and a massive lost opportunity. (Peter Batey, in his previous role as head of the British Chamber of Commerce, had to break up a fight by British insurance company executives over the seating chart at a similar event.)

The commute in from Beijing's airport and the fifth-ring expat enclaves to the city center begins with a series of billboards: Lucent, Motorola, Siemens—enormous symbols of corporate intent rising above rows of scrub trees. Behind these dust catchers for Mongolian sandstorms are single-story brick buildings, bicycles and underpowered bread-loaf vans, the dregs of an older Communist China. Then, beyond the fifth ring road and the fourth, patches of concrete apartment blocks begin to loom up ahead, resembling a once-great city rebuilding after massive carpet-bombing. A few are expat-worthy apartment complexes, featuring vast stretches of pea-green apartment blocks differentiated by primary color accents, in homage to Hong Kong. On the edges are little shops, Italian restaurants, and coffee bars that stay open late, all run by Chinese, all working hard to cater to the strange habits of the foreigners. These are the homes of the worker bees, the aspirants—the young American expats who hope some day to become captains of industry too. Yet their ambivalent positioning between the airport and the Forbidden City shows that they are not committed to Beijing; they like the efficient modern New China, yet many would just as soon be based in New York, Tokyo, Hong Kong, or at the very least Shanghai. Because they are below the management level, most American worker bees of the fourth ring road have little to prove, and like their youthful Chinese counterparts, they have an aversion to strong political beliefs and take their cues from the top of the corporate hierarchy. Consequently, of all the expat groups, they have the most freedom: Ed and his ilk do not follow them.

But if you step across the third ring road, a different Beijing takes over, the Beijing of totalitarian kitsch: vast complexes with titles such as the International Oriental Cultural Exchange Trade Center. Paramilitary guards signal points of interest: Princeling drive-in restaurants, pedestrian subways-*cum*-bomb shelters, warehouse sex clubs with names like "Success," Communist Party headquarters with Dr. No steel gates, and state-run foreigner compounds. These are Beijing's wild-wild-East neighborhoods, with their easy humor and impermanence, their corruption and political intrigue. You can feel it particularly late at night: buildings lit blood red, tank parade practice for special occasions, the destitute North Korean embassy's after-hours cold noodle shop, and the Deep Space Nine claustrophobia of the Russian discos. Poverty and crudeness—even the occasional outbreak of malaria—still lurk along the unpoliced edges, like the jungle encroaching upon the crumbling squares of Brasilia.

This is where the majority of the long-term expats reside, the real friends of China: the businessmen, lawyers and consultants who run AmCham and the U.S.-China Business Council, who lobby in Washington and keep investment moving in. They live here in newly built high-rises, some of them even receiving small rental discounts for letting their names and pictures be used in brochures aimed at attracting the Chinese nouveau riche market. Their apartments are furnished with the latest electronics and oversize wafer-thin televisions, side by side with heavy antique Chinese furniture such as four-poster beds in the imperial style, mirroring the expats' permanence and dedication to being in China. Journalists and embassy personnel live here as well, many encased in the diplomatic compound, the same buildings that were pitted with fire from automatic weapons during the Tiananmen crackdown. In spite of being rather ugly on the outside, the apartments are actually quite spacious, with a good central location, sweeping views of the city and abundant listening devices.

There were a few in the third-ring world who preserved a critical sensibility, who made China their business but had a solid academic base to operate from: Internet analysts such as Peter Lovelock, art historians such as Freda Murck, and a few journalists. And of all the expat groups, one would expect to find that the long-term journalists would muster the strongest collective resistance to being a friend of China, the most razor-sharp skepticism toward the feel-good interpretations of China as changing for the better and American business and culture as being a key factor driving the change.

Yet in Beijing, I noticed far less adversarial and investigative reporting than I had expected. Jasper Becker, formerly Beijing bureau
chief of the *South China Morning Post* and one of the more critical-
of-China hands, wrote a book titled *Hungry Ghosts* on Mao's creation of the Chinese famine in the early 1960s, in which it is
estimated that up to forty million Chinese peasants perished. He
went over official documents, examined interviews of Hong Kong
refugees, but most critically, to hammer home his thesis that the
famine was created by Mao's policies, he traveled to the hardest-
hit provinces for months on end to interview the survivors. When
I first met Jasper, I praised the book effusively. Yet he seemed genuinely nonplussed, almost dismissive: "Any of my colleagues could
have written it. They just didn't choose to."

The roots of not choosing to may be as individual as the journalists on the ground in Beijing, but a few generalizations can be
made. Reporting in China may not be as difficult as it was, say, in
Saddam Hussein's Iraq, but CNN occasionally has its transmission
blacked out, journalists are still denied visas, and media conglom-
erates that want to make inroads in China watch what they say.
(For example, Jasper Becker and Willy Lo-Lap Lam, both top China
columnists, were dismissed when the *South China Morning Post*
decided to go after the mainland market.) Thus, news organizations in Beijing become paragons of journalistic "integrity." They
balance bad-China stories (the *New York Times* exposes the spread
of AIDS in a Chinese province) with good-China stories (the *New
York Times* reports on the first local Chinese beauty pageant). They
edit out language that seems to apply Western conceptions of
human rights and democracy to China. (It's not "objective.") One
AP China reporter bragged to me that he rejected any investigative story if the whistleblower had a "motive," such as anger or
revenge. But in China that means the most interesting stories are
never examined.

The journalists in Beijing not only had to deal with their
bosses' editing and state surveillance, they had to operate in an
environment where it was hard to get real information about anything—statistics, public attitudes, ownership, levels of investment,
profits and losses, even regulatory language—the most basic report-

ing requirements. As well as going through the motions of talking to Chinese government representatives, journalists ultimately would have to approach American corporate representatives, hat in hand, just to get the news of the day. Yet they ran into a shared culture of discretion. After a Western business lobbying triumph (the Chinese government had relaxed its policy on encryption), I asked Tim Stratford, AmCham's president, why my public affairs company (which had done most of the legwork) was being given so little public credit. "In this town, it's usually better if people don't know what you did!" Stratford shot back. At a U.S. embassy function not long after the Loral-Hughes satellite scandal, I listened to a Hughes representative openly bragging—okay, practically shouting—about blacklisting a *Washington Times* reporter who had written something he didn't like. Indeed, positive or negative, a hard-hitting investigative report that threatened either the Chinese government or the American corporate community would be quickly rewarded with a withdrawal of access for the reporter.

As you step inside the second ring road, you are stepping inside Beijing's Old City. The roar dies down, particularly in the remnants of the *hutong* neighborhoods, and the quest for authenticity deepens.

Chinese housing was forbidden to foreigners until very recently. Yet throughout the nineties, enterprising young foreigners in search of lower rents and a *real* China experience risked occasional visits from the police to colonize small sections of shabby apartment buildings, neo-*hutong* complexes, and even ancient coldwater courtyards. These are the domain of the neophyte expats: the young man earnestly learning Chinese, the mixed-nationality couple, the avant-garde artist, wannabees of all description. Without an expense account for taxis, some claim that they find meaning in the transportation of the people—buses, subways and old bicycles. Many young expats actually make their living promoting art, music or other aspects of Chinese culture, such as the Beijing Olympics, as objects of both veneration and exploitation. These young questing-for-authenticity expats came largely from a generation of Americans who had been rigorously trained in their universities to avoid using Western perspectives—or often, any kind of judgment whatsoever—when confronted with anyone who could claim victim status. The Chinese claimed it, so it was okay to embrace a changing China and even the American role in transforming it. But as long as China was weaker than the United States, a line was drawn at too much criticism of their adopted country's government policies or questioning whether a stronger China was really a good thing for the world. Such suggestions could be construed as imperialism. In the daily pressure of getting along with their Chinese friends and lovers, young Americans in Beijing quickly developed a remarkably subtle, almost Chinese sense of what could trip the fragile sensitivities around them. It was best to adopt an easy posture of tolerance, punctuated by cross-cultural amusement—embrace the floating world or end up alone.*

As a neophyte myself, I wanted in. Shortly after I started working for the public affairs firm, my salary increased to the level where I could afford *it*—adjacent to the Drum Tower, just north of the Forbidden City. The compound, Ju'er Hutong, was about 10 percent foreign, a legacy of being an early experiment in China's opening to the West. Financed by Swedes and promoted by the former mayor of Beijing, Ju'er was built as an attempt to square the human-scale *hutong* style of Old Beijing with modern apartment living. The rambling compound was only three to four stories high, with self-

---

*The other boys—the odd expatriate Americans who had made good purely in the Chinese system—thrived in the second-ring rarified environment of government ministries, PLA commanders and Princelings. There was the young British adventurer who spoke to me obliquely about his successful business smuggling weapons components to North Korea; and the American who feigned complaint about how much time he spent on international flights, bringing in promotional copies of Hollywood's latest film releases for the Chinese to pirate onto VCDs and DVDs for mass distribution. Some of them had done so well that they moved back to North America: Dashan, the Canadian student turned Chinese entertainer, beloved by cab drivers throughout China as a foreigner willing to don a monkey tail on TV and beloved by the government for his willingness to appear on the CCTV New Year's show following the Tiananmen crackdown.

conscious neo-Orientalist architectural elements. Most of the original toilets were Chinese squat style. The result was Ikea-socialist
charm with Chinese characteristics: mainly decent family living,
but in the middle of the compound, a surreptitious restaurant that
specialized in hotpot made from puppies.

To find our place, it was necessary to walk through several
ancient *hutong* alleys to the Ju'er entrance—a courtyard crammed
with old bicycles and hanging laundry. You took a left onto the
stairwell. If you mistakenly descended the stairs (as I did only
once), you entered a series of dank chambers completely packed
with metal bunk beds, like the hold of a slave ship—home to the
Chinese migrant workers, the wealthier ones who didn't have to
sleep in tents on the construction site. From time to time I would
surprise a worker standing on the stairway giving himself a sponge
bath from a tin bowl. If you ascended the stairs, the first floor was
a kind of shoddy hotel, not much better than the basement. The
second floor was a slightly more upscale rooming house (although
they still had to move the beds out at night, scraping them across
the floor). The third and fourth floors, well, that was ours: a duplex
with wood paneling, two open-air porches and a greenhouse. It
was small and tidy, but the main element was the view. Beijing
was a city that was systematically being destroyed and rebuilt, yet
other than some telephone poles and a police station with a few
satellite dishes, our sweeping view of the ancient Drum Tower and
its sister, the Bell Tower, which defined the outer boundary of the
Manchu city, had not changed since the fifteenth century.

One night after moving in, we threw a small get-together on
our porch. The industrial haze had gone south that day, revealing
Beijing's true geographic nature: a desert city with little in the way
of trees or living things to hold the temperature constant. As the
sun set behind the Drum Tower, the midday heat rose above the
clay roofs and a cool breeze picked up. A few bats, good luck in
China because their name sounds like the word for wealth, circled
above the porch. Below, stray cats gathered on the rooftops, responding to the scents from the cook-stoves and a female cat in heat.
Steaks sizzled on the grill, my wife was reloading the martini shaker,
and there were even decent cigars around. A recording of John

McCormack's nostalgic Irish ballads wafted out onto the balcony.

Rex, a young friend of mine, was hanging out having a drink. In his spare time, he had become a kind of neighborhood master snoop. So when I asked him if he liked the view of the Tower looming over the Chinese rooftops like a sentry, he answered that it was an accurate depiction of my neighborhood; then he proceeded to point out five different military installations and dormitories clearly visible, and mostly within shouting distance of our romantic perch. The nearest one belonged to an air force general. For security purposes they had no signs, labels or identifying characteristics.

We were close to the center of power here, a point that was brought home to the Chinese leadership during the Tiananmen uprising in 1989. The people in neighborhoods like Ju'er had provided significant logistical support for the uprising, delivering food and other goods to the protesters daily, while people from similar neighborhoods on the outskirts successfully persuaded wave after wave of troops not to act. (When their appeals failed, they built roadblocks out of anything they could find to stop the assault.) Eventually the Chinese leadership resorted to crushing the rebellion using non-Chinese military units from the far west of China: Muslims who might even have enjoyed slaughtering the urban, by-their-standards-wealthy Chinese after years of Beijing's oppression.

Out of the Tiananmen disaster, the authorities had learned not to rely on any single PLA unit, but instead to infiltrate the neighborhoods surrounding the center (essentially, anything within the second ring road) with small, diverse military groupings of the most elite troops, military police and officers. The redundancy would ensure that enough units would stay loyal long enough to suppress any new threat to "social stability."

I hadn't realized this when I moved in. Living in the *hutongs*, shopping in Chinese stores, having every meal at local Chinese restaurants—it was a great adventure, but I began to sense that it didn't allow much of a buffer. There were the old ladies with their red armbands, officially authorized to report the most innocuous trespasses of the rules. There were the police marching down the alley. There was the strange click on my phone. Rex was right about the military presence; at first light every day, my wife and I would wake to a resident PLA unit roaring out ritual slogans from what sounded like just a stone's throw from our bedroom window. (As well as setting your watch by them, you could even gauge China's position in the world by the unit's mood; for example, when the American EP-3 crew was being held on Hainan Island, their cries became considerably more triumphant, more wolfish.) Rex and I laughed and called them "boyz in da hood," but we knew it was their world and we were just living in it.

There was no crime in my *hutong,* no garbage on the streets. The soldiers rose early, announced their presence, and the neighborhood got on about its business. But once I got past the novelty, there was something insidious about the daily combination of poverty and rigid security that began to seep under my skin, poisoning my attitude toward the way I was headed, the way of Laurence Brahm. No matter how much active mastery Brahm displayed, I reflected, he was still submitting to the Chinese central power as surely as the old ladies with their red armbands. At work, I started slipping, sometimes blurting out "police state" in discussions of China as if I had expat Tourette's syndrome. I was subtly, respectfully reprimanded for doing so, but they shouldn't have bothered; I knew it was bad business practice to express contempt for the product—China—that we were trying to sell.

Yet being a friend of China grated. Across the expat castes, I kept hearing the same refrain: China was changing, and to help China progress, you needed to understand that it wasn't just growing economically, it was converging politically with the West. Of course, other than NGO types, few of us bought into the village elections, or any of that window-dressing. Again and again, I heard that this was taking place *in Beijing* in the form of Chinese factionalism. Prior to the recent leadership transition (where fantasies about Hu Jintao as a reformer and the line "the first peaceful transition in PRC history!" were endlessly bandied about), China was ruled first and foremost by Jiang Zemin, president and chairman of the Communist Party. Next in the hierarchy and presumably in competition were Zhu Rongji, premier of the State Council, and Li Peng, chairman of the National People's Congress (NPC).

Being a good expat meant quietly loathing Li Peng, maintaining a studied respect for Jiang, and praising Zhu.

Zhu was not only articulate and savvy (by Chinese political standards), but also regarded as beyond corruption. Don St. Pierre, the normally crusty former head of Beijing Jeep, told me in reverent tones (although it's probably a story that has expanded in the retelling) how Zhu saved his business by slapping down his Chinese joint venture partner, how Zhu had been the one Chinese official he could trust, how he traveled with Zhu and, following a meeting with a bunch of regional officials, Zhu had confided in him his own visceral disgust for the Chinese bureaucracy. "What can I do with these people?" Zhu supposedly asked.

I didn't respond; I knew that Zhu was relentless in attacking petty bureaucrats and corrupt officials on a case-by-case basis, but I also knew he was equally relentless in supporting and expanding the powers of the police state: to conduct surveillance, to encourage informants and to carry out executions speedily. He may have exhibited a relatively pro-American attitude on the surface—based on his assessment of the direction of economic reform, technological transfer and a whopping trade balance that favored China—but I suspected that he simply understood the American corporate mentality, and in the negotiations over China's entry into the WTO, he had learned something about how to game the American political system. In response to the new aggressiveness of the incoming administration of George W. Bush, Zhu authoritatively advocated employing the "business card," that is, using the threat to fix the competition between European, Japanese and American businesses against American interests unless American businessmen agreed to lobby the U.S. government to come up with a more pro-China Taiwan policy.

I was also endlessly told that Jiang was "pro-American," that he had bet his career on rapprochement and strategic partnership with the United States. Yet a defense analyst at the embassy pointed out to me in confidence that in internal meetings and speeches to the PLA, Jiang could be as aggressively anti-American as Li Peng. So I saw Jiang's partnership with the United States from a more cynical standpoint: he had only been interested in equating China with America, thus promoting the internal perception of China's superpower status, and thereby boosting his personal legitimacy.*

Why did we insist on seeing good guys and bad guys in the Chinese leadership? A friend of mine, a top member of the AmCham board and a fairly savvy guy, explained to me that it mattered because below the surface, China was actually converging with the United States or any other modern democracy. What was his evidence? Well, he had recently dined with Sidney Shapiro at Laurence Brahm's Red Capital Club. Shapiro, a longtime Maoist and a Chinese citizen since 1963, was now serving as a member of the Chinese People's Political Consultative Conference as an adviser on economic policy. Shapiro told my friend that in America, there are Democrats and Republicans, so everyone thinks of it as a democracy. In China, there are parties as well, they just aren't called parties. But there are reformers and hard-liners. Shapiro could tell if he was dealing with a reformer or a hard-liner. So what if they don't have symbols like donkeys or elephants? They still compete.

I asked my friend if what Shapiro was describing was any different from, say, rival gangs such as Bloods and Crips. *They* compete. And one might even be able to figure out—by his tattoo or the color of his bandanna or something—whether it's a Blood or a Crip who's kicking you in the teeth. But are these gangs accountable to the ghetto? And who elected them to run the ghetto by fear in the first place? My friend quickly conceded the point, but I was unsettled at how Shapiro's argument could have won him over so easily in the first place.

---

*One of Jiang's former aides, in the safety of a Washington hotel, related to me a story of Jiang's faintly ridiculous attempts to straddle opposing sides. Early in his career, Jiang was preparing to meet a small delegation of Western businessmen, a first for him. He was nervous about making a strong and confident impression, his tension centering on what he would wear. Jiang, coming from the forward-looking Shanghai faction, tended to feel most comfortable in Hong-Kong-style business suits. But Deng, the Supreme Leader of China, made a point of wearing Mao suits and he didn't give a damn whom he was meeting. Jiang dithered. Finally, he kept the Mao suit on, but pulled his suit jacket on over it.

As my doubts were gathering, an incident occurred that dampened my friendship with Laurence Brahm. From 2000 into 2001, he was working on a new book called *China's Century: The Awakening of the Next Economic Powerhouse.* He planned to combine briefs by top Chinese ministers on China's economic and political future with essays by top names from across the Western business spectrum. To provide context and background, he would write the opening to each section.

On both sides it was an impressive list, particularly on the Western corporate side, which included CEOs from top American companies. There was also a smattering of NGO heads, along with Michael Furst, executive director of AmCham; Claude Smadja, managing director of the World Economic Forum; and the China-friendly Canadian ambassador Howard Balloch. The Chinese side included ministers from the State Development Planning Commission, Foreign Affairs, Foreign Trade and Economic Cooperation, Information Industry, State Economy and Trade Commission, State Council News and Information Office, plus the chief justice of the People's Supreme Court, the governor of the People's Bank of China and, just for kicks, Sidney Shapiro.

Zhu Rongji himself would write the foreword. Given the legitimacy flowing from this extensive East-West cast of characters, it was predictable that Laurence finally had a major publishing house behind him, John Wiley & Sons of Hong Kong.

In the fall of 2000, Brahm contacted Peter Batey, inviting him to write a chapter. Batey was a natural choice if you were looking for a representative from the consultant community; as a long-term resident of Beijing, he spoke Mandarin fluently and had an unrivalled understanding of the Chinese government. As political private secretary to the former British prime minister, Sir Edward Heath, Batey had been influential in setting up the first seminal trade contacts between China and the United Kingdom. He had also been chief rep for Arthur Andersen during the 1980s; had founded his own company, Batey Burn, in 1989; had served as chairman of the British Chamber of Commerce in China during the 1990s; and now was chairman of APCO Asia, a leading public affairs firm in China. He was also vice president (soon to be president) of the newly formed European Union Chamber of Commerce.

With a bit of pressure from his staff, Peter produced a draft: "China Opening the Window," a historically based essay on "China's economic rebirth and the challenges lying ahead in sustaining the momentum of economic reform and mega-growth in the new century." Batey discussed the rise and fall of the Chinese empire, explicitly posing the question of whether China could recover its leadership in the twenty-first century. How much has opening trade also opened China to the world of ideas? China's greatest periods have also coincided with its periods of greatest openness. Will this one last and expand? Probably yes, according to Batey. WTO accession will bring in not just reforms but ideas: China's pragmatic leadership has already dismantled many of the state-owned enterprises and continues to reform the economic system. If China allows the Window of Ideas to stay open, Batey concludes,

> China's future should be bright. Her leaders face a formidable task ... but it is not one that should defeat a government of the caliber of that currently headed by Zhu Rongji. Especially not if they heed another of the great Deng Xiaoping's maxims and bear in mind that "opening the window inevitably lets in the flies."

Nothing too controversial about that, I thought. Having fallen into the middleman role because of my relationship with both men, I read it, marked it up a little to bring down the word count, and e-mailed it to Laurence. He replied: Looks good.

A couple of weeks later, I called Laurence. Had he edited the piece? He had done a little cutting, something about fitting it in the galleys, but not to worry, everything was fine. Something in the pace of his response concerned me. I politely said that I needed to see the current draft. With some tension in his voice, Laurence agreed to send it to me.

When the edited essay appeared on my screen, I understood. Right at the beginning, Peter had a line explaining the rise of China's imperial power during the Tang Dynasty:

> It was successful in colonizing or making vassal states of many of its neighbors.

Laurence wrote (my italics are added to highlight the additions):

It was successful in *both diplomatic and trade efforts, in that* many of
its neighbors *became* vassal states recognizing *China as the central
kingdom.*

This accorded with the official Chinese interpretation of history:
China was not a colonizer (it was the colonized, a victim; only
barbarians and Westerners were colonizers); instead of armies,
China used diplomacy and trade to be voluntarily recognized as
the "central kingdom" (or "Middle Kingdom"). This was a projection of Chinese historical continuity and legitimacy backwards in
time.

A bit further on, Peter had written:

China has long envied the Singaporean synthesis of a dynamic market economy and a one-party state, even if disguised by democratic
trappings. It must have come as a blow to some of Singapore's Chinese admirers when the architect of that system, the remarkable
Lee Kwan Yew, recently admitted that further democracy and an
end to the monopoly of power of the People's Action Party would
eventually come.

Laurence wrote:

China has long *admired* the Singaporean synthesis of a dynamic
*State-guided market economy, but recognizes that the Singapore economic
miracle has occurred in a country a mere fraction the size of any major
city in China today.*

Peter had written:

Modern technology in the era of instant communication over the
Internet poses a terrible dilemma for the Party.... Can it find the
means to block political exchange and organization using the new
technology without at the same time strangling the exchange of
economic, technological, scientific, management and other information.

Laurence wrote:

Modern technology in the era of instant communication over the
Internet *poses a series of dilemmas. ...* Can it find the means to block
*the negative political and pornographic exchanges, the commercial and
credit card fraud,* without at the same time strangling the exchange

of economic, technological, scientific, management and other information. . . .

After that, Laurence's edits simply slashed and burned through entire sections, utterly transforming the thesis into the standard Party line. I printed out a comparison of the documents, headed to Peter's office and handed it to him wordlessly. As he read, he began to shake his head slowly. Then he smiled. Then he began to laugh. Then tears, actual tears of laughter, started to roll down his cheeks.

After a couple of compromise drafts and an extended negotiation session between me and Laurence at the Red Capital Club (Peter and I caved, Laurence stood firm), followed by more last-minute edits on Laurence's side (which he refused to show us), Peter pulled the chapter from *China's Century.**

The list of luminaries who didn't pull their chapters is an impressive one: George M. C. Fisher (chairman of the board of Eastman Kodak), Heinrich von Pierer (president and CEO of Siemens), Don Davis (chairman and CEO of Rockwell International), Charles Pryor Jr. (president and CEO of Westinghouse), Dr. Manfred Schneider (chairman of Bayer AG), Peter Sutherland, (chairman and managing director of Goldman Sachs International), and James Murdoch (chairman and CEO of Star TV). As a reward

---

*When Laurence Brahm was asked about the editing process in a promotional interview, he responded:

"There was no Chinese government involvement in the preparation of this book other than the chapter essays contributed by different ministers and the foreword from Premier Zhu. Likewise, each of the other contributors, whether a multi-national corporation CEO, academic, or media commentator each had the freedom to write their own piece. In the preparation of each chapter essay, no author was aware of what the other was writing, except me as I was coordinating the project. This was intentional to create complete independence of ideas. Many of the comments provided by business leaders provide constructive criticism of policy changes and measures which these individuals feel from their own sector expertise China will need to adopt to achieve its development goals. Likewise, many of the Chinese contributors to the book who are media commentators were especially outspoken concerning the need to further liberalize this particular sector in China. So there was no 'sugar coating.' I did request contributors, however, to be cool-headed and constructive in their comments so that they would be of value to both foreign as well as Chinese readers."

for their labors, they all received a meeting with Premier Zhu—
an invaluable exercise in *guanxi*. The book launch itself, held in
the Great Hall of the People, was a reminder that the days of old
Maoists Shapiro and Rittenberg were not over, just changing with
the times. The right man could still pull the fifth-ringers back into
the Chinese government's orbit.

I'll confine my review of *China's Century* to Laurence's first
paragraph. As is the editor's prerogative, Brahm begins every section of the book with a nuanced statement of the logic behind
the Chinese leadership's positions and adds some local color. His
introduction begins:

> Beijing, October 1st, 1999. A heavy rain had poured from the sky
> the night before. By dawn the rain had stopped. Mist evaporated
> quickly against a sharp Autumn wind. As I arrived in Tiananmen
> Square to attend celebrations for the 50th anniversary of the Peo-
> ple's Republic of China, the sun had already pierced through clouds
> overhead. Red flags flew from the mammoth buildings—the Great
> Hall of the People, the Museum of Revolutionary History—lining
> the square. It promised to be a bright, sunny day.

This is just one tiny example of the "positive propaganda"
that has been the guiding principle for all Chinese journalists for
over half a century. Brahm's paragraph betrays his American roots;
one can almost hear an echo of *by eight, the morning fog must dis-
appear* in the prose. Yet he is kicking off with a bright, shining lie.

It *had* rained hard the night before, uncharacteristically, thus
leading to rumors that the Party leadership had seeded the clouds
to stop them from raining on the parade. But on October 1, 1999,
I was standing on a balcony at the diplomatic compound, beer in
hand, watching the armored vehicles gathering on Jianguomen
Avenue—and the sky was uniformly gray, overcast and utterly
uninspiring. That the sky itself should perform to Communist
Party specifications is laughable. Like the authorities spray-paint-
ing the lawns a vibrant green when the Olympics committee visited Beijing, it also seems harmless. But in the context of the book
(with essay titles hinting at the breathless tone: "Unprecedented
Experiment," "China, Unlike Its Famous City, Is Forbidden No
More," "Kodak and China: Seven Years of Kodak Moments"), is

Brahm's little fib just foreplay? Is it the editor's duty to warm you up to accept much bigger lies?

Does it matter? The parade (and the sky) was filmed for posterity by countless cameras that day, but perhaps things looked different from where Laurence sat—in the reviewing stand, overlooking a hundred thousand smiling Chinese faces. He had crossed over a long time ago and he had done it alone. Now his home was no longer in the States, perhaps not even in China, but only here, inside the second ring road, in El Dorado.

5.
How to Succeed in China without Really Succeeding

I really didn't have a background in business, much less an aptitude for it. I suspect that my public affairs firm hired me because a little political acumen, combined with some backslapping, networking mannerisms, was confused with an ability to actually make money for the company. This, however, doesn't fully explain why the company kept me on, as I was probably a financial wash. Theoretically, my job was business development. As an occasional writer I was expected to create sparkling copy about our government relations capability for our glossy brochures (a task that I would shuffle around my desk for months on end). But my main responsibility was to keep a finger on the pulse of the American Chamber of Commerce in Beijing (AmCham) and act as a kind of personal advertisement for my firm's peerless government relations capabilities.

In the beginning, I had to work hard at networking, gearing myself up to reach the sweet spot—a caffeinated, nicotine-saturated state where I would come across as personable, focused, yet sublimely relaxed. There were good days and bad days. On the good ones I felt like a fuzzy mascot, beloved by the business community, all easy smiles, pumped-up handshakes and beaming my card into Palm Pilots. On the bad ones, I felt as if I were wearing a heavy wooden sandwich board to my daily routine of meetings, lunches, drinks, gossip and more drinks. In any case, by the beginning of 2001, it became clear that the top guys in AmCham liked having me around. I was increasingly included in the informal strategy sessions of the inner circle and asked to take a formal role as the vice chair for AmCham's Government Relations Committee.

It all looked respectable, yet on my way up, I increasingly felt like a fake. The sense that something was wrong started with my business card. If you just browsed through one of those glossy brochures that I was supposed to be writing and made a quick comparison with our home office in Washington, D.C., you would discover that my title, Senior Counselor, was identical to that of two highly respected former congressmen and the former national security advisor to President Reagan. But it wasn't just me. The more I learned about commerce in Beijing, the more I scratched under the veneer of order, hierarchy and sobriety, the more it began to resemble a looking-glass world. AmCham committees, corporate logos and Brooks Brothers rep ties covered an inflation of skills, business failure, the opacity of the China market—and a creeping Chineseness to some companies' business dealings, including the systematic use of bribes.

In writing this book, I resolved to avoid quoting Chinese proverbs, particularly if they involve dragons, monkeys or the art of war; but there is one old Chinese saying, still in use, that strikes me as relevant to the American way of business in Beijing: *Heaven is high and the emperor is far away.* The original meaning of the phrase seems to have been that it was difficult to get justice in the provinces. In the modern Chinese context, it often means the opposite: if you aren't based in Beijing but, say, in distant Chengdu or in flat-out capitalist Shenzhen, you can run your business, maybe even your life, in the way that you choose. In the American expat context, in Beijing the heavens were high (or at least so we told the home office) and our emperors—the U.S. government and the home office—were far away. To a surprising extent, we could interpret standard business practices and concepts as we pleased. The first one that we reinterpreted was the concept of success.

■

After I had been working in the office for about a year, I began to notice a new pattern among our clients—one that related to our business. We were known as a full-service, comprehensive, soup-to-nuts kind of public affairs company. Our bread-and-butter was market entry, making sure a workable license emerged from the cogs of the Chinese bureaucratic machinery. But we were also good at the midstream stuff: ironing out problems with Chinese officials on an ongoing basis, finding ways around advertising restrictions, devising strategies against unfair competitors, and fighting smears in the Chinese press by using our journalist contacts. At the end of the day, we could always use our well-paid former Chinese government officials (some of whom were members of the Zhongnanhai club) to lean on their friends in the Chinese ministries. To prepare for CEO visits such as the ones I've described previously, we could give companies various fig leaves (for example, we could generate the appearance of a business plan for e-commerce, something the home offices were always pressuring them on). Additionally, we excelled at the mature company requirements: branding new products, expanding into regional markets, correcting corporate images with devices such as corporate philanthropy, and giving companies at least the optics of an anticounterfeiting strategy.

We literally presented it as the arrow of progress: our potential client would go from market entry, to midcourse correction, to maturity and profitability. One of our sales devices was a graphic of a large arrow with notations suggesting how we could solve the inevitable problems of doing business in China along the way. But where did the arrow of progress for American businesses in China end? What if firms never achieved profitability?

Over the year 2000, as I settled into my job, I began to suspect that for a lot of companies, our imaginary arrow was better represented by what health officials call an "epidemic curve," a bell shape of success and failure over time. When a corporation first invested in China there would be a slow start, followed by gradual market penetration and slow movement up the curve. Then, like an epidemic spreading through a susceptible population, the firm's products would briefly catch fire, usually among the wealthiest Chinese. The company would fuel increased sales, doubling the bet, reinvesting, hiring staff, and writing grandiose business plans to expand beyond the markets of Shanghai, Guangzhou and Beijing. Then—again, like an epidemic running out of victims to prey on—the sales volume would start to level off and the curve would begin a rapid decline.

Sometimes the sales concept had been flawed in the first place.* However, the usual cause of trouble for retail operations was counterfeiting. As much as 30 percent of Chinese manufacturing was dedicated to producing counterfeit goods—anything you could imagine: Rolex watches, American Standard toilets, Pfizer's Viagra, Chrysler brake shoes, even entire Audis. The Chinese counterfeit manufacturers produced at high volume, operating out of state-owned enterprises, barracks and homes, without business plans, consultants or any sort of overhead (other than armed guards). They sold the goods throughout China and abroad, with perfectly reproduced labels, for a fraction of the price.

For companies such as Microsoft there was an opportunity cost to losing over 90 percent of the Windows market to the ten-dollar CD-ROMs sold on the street corners of most major Chinese cities. But the assumption was that over the long term, Chinese consumers would recognize the value of Microsoft's innovative and comparatively glitch-free products, and at some point in the future there would be a payoff. But American companies such as Procter & Gamble and Phillip Morris did not have the same luxury. Not only were approximately 25 percent of Procter & Gamble products on the shelves outright fakes, but informal studies of Chinese regional markets suggested that some customers had never been exposed to the real product. Shampoo that not only dried out hair but contained high levels of bacteria, and Marlboros that tasted like sawdust and led to immediate respiratory problems— such counterfeits destroyed the reputation of the product and the

---

*As expats, we spent a lot of time passing around stories of Western corporate naïveté, such as slogans that didn't translate well or companies trying to sell products that were prematurely luxurious in a still-immature Chinese market: fancy beers or microbrews (beer is more like a staple food in China), environmental industrial devices such as coal scrubbers (no Chinese factory wanted these unless they were being forced to use them), and breakfast cereal to a population that is largely lactose-intolerant. In my experience, these were colorful exceptions. The greater problem was that the home office had unrealistic expectations based on China's annual GDP growth rate (which tended to hover officially around 7 percent). Most Chinese individuals were emerging from such a low base income—just over $900 per year on average—that a 7 percent annual growth rate could not lift their disposable income to permit much more than an occasional Big Mac.

brand. Johnson & Johnson had to deal with fake baby oil that caused rashes and had closed several production lines. Even more frightening, high-tech American corporations had to cope—as quietly as possible—with Chinese manufacturers' counterfeiting of specialized products, such as automobile airbags, for export.

Copying an American product for sale under a Chinese brand name was not really considered illegal by the Chinese state authorities.* Instead, it was quietly encouraged. High-tech corporations such as Cisco had little recourse if Huawei, a Chinese version of themselves (but with massive state backing), chose to reverse-engineer Cisco routers and duplicate them. (In Huawei's case, they even duplicated Cisco's serial numbers, leading to legal action.)

In response, American companies would try to lower their prices to a competitive level. For example, a Big Mac cost less in China than anywhere else in the world (partly an effect of China's artificial exchange rate, but also a McDonald's sales strategy). But in any area that the Chinese leadership considered to be a "pillar industry," such as automobiles, Chinese government regulatory bodies used arcane licensing procedures to block U.S. corporate expansion, thereby allowing Chinese corporations a chance to catch up and seize market share. The American firm could talk about superior quality all it wanted, but to actually make a profit it needed access to the Chinese market allowing economies of scale. But access was easily stymied by tariffs, customs and various legal maneuvers. If the American corporation wanted a larger share of the market, the Chinese leadership might grant such "concessions" in exchange for the Americans' Washington connections. Suggestions would be made: lobby against arming Taiwan, against human rights linkage, against dual-use export controls, whatever the leadership issue *du jour* happened to be. Even that didn't always work. In my first personal meeting with the former

---

*Although it may be apocryphal, here is a horror story that made the rounds: A foreign businessman set up a joint venture and built a modern plant to exacting specifications in the Chinese countryside. The foreign businessman checked up on the plant regularly, but one day he took a wrong turn and got lost. Coming over a hill, he saw the plant, though in the wrong location; apparently his Chinese partner had duplicated the entire plant and was already selling the product under a Chinese brand name at a lower price.

Beijing director of the U.S.-China Business Council (the USCBC is, arguably, the most effective lobbying organization for Chinese interests in Washington), she complained to me that Chinese government officials "just didn't seem to understand" that American companies needed to sell in bulk also—as if it were some sort of communication problem.

I had a sense of the difficulties on the micro level too, having worked on both sides of the aisle, even acting at times as a go-between for American venture capitalists and independent Chinese companies looking for investment. So I had been through the process: a lunch featuring a fish swimming in sesame oil and scallions, endless meetings, cab rides back and forth, faxed proposals, revisions, and tense cell phone conversations. But it seemed always to come down to the fact that the Chinese side had things to hide: usually a combination of debts (it's common in China to borrow without a written contract) and accounting—concealing the company's profits from the state tax collection apparatus. The Chinese accounting trick is to declare every dividend paid out to the company's investors not as a profit but as an expense. Thus even fairly lucrative companies in China will often show paper losses year after year. The Chinese business culture—conditioned by one-party leadership and centuries of xenophobia—believes that to reveal any liabilities to the foreigner is a major concession, so instead of the bottom line, negotiations would often bog down around irrelevant issues of respect, style and tone. As a friend of mine pointed out, "The Chinese will never get rich, because they would rather lose money than lose face."

The Chinese fetish for secrecy could be a disaster in a joint venture. A former manager of the American side of Asian-American Communications told me that the American engineers on his staff had the responsibility of overseeing the design of the communication systems in which they had invested, but they spent most of their time making elaborate castles-in-the-sky business models. Yet the home office was telling him to screw the business models and concentrate on billing: "But the Chinese said no. The billing system is our business. . . . So we got into a situation where we didn't know exactly how much money was coming from the network except for a report that was prepared by the Chinese accountant, because in the contracts, the Chinese were granted CFO status. American companies, in this regard, were just screwed royally. I was the chief representative officer of a company that invested a hundred million dollars—and to this day, I have never seen the raw statistics: the number of calls made, the number of roaming calls made, any of it."

No financial analyst that I knew of could claim to have a definitive figure on how many American companies were turning a profit, particularly in relation to their initial investment. Few corporate leaders in Beijing would assert in private that China was a profitable market. Feel-good embassy reports—suggesting that 50 percent of American companies in China could be making a profit—were contradicted by conversations with the U.S. embassy commercial officers, who suggested to me that less than a third of American companies, at best, were making quarterly profits, and only about 5 percent were making a profit if you factored in their original investment. Yet it was risky for American companies to emphasize losses in China because the perception in U.S. financial circles was that China investment—investment in the last great untapped market on earth and all that hype—was indicative of the corporation's confidence in its future. You could close a line or sell a factory, but pulling out of China completely could damage the overall corporate image way out of proportion to the actual investment.

The American perception couldn't change the facts on the ground, though. For many companies hit by counterfeiting, reverse-engineering, government restrictions, or any combination of these factors, the business curve would start to plummet and the losses would begin to accumulate. The local rep's temptation at this point was to prove to his Chinese hosts that they were "here for the long term" by reinvesting. Yet unless you were at the forefront of technological innovation, like Cisco or Motorola, and therefore at least half a step ahead of the reverse-engineers, this would not prevent the slide. A brewery, for example, could keep a low-level operation going and perhaps rent out the rest of the factory, but it still wouldn't break even, and the curve would stay depressed.

It was at this point, somewhere near the bottom, that the representatives of the company, the potential clients, would appear on my radar. I looked for the personal clues that didn't appear in the annual reports: they would pick at their food, nurse their drink too solicitously, get a faraway look, and finally slump a little when they came out with it. They wanted to cut their losses, sell their carefully constructed manufacturing plants and the attendant assets. They had nasty joint ventures with nasty Chinese thug-partners and they needed divorce settlements they could live with. They had been hemorrhaging money for five or ten years now and no matter how they had adjusted their burn rates, it was late in the day and the home office had finally said, Enough.

Now, for a few of these potential clients, China, rather than being their career break, could be their career graveyard. They had to find their way home. But to be welcomed back ... well, it was suddenly occurring to some of them that America wasn't all that different from China in some respects. In China, if you screw up, you bring a gift; likewise, wouldn't it be nice to bring home a bit of the company's money? So they needed to take a portion of the assets—factories, offices, IT equipment—and somehow make them liquid again. This was harder than it sounded; even routine business such as repatriating funds (because the *renminbi*, the Chinese currency, is not fully convertible) had to be handled by a third party. Even more difficult, their Chinese joint venture partners seemed to assume it was their right (as maltreated little brothers) to inherit the lot. Many of the Chinese partners that the Americans had drunk with, banqueted with, and spent so many hours in karaoke dens with, would—not just in the closing days of the enterprise, but often at the first sign of trouble—simply strip and cart off anything they wanted from the company without even so much as a *fuck off!* to remember them by. Regional Chinese officials prevented any kind of open-market auction of the assets unless they were given enormous kickbacks, and if you didn't like how it turned out, going to the Chinese legal system guaranteed you wouldn't see the money until every machine in your plant was obsolete or covered with rust—and that's if you won. This kind of unhappy ending is not unique to China; it's endemic throughout the third world and many emerging markets. But the scale was so much greater in China, the investment so supersized, and that fact provided a huge opportunity for our company.

It required shrewd negotiation with Chinese jackals to recover a fraction of the plant's value even at fire-sale prices. But with our government connections and our ability to find Chinese competitors in a given market area, we *could* do it. And although it was demanding, frustrating work, we could cut the deal with the client on a commission basis. Even if it was a small percentage, on the order of 10 to 15 percent, this still meant potentially huge money for us.

"Our clients need exit strategies," I brightly explained to my boss. Why couldn't we put that in the brochure along with market entry and everything else? Right at the end of the arrow? My boss glanced at me, fiddled with some papers, looked back, and seemingly couldn't suppress a knowing smile as he said, "No, Ethan. It's just *too* depressing."

Every American expat strays into the Other China at some point. For me, it was early in 1999 on a midweek visa run to Hong Kong. In Guangzhou, my poor Chinese skills led me to the wrong bus and, at the end of the line, the wrong train station. Spread out over a massive square were literally tens of thousands of people simply sitting passively in the midday sun. Their hair was uniformly matted as if unwashed for months. As it was dawning on me that this station only serviced China's interior, a policeman grabbed a peddler woman crouching a few yards from me. Peppered chicken legs tumbled out of her plastic bag while the policeman began pulling her by the pigtail, cracking her head against the concrete pavement. A few people looked up impassively, but most remained hunched over as if occupying tiny cubicles.

I stared, but I didn't pull out my camera. The responsibilities of my own Beijing cubicle dictated that I get a return visa, not evidence of runaway unemployment and human rights abuse. I threaded my way back through the crowd, found a taxi, and got out of Guangzhou as quickly as I could.

The incident left an impression, but by the end of 1999 I realized that I wasn't going to see something like that again, not in Beijing anyway. A kind of gauze curtain had dropped over China. Train tickets for ordinary Chinese between cities such as Guangzhou

and Beijing were again subject to tighter control. Hordes of unemployed migrants were being kept out of Beijing through a periodic
dragnet on the highway approaches. (Visiting Americans tended
not to notice because police rarely stopped vehicles carrying foreigners.) Unemployment figures were increasingly suspect. My
Chinese co-workers and my maid were quietly but regularly asking me to change *renminbi* into dollars. When I asked them why,
they said they were planning against devaluation, massive inflation through the government simply printing a lot of money, a
bank run, or all of the above. Given these fears, they weren't spending, and the enforced one-week "vacation" that the government
suddenly announced just before National Day had not produced
the desired jump-start.

Anecdotal evidence? Of course, but the real stuff was becoming sketchier by design. The National Bureau of Statistics (the
NBS—at the time, the State Statistical Bureau) announced new
regulations that forced all foreign market research companies to
register and go through a certification process. Following registra-
tion, every survey, no matter how innocuous—Coke versus Pepsi
and the like—would have to be cleared by the NBS. Any questions
deemed sensitive to national security could be censored, surveys
could be cancelled, and the firm could permanently lose permission to operate if it didn't cooperate. The regulations were vague
yet stern enough that it was possible that asking a Chinese respon-
dent about his occupation (or lack of one) was no longer a legitimate inquiry. Consumer confidence was a particularly taboo line
of questioning.*

Some Chinese sources told me the NBS was reacting to a Tai-
wanese-connected market survey project that was suspected of
spying. A few analysts at my firm theorized that the government

*The NBS policy left firms like Gallup China, whose reputation was built on its
ability to accurately survey big issues such as consumer confidence, in serious
trouble. It is interesting to note that a few days before the regulations were
supposed to take effect, Gallup rushed out a new national survey. Chinese
national consumer confidence had risen dramatically—from a position of low
confidence to a majority expressing confidence in the Chinese economy—all
within the space of several months. It was difficult to see anything in the news
or in the business cycle that could account for such a shift. Had Gallup changed
the methodology? Were the questions phrased differently? There was no

campaign against Falun Gong was to blame. Some highly placed executives in the survey field whom I spoke to about the issue felt that the explanation was simpler: the Chinese leadership simply wanted to control the dissemination of public attitudes and indicators that could be used as clues to the current state of the Chinese economy.

During the early nineties there was less to hide. Following Deng's order to remove market restrictions, China's reported GDP growth had been phenomenal: 14 percent in 1992, gradually decreasing to 10.5 percent in 1995 with inflation hovering around 10 percent. Investment flooded in, but the Chinese growth spurt showed signs of coming up against the intractable problem of China's state-owned enterprises and the Asian economic flu. China's GDP figures began a predictable trajectory: by 1997, growth was 8.8 percent, down from 9.6 percent the year before. As Asian exports collapsed, the Chinese leadership faced the danger of economic stagnation. The leadership believed that its survival was contingent on social stability (preventing workers from forming an organized opposition), which was contingent on keeping urban unemployment below double digits—which, in turn, was believed to depend on Chinese GDP growth at an annual minimum of 7 percent.

In 1998, Zhu Rongji exhorted Chinese enterprises to surpass a growth rate of 7 percent. The NBS responded by declaring China's GDP growth for the year to be 7.8 percent—even though the year was not over yet. But the farce went beyond that: every Chinese province with the exception of Yunnan reported a growth rate *surpassing 7.8 percent.* Embarrassed, the NBS pledged to stop using provincial reports to arrive at China's GDP figure and pledged to switch to a system of independent calculation (although the new system was never made explicit).

---

explanation, leading me to suspect that Gallup simply cooked the new survey, hoping for mercy from the NBS. If that was the strategy, it failed; the NBS put the regulations into effect shortly afterward. Gallup now claims to have reached an understanding with the NBS, but there is little question that the NBS's selective enforcement of the new rules is a strong incentive for market research firms to comply with government objectives and self-censor both their surveys and their findings.

The growth figures that the NBS reported following 1998 showed an impressive and stable trajectory: 7.1 percent GDP growth in 1999, 8.0 percent in 2000, 7.3 percent in 2001, 8.0 percent in 2002. But the numbers were so perfect, so in line with Zhu's exhortation, that they were bound to be challenged. Several economists— Thomas Rawski, from the University of Pittsburgh, and Lester Thurow, MIT—noted that a simple comparison of NBS economic indicators painted a strange picture. Official GDP growth had leveled out but not dropped appreciably, yet energy consumption— the stuff that factories run on—mysteriously continued to decline, even though there was no widespread energy conservation policy in effect. Specifically, China's GDP had grown by over 34 percent in the years 1998 to 2001, while energy use actually declined by over 5 percent during the same period. Every other Asian Tiger economy had seen a corresponding rise in its energy consumption during growth spurts. How could China—a society that believed in coal, not conservation—have pulled off such a trick?

Other economic indicators showed similar mysteries. Job creation was flat. In the rural areas, where 80 percent of the population lives, there appeared to be no growth at all, while Hong Kong, the key economic and financial platform for southern China, had experienced negative growth. Consumption numbers didn't fit. While the Chinese economy was supposedly growing at a rate of 7.8 percent in 1998, air travel had increased by only 2.2 percent, even while ticket prices were falling. The rate of inflation had somehow, without a recession, gone from 10 percent to zero. And while export growth had fluctuated wildly, China's economic growth had somehow remained flat and predictable for four years running.

Some economists, like Thomas Rawski, looked at the statistics—particularly the drop in energy consumption—and saw a picture of an economy that had been experiencing low or even negative growth in the late nineties and by 2001 was growing at a rate of perhaps 3 percent. Zhu commented that it was obvious that Rawski had never been to China. Stephen Roach of Morgan Stanley went on about how China was "the only place I have ever visited where you can see the growth unfolding before your eyes." *China Economic Quarterly,* a respected business journal, preferred to split the difference by allowing that the NBS cooked the numbers in 1998, which was clearly a year of recession, but maintaining (with scant evidence) that current GDP figures were accurate, give or take a percentage point. A professor from the Hong Kong University of Science and Technology accused Rawski of relying "heavily on other NBS data to reach his conclusion"—essentially saying that Rawski was operating in a hall of mirrors.

He was. We all were. Foreign investment was flying blind at precisely the time when investment in China should have been moving in the direction of science. But personally, I didn't believe Rawski's estimate of 3 percent either. Over time, I was beginning to sense that there were two Chinas and any attempt to reconcile them in a single figure would be nothing more than a guess. In the New China, the coastline and the large cities of China where I and most expats lived, growth was indeed unfolding before our eyes, and something close to 7 percent seemed plausible—particularly because the growth was partially fueled by spending and debt that was about 16 percent of GDP. (If you included what many analysts believe to be insolvent debts by the state-owned banks, the figure rose to 70 percent or above.) Yet the anomalies that Rawski pointed to made me strongly suspect that the Other China, the one that I had stumbled into in Guangzhou, that few expats would choose to live in, was failing. From the look of the energy consumption figures, which could well represent the vast state-owned factories, it was collapsing. And while I didn't have the space in my brain to try to make a composite figure of the two Chinas, market research firms were beginning to explore the Other China, to weigh it in their surveys, and that was something the Chinese leadership could not allow. Foreigners were expected to let the Chinese government take care of the international perceptions while they simply invested on faith—faith that the Chinese had enough reserves to muddle through the potential banking crisis, and faith that the New China could keep the Other China out of Beijing.

■

Was the whole game an illusion then? Given what I have been describing—a sinkhole market for the majority of American companies in China, duplicitous Chinese partners, a tedious and intrusive bureaucracy, a counterfeiting operation that is so deeply entrenched that, according to some estimates, it constitutes nearly a third of the Chinese economy, and an economy where even basic numbers such as GDP growth are suspect and driven by political wish fulfillment—with these kinds of problems, why was there continued involvement in the China market? If we couldn't turn major profits, what sustained America's Beijing Boot Camp in its belief in a glowing economic Chinese future?

I puzzled over these questions throughout my time as a business consultant in Beijing. Coming from a free-enterprise stance, perhaps I should have figured it out earlier. But here's how I made some sense of the apparent irrationality of my clients.

As I mentioned, my public affairs firm was truly global in reach: headquartered in D.C. with offices all over Europe, including Russia, and even small offices in Indonesia and Africa. Our corporate ethos was to think big. Our clients have global problems? Let's solve them using our global capabilities. It sounded good and it sounded profitable; but in point of fact, most problems in China are local. Yet I thought I had found one problem that could use our capabilities in both China and the United States: for several years, following the investigations of Nike's sweatshops in Indonesia, I had been watching a perceived failure of trans-Pacific corporate responsibility mushroom into a potent political movement made up of American unions, antiglobalization leftists, socially concerned working-assets-type liberals, and American college students who craved political activism against the Sinister Corporate Machine. Their collective focus was third-world worker hellholes run by prominent American corporations in Latin America, South Asia and, most of all, China. Ad hoc groups had sprung up, multiplied and formed broad coalitions: United Students against Sweatshops, National Labor Committee, Co-op America, Sweatshop Watch, UNITE USA. They had created checklists of corporate behavior backed up by congressional hearings, daily blast-faxes and fellow-traveler journalists. Labor activists posing as investors had traveled through the dark satanic mills of China, taking pictures of compounds with guard towers and barbed wire, earnestly recording how many young women were stuffed into a single barracks (way too many), how many vacation days or sick days were allowed (almost none), whether union activity was allowed (of course not!), and how much they were paid (about 25 to 35 cents an hour).

Living in the *hutongs* of Beijing, I confess, I sometimes found it difficult to work myself into a lather about all this. Perhaps daily exposure to China makes you callous or, to put it more grandly, exposure to China heightens one's immunity to existential tragedy. Or perhaps it was just that the sweatshop girls—miserable and exploited and all—were making roughly twice as much as the Beijing construction workers who slept in the basement of my building. The difference between 30 cents an hour and 15 cents (a construction worker's salary when you figure in their full hours) was of vital interest to my Chinese neighbors, as they struggled hard—and I must say, quite decently, under extremely difficult circumstances—to make a living. I sometimes felt that the anti-sweatshop movement cared little about what they considered minuscule salary differences or, for that matter, about how the majority of Chinese people would make a living at all in their imagined world.

Several China activists had told me that American companies on the ground in China were actually supporting the Communist Party system of worker control by giving cadre leaders special luxurious offices where they carried out the Party's business and controlled the Chinese workers on the company dime (for example, in Motorola's plant in Tianjin). This kind of collusion irritated me and I quietly supported the right of the workers to organize independently; but what did it matter what I thought? Or what American corporate chiefs thought? Given the Chinese leadership's unholy fear of Chinese workers in the Workers' State, what possible impact could we have? The Chinese regime briefly promoted the guild system as a fig leaf for actual labor organization, but few American corporate leaders took the final cynical step of parroting the government's line in this regard.

Ultimately it didn't matter what consultants thought about the sweatshop issue either. But it had to matter to our potential clients; over half of them used Chinese labor to make clothing, shoes, fashion items and other high-profile consumer goods such as toys for the American market. They had to be acutely aware of the damage that a television investigation on *60 Minutes* or a *New York Times* report on failing the sweatshop standards could do to their corporate reputation. And it seemed to me that there was a vast public affairs opening here for anyone with the imagination to come up with a creative solution to the problem of working standards.

It was to our firm's benefit if we could actually grow a client organically—that is, "proactively" identify a problem, work out a plan, and then get the client to agree to pay us to implement it. Through the grapevine I had heard that one company in particular, a venerable and well-known American clothing manufacturer, was considering setting up mass production in China. Yet the company was already under close scrutiny by anti-sweatshop groups and the founder of the company had expressed deep concern about China's anti-labor policies. The founder's views were no secret. He had actually gone public with his concerns over Chinese labor laws and human rights policies. Yet his company was losing money and needed to bring its production costs down quickly. That meant cheap labor, that meant China, and that meant the company could be in a terrible fix.

I got together with a colleague who specialized in corporate philanthropy and we sketched out a plan: a model factory where the peasant girls would live in decent dormitories, with on-site health care and safety regulations second to none. Most of all, we tried to think about the factory's operations as if there were a union present. That meant overtime and dirty-work rates, healthy cafeterias, day care, a grievance system, and actually making the effort to educate and promote workers to junior management, not just kicking them out the door when their reflexes slowed and it was time for them to get married at age twenty-five or so. If we had to give a special office to the in-house cadre, so what? At the end of the day, the workers would play pickup basketball wearing the company's clothing (artfully torn) while the cameras rolled. Think of the TV ads—some Madonna-esque world music background, slo-mos of the Chinese workers doing high-fives, maybe we could even get Michael Jordan to visit.... *This,* I thought, is corporate philanthropy.

We invited in the Asia representative of the company to try out the idea. After the usual introductions, boilerplate on our backgrounds and unique capabilities, we dropped a phrase or two about our corporate responsibility and philanthropy programs in China. "You're speaking our language," he replied enthusiastically. His body language indicated receptivity, so I cut to the chase. We knew that his company was thinking of ramping up its manufacturer capability in China, and we had come up with some proactive plans to add value to manufacturer reputations in China. He suddenly stiffened and with a poker face said firmly, "We are not a manufacturer in China; we are a *retailer*."

A retailer? Yes, of course . . . in that any clothing item they manufactured somewhere in South Asia eventually made it onto a few Chinese shelves—in clever facsimile form, of course—in any of the numerous counterfeit retailing markets that blossomed throughout Guangzhou, Shenzhen, Shanghai, Chongqing and Wuhan. The fact that the company's authentic apparel had never made a perceptible dent in the China market—well, there really wasn't much more to say without directly contradicting the company rep, and so the meeting came to a quick, dead end.

I had never really come face to face with the Basic Bullshit so clearly before. "We are a *retailer*." What company wants to say openly that they are in China for the export platform—a very successful export platform consisting of well-controlled, incredibly hardworking labor that costs next to nothing? What company wants to trumpet that they are moving factories out of the States at record pace? Or that they don't care about our spectacular trade deficit with China? So instead, you subcontract the actual running of the factories to the Taiwanese, who drive the meanest wage bargain in the business and are known for running a tight shop. You set up a highly visible sell-to-the-Chinese market operation with a nice office and a fancy showroom in China World or Kerry Center, with a prominent square-jawed American rep who makes the rounds in AmCham and is a member of USCBC. You hobnob with the ambassador at a luncheon or two and make sure your CEO testifies at congressional hearings in favor of China. You follow all these steps and somehow you are a retailer, not a manufacturer.

Not that there is anything intrinsically wrong in using China as an export platform—particularly if you say that's what you're doing—but it certainly changes the equation. For example, why should you care about the Chinese GDP numbers? You might even benefit if they are exaggerated; a slowdown in Chinese growth would lower the costs of creating plants and hiring workers to make the products that would then be exported to America.

Was the whole game of selling to the Chinese market an illusion then? Not completely, but it did mean that doing business in China was a bit like the psychology of adolescence. The export platform is your parent: it feeds you, puts a roof over your head, even buys you an education. As long as you stick with the retailer pose and don't do anything to offend the Chinese leadership, it feels as if you can try anything, make mistakes, screw up and start all over again because it's *China*—and reinventing yourself while preserving appearances is an art form in Beijing.

The Communist Party had reinvented itself as the party of state-controlled capitalism, and to avoid having to admit they were wrong for over thirty years, they called it "socialism with Chinese characteristics." As expats, we found a double-edged irony in that phrase. When it came to business, the Chinese characteristic was usually outright corruption; and I began to notice some remarkably Chinese patterns inside American companies, cases where corruption became internalized. At first it seemed to be just around-the-edges stuff: a few drinks too many on the expense account and as long as you talked about business on the first round, you submitted the receipt to the accounting department. Americans in America do that, Americans in China do that—and yeah, I did it too on occasion. But it can also become systemic.*

---

*For example, a former executive gave me a detailed briefing on what he believed to be the misuse of expense accounts by Asia Global Crossing president and COO William "Bill" Barney. According to the former AGC executive, there were several revenue streams for kickbacks. Travel agents: accounts payable were used to produce perks such as free tickets. Search firm fees: headhunters were bringing in former WorldCom employees with inflated bills. There were free cars, and there were apartment deals: "relocating" bonuses and an apartment for the administrative manager in Bangkok (although there was no AGC office there). "Mysterious legal fees" came in from an Australian law firm. There were employment contracts that cost up to 20K; one bill even exceeded that, the

In meetings, and in conversations with top members of AmCham, I occasionally made little snipes comparing the ethical standards of the American corporate world with what we did on the ground in Beijing. What bothered me was not the occasional improvised bribe, but the fact that the normalization of illegal activity was already an accepted part of business. I can still see my former colleagues at AmCham rolling their eyes. After all, they had encouraged me to get involved in the AmCham committee structure, even asking me for suggestions on their lobbying trips to Washington. They felt that even if I was a bit of a bastard, I had good Washington connections, and ultimately I would be *their* bastard. I did not have a reflexive view of the Chinese as a bunch of Chi-Coms planning the next cold war. Nor was I some kind of spoiled hypermoral child, blind to the necessary compromises of running a successful business in China.

They read me correctly in part. I acknowledge the faint absurdity of running a straight-shot comparison between American business ethics and laws, and what we did in Beijing. We operated in a deeply corrupt environment. And although they compromised, American companies were paragons in comparison with, say, the French. But in the final analysis, to be a success in China may require that you do things that would be difficult to explain in the West. Gifts to officials, for example, also known as bribes, are commonplace in China. In America they're illegal, and the Foreign Corrupt Practices Act applies to what we do in China. A Chinese teacher whom I met in Shenzhen, referencing various

---

former AGC executive recalls. Yet all of these kickbacks paled beside the possibilities created by a sea of bad debt and a capacity market shot to pieces. According to the former AGC executive, various companies, usually dot.coms, were saddled with high amounts of bad debt; they needed to improve their image and their stock options by buying capacity from AGC. If they could provide approximately a 50K kickback per circuit, the payment schedule was expanded, and late payments were pushed far into the future, even though the companies would clearly be bankrupt shortly.

One fact is beyond dispute: AGC was in deep financial trouble throughout the time period that the former AGC executive describes. Yet even if the story resembled an Asian Enron, what struck me was that it was unlikely to be reported or investigated as an Enron-type scandal, simply because—far from the emperor—this kind of behavior was not that unusual.

small-scale bribes by firms like IBM and Dell, had a name for firms that engaged in this kind of activity: "American companies with Chinese characteristics." Then he identified the larger problem: "Not all of the [American] companies have Chinese characteristics. But some of them without Chinese characteristics will fail in the market competition."*

■

There was one company that unequivocally had not failed in the market competition: Motorola. I learned about how they became one of the top American corporations in China from a former Motorola manager, a man I'll call Buster.

Normally, it's hard to get people to talk about corruption in Beijing. There are confidentiality agreements that keep people in check, but it's simpler than that: if they want to stay in business, they had better be discreet. But with a golden parachute and enough money to live comfortably for the rest of his life, Buster decided that "it needs to come out" and that this afternoon, at least, he could talk about whatever he wanted.

He suggested drinks at the Capital Club, the apex of expat achievement with its soaring view of northeast Beijing. He had a favorite spot, something that looked like a small opium den: all silk throw pillows and an elegant Chinese teakwood table loaded with whiskey and ice. It was reasonably discreet and he didn't mind the tape recorder.

Buster was a senior operations manager for Motorola in China from 1991 to 1995. Those were the big years, which saw the construction of the greatest American success story in the New China. Buster was privy to it all because he had to deal with all the

*When his school wanted to buy two hundred Dell PCs, the institution saw a way to make a little extra money. The direct price for a Dell is 10,000 yuan (approximately U.S.$1,200). The teacher described how "Dell computer will sell them to the Chinese companies—who have a relationship—to sell them to the school at a price of 6,000 yuan. They give the school a receipt for 10,000 yuan ... and that extra 4,000 yuan is not normal profit; that 4,000 yuan is Dell's understanding of how to use the money to bribe some officers to hold the market." He added, almost as an afterthought: "Dell takes nearly no profit for the market."

functions: paging, PCS, cellular infrastructure, cellular subscribers. Internet wasn't big yet back then.

Buster had private access to all the revenue figures. Paging accounted for $1.5 billion of revenues back in the early nineties and Motorola had 98 percent of the business, making about $1.5 billion a year in the early nineties, $2 billion a year by 1995.

Yet Motorola paging did not even have an office in the mainland. They set up what Buster called a "finder's system," working exclusively through Hong Kong and Taiwanese businessmen. Motorola had a contract with the finder: you get 3 percent if we win the award, but you've got to "lobby" on our behalf. To "lobby" meant that the finder would cut a deal with government officials, find out exactly who should receive the money, then pass the 3 percent award directly to the appropriate Chinese officials.

Did other American companies make similar contracts? Buster thought so: "But for Motorola at least, it was 3 percent. . . . It was kind of a standard by the time my division got into China. It was clean as a whistle. Just figure 1.5 billion; 3 percent of 1.5 billion a year went into the government officials' pockets. Thanks to Motorola."

That works out to $45 million a year in the early nineties, $60 million a year by 1995. It sounds like a lot of money. But consider it from Motorola's vantage point: although the company had excellent connections with the central government, its real success was built on playing the regional card, influencing local officials and city bosses far from the emperor. The Chinese bureaucracy is touted as being two thousand years old. And it's never been bigger. The raw numbers, the mass of provincial officials who needed a cut was staggering. Not to mention things like paying off the PLA signal corps for frequency access. Think also of the banquets, the business trips to the United States for Chinese regional delegations, the petty local officials underneath the regional officials who needed to be taken care of, the services rendered—and $60 million a year in bribes doesn't seem quite so large.

The usual strategy, buying goodwill from the jaded central government in Beijing, paid off at times. For example, Motorola was able to cut a contract with the Ministry of Posts and Telecommunications whereby the ministry was actually distributing its handsets. But going to the center involved slightly more risk and cost than at the provincial level (in part, because the central officials were more carefully monitored).

I had noticed this problem myself: if an American company wanted to ease potential friction with the Beijing bureaucracy, yet avoid paying out possibly risky "lobbying" fees, it would have to consider various pass-throughs. One method was to commission a study from a state-run think tank. To make sure that the academics in the think tank did not actually have to think for their money, you could suggest the length of the final report—say, five pages. Every think tank had five pages of party-line boilerplate on various industries in the can. All they had to do was add a paragraph referencing the positive contributions of the American company to China. Such a study could cost U.S.$20,000 (or much more). You could then inform the government officials you were trying to influence that you had commissioned a study with a noted Chinese think tank—and assume that the official would take a cut. Yet the process was frustrating: you had to waste money on lazy Chinese academics and the pass-through had so much deniability built in that the official that you were attempting to sway could pretend that he never got his cut. In the end, it wouldn't be clear what tangible favors or goodwill you had bought for your money.

The other way was to hire a Princeling, a son or daughter of one of the top Chinese leaders, to lobby your case. Most of the Princelings had attended top universities in the United States and were viewed by American businessmen as charming, Westernized, and possessing amazing access to the top leadership. ("Almost like hiring a spy," Buster said.)

The Princelings are an interesting, almost tragic, group—a mirror of the New China's history. Some Princelings nurtured idealistic ambitions to reform China during the eighties, ambitions that collapsed with the Tiananmen movement. To buy their loyalty back, the government engineered key positions for them throughout Chinese politics and business, with mixed results. (For example, several Princelings were implicated in an attempt to sell Norinco AK-47s to street gangs in Los Angeles.) Ultimately, their growing ambitions were slapped down by Jiang Zemin himself, and the impression that one gets in Beijing is that the Princelings are like an aging aristocracy, holding on to the appearance of power and legitimacy, though bypassed by the new, more entrepreneurial China.

Buster had worked briefly for Asian-American Communications in the latter half of the nineties, and the company had hired a Princeling, Lloyd Song (whose father built the Mao Zedong mausoleum and the buildings surrounding Tiananmen Square). Song was given $50,000 a year, and the company arranged for his daughter to be sent to college in the States. Buster disagreed with this approach:

> You almost have to enslave yourself to Princelings and the like. And in doing so, what you miss is what's happening at the street level.... Lloyd Song knew what was happening on the inside of the Politburo—what Zhu Rongji had to say about telecoms. Lloyd would divulge every single minute from every single meeting related to telecoms to us. Yet at the top level they talk in very vague terms: "We support the second operator." And the decisions are made at the provincial or city level. And this is where the problem came in.... The Princelings, of course, know shit about telecoms and technology. The advice that they give you oftentimes is at odds with what is being told to you by the provincial or city officials, and therein lies the dilemma—who do you trust? At every step, Song would thwart what were solid business decisions.... The Princelings' function is to report, not to influence, because they are out of the influential sphere. To hang yourself on the Princelings is a mistake.

According to Buster, Motorola never had a Princeling:

> If you want to influence policy, you have to do it from the provincial level. The best investment that American businessmen ever made was in Hong Kong businessmen who wined and dined the local officials—who got the local officials laid.... The Chinese have a saying: *If there's a policy above, then there's a strategy below.* The strategy below is to find loopholes in the policy above. And the Chinese are very adept at doing that. So Motorola, by localizing, with Taiwanese and Hong Kong businessmen—they're the reason for the success at Motorola.

Princelings were also potentially too indiscreet for Motorola. Buster pointed out that the closest the finder system contract with the Hong Kong businessman got to being explicit was the use of the word "lobby." But the contract was purposely left vague to give Motorola legal deniability and a kind of ethical buffer zone:

> It wasn't as if we could say: I've got this Hong Kong businessman ... who will take care of you. Because, no—I don't want them to know.... So it was all done through Hong Kong businessmen. Ask anyone at Motorola, they'll tell you: *I don't know. Never heard anything about it.* ... But you want to make money in China? Swiss bank accounts have to be involved.

When Buster left Motorola in 1995, the company was pulling in over $2 billion of revenue a year, but it was beginning to slide. "Localization comes at a price," Buster said. It wasn't about the technology. Every time the boys in China had a technical issue, they called in the boys from Schaumburg, Illinois, and they were "world class." Every time the Chinese had an issue with a product, Motorola was there in three days. Motorola was flawless, but insisted on pushing the CDMA standard. China had always been a European-standard country (GSM). In the analog market, Motorola at one point had boasted of 70 percent market share; as China moved to a digital standard, Motorola would ultimately fall to 30 percent, losing out to Siemens, Ericsson and Nokia. Why? In part, because the price of influence had gone up.

The issue of which standard to use was ultimately a central government decision, controlled by Beijing; and this meant that the weakness in the regional strategy was exposed. Motorola realized it. A shadowy expat who had formerly made some successful deals for Ericsson appeared on the scene, shopping his résumé around. Buster says he approached Motorola and candidly laid out a strategy:

> The terms of the deal was ... a ten-million-dollar discretionary fund. Hands off, no questions asked. Don't ask me where the money goes, and on those terms, "I'll work for you." We knew exactly what he was up to, and exactly how successful he would be, and how important and crucial it was.

Buster explained that the "slush fund," $10 million, was simply too large a package this time. Motorola watched the deal slip away and the standards war go to the Europeans who were willing to pay. The victory was worth at least $1 billion, so the $10 million would have been—and was for the Europeans—a good investment.

Motorola was shaken by the CDMA loss, but its ongoing technological edge over European competitors, its ability to innovate faster than Chinese domestic companies could copy them, and most of all, its willingness to transfer advanced technology to the Chinese authorities allowed the company to persevere long after Buster had left for another company and an even more golden parachute.

Motorola is a success, but the company doesn't want to talk about how it became one. I had a longstanding social and professional relationship with the current Motorola VP for public affairs, Jim Gradoville. But once I made it clear that I had some questions for him, he did not respond to my calls. I met informally with a top Motorola exec for coffee, trying to get Motorola's side of the story; he politely clammed up. I took Jim's public affairs partner to an off-the-record lunch at an upscale Sichuan restaurant. She put me through what felt like a litmus test over Jiang Zemin's speech to the Communist Party Congress. I must have failed the test because she never got back to me on a formal interview. And Motorola simply ignored my e-mails.

And as a Beijing business consultant, that's what I would have advised them to do.

6.

Case Study:
Who Lost China's
Internet?

It's not easy being the father of the Chinese Internet. Children are running by, boats are paddling, the smell of roast lamb fills the air, and Michael Robinson, a young American computer engineer, sits rigidly facing the empty café on the shore of Qianhai Lake, speaking in a low voice about the Internet crackdown. "What is better? Big Brother Internet? Or no Internet at all?" he asks.

Michael was hired as the lead support engineer in 1996 by the Chinese government and Global One (a Sprint/France Tele-com/Deutsche Telekom joint venture) to build the first network in China providing public access to the Internet. One day sticks in his mind: The Chinese engineers working with him suddenly convened a special meeting, demanding to know if it would be possible to do keyword searching inside e-mails and Web addresses on the Chinese Internet. Not really, Michael replied; all information that travels the Net is broken up into little packets. It's hard to "sniff" packets of information, particularly coded packets. You would need to intercept packets as they travel, and then there's the problem of collating the information they contain, actually making sense of it. Yes, yes, they said, but can you do it? On the third go-round, it dawned on Michael that his fellow computer geeks wanted to end the meeting too. But at a higher level, someone required assurance. Before Internet construction could proceed further, they would need to monitor what Chinese users did with it. For the engineers, this was just cover-your-ass stuff. As long as the foreigner assured them that down the road, the Chinese would be able to build an Internet firewall to keep the world out and conduct surveillance on their own citizens, the engineers could continue working with him. Yes, yes, it can be done, Michael told them, and they went back to work.

Americans make dreams, and every generation carries new ones to China. Since 1979, that dream has been the fall of the Chinese Communist Party and the rise of the world's largest market, an event that U.S. businessmen and China hands repeatedly predicted was on the horizon or even imminent. Yet Michael was not naïve. He understood the self-serving nature of much of the democracy-is-just-around-the-corner rhetoric. Working inside, he sensed the Chinese leadership's true motives in building an Internet. Michael's friend Peter Lovelock, who heads up the Insight Division at Made for China, a Beijing-based IT research consultancy, puts it this way: "These are Marxists. Control the means of communication; embrace the means of communication. Fill it with Chinese voices. If they can block the outside, and block relationships between Chinese forces, no one will listen."

But for Michael, any reservations over complicity with Chinese government objectives were outweighed by a bedrock faith in the Internet's ingenious architecture. A system originally conceived by a RAND researcher as a way to relay U.S. command messages over a damaged network after sustaining a Soviet nuclear strike could surely find a way to get messages through, securely, amid the white noise of millions of Chinese users. Resistance would be futile—even the Chinese Borg could not stop it. With the genie of free speech out of the bottle, it would just be a matter of time before all those predictions of democracy in China would come true.

That vision has now been called into question, not by a failure of the Internet's architecture, but in several cases by a failure of American corporate values. Let's start the story where Michael left off, with the expansion of the Chinese Internet—a story told to me by a top Chinese engineer, Wen, during a thirty-course imperial meal by the shores of Beijing's Beihai Lake. The shark's fin soup loosened Wen's tongue on the subject of Cisco Systems. In the United States, Cisco is known for, among other things, building corporate firewalls to block viruses and hackers. In China, the government had a different problem for the company: how to keep a billion people from accessing politically sensitive Web sites, now and forever.

Here's how: If a Chinese user tried to view a Web site outside China with political content, such as VIP Reference (also known as Dacankao Daily News, a Chinese dissident information source based in the U.S.) or any of the other Chinese-language Web pages advocating democracy, independence or human rights, the address would be recognized by a filter program that screens out forbidden sites. The request for the forbidden Internet page would then be thrown into the electronic equivalent of the trash, with the user receiving the bland message: "Operation timed out."

Great, but China's leaders had a problem in implementing this maneuver. The financial excitement of a wired China had quickly led to a proliferation of eight major Internet service providers (ISPs) and four pipelines to the outside world. Smaller Chinese ISPs were already looking around to buy unused capacity on corporate networks with connections to the United States. And there was a gold-rush pattern of Western investment—precisely the genie that Chinese authorities had wished for by rubbing the Internet lamp in the first place. At the same time, Chinese government oversight seemed curiously flatfooted, split between several competing ministries bickering over their jurisdiction, creating what the Chinese refer to as a "Warring States" decision-making process.

Yet at the highest levels of the Chinese leadership, there was a growing awareness that once out, the Internet genie could also do great damage. In an oft-repeated story among Western expats, a well-connected People's Liberation Army general surfed the Web for a weekend and, after finding that he could access not only heretical Western news but *Playboy* centerfolds, told the leadership that this new technology presented some problems. The Chinese authorities found themselves uncomfortably torn. They needed Western investment to keep the urban unemployed at manageable levels. They needed to keep Chinese-owned monopolies growing (along with kickbacks from their controlling interests and investments in entities such as China Telecom). But political survival demanded technical control over the content of this new and powerful medium, using technology they did not have.

To force compliance with government objectives—to ensure that all pipes lead back to Rome—the Chinese authorities needed to standardize the Chinese Internet and equip it with firewalls on a national scale. Public Security Bureau (PSB) officials had been overseeing keyword searches, tracking down perceived Internet malfeasance (such as Tibetan independence sites) by hand on a case-by-case basis, and communicating lists of forbidden sites to the ISPs. But the problem was one of exponential growth in volume; by 1998, it was estimated there would be over 2 million accounts online in China, which translates to roughly 4 to 5 million actual users, and the number of Chinese users was *doubling every six months*. Given the rapid expansion of traffic, the filtering and keyword-search demands on the PSB and the ISPs had already become overwhelming. Rationalizing the system—and the terms "firewall" and "censorship" were already synonymous in China— required not just outside help, but specialized equipment that would allow the mainland to route and intercept the traffic internally, particularly e-mails.

When it came to building an electronic equivalent of the Great Wall, the Chinese ministries, led by the Ministry of Information Industry, were considering at least three companies in 1997: Bay Networks, Sun Microsystems, and the networking superpower, Cisco. By 1998, Cisco had trounced the competition, taking the lion's share of China Telecom's CHINANET contracts.

Cisco was known in the industry for its ethos of customer satisfaction and "end-to-end" solution capability; among industry experts in Beijing, Cisco was known specifically for creating the Chinese firewall. How had Cisco gained such a dominant position? According to the Chinese engineer Wen, Cisco came through by developing a router device, an integrator and a "special firewall box," designed for the government's telecom monopoly and its need to comply with government censorship objectives. Cisco also offered a significant initial discount on the price of the firewall boxes. Wen claimed that in the West, a similar Cisco product could sell for as much as $50,000; in China, at approximately $20,000 a box, China Telecom "bought many thousands."

Following IBM chairman Lou Gerstner's meeting with Jiang Zemin in October 1997, IBM arranged for the high-end financing. Accordingly, about 80 percent of all Chinese firewalls have Cisco routers. Michael Robinson concurred: "Cisco made a killing. They are everywhere." And all across China, as users searched for the forbidden Internet, operations timed out.

Cisco did not deny its success in China. Nor did a Cisco rep— initially, anyway—deny that it may have altered its products to suit the "special needs" of the Chinese market, a localization process that the company did not engage in elsewhere in the world. (An executive within the Cisco hierarchy later confirmed to a close friend of mine that China's special treatment had been a controversial issue within the company.) But Cisco categorically rejected any responsibility for how the government uses its firewall boxes. David Zhou, a systems engineer manager at Cisco's headquarters in western Beijing, told me flat out, "We don't care about the [Chinese government's] rules. It's none of Cisco's business." I acknowledged that he had a point: It's not the gun but the way it's used, and how can a company that builds firewalls be expected to, well, not build firewalls? Zhou relaxed, then confidently added that the capabilities of Cisco's routers can be used to intercept information and to conduct keyword searches: "We have the capability to look deeply into the packet." Did that mean they could do keyword searches throughout the Chinese Web if they wanted to? Yes, that's what it meant, Zhou confirmed. When I asked him which Chinese government agencies Cisco reports to, he admitted that the company is under the direct scrutiny of State Security, the Public Security Bureau and the People's Liberation Army.

Does Cisco allow the PLA or State Security to look into the packets? Zhou didn't know or wouldn't say. But minutes after printing out pro-democracy materials from a Web site using a friend's computer on April 18, 2001, veteran activist Chi Shouzhu was picked out and detained in a crowded train station in the northeastern city of Changchun. Because Chi was carrying the writings of pro-democracy activist Leng Wanbao, the police in the northeastern province of Jilin swiftly detained Leng as well. Arrests based purely on Web activity—from the transfer of e-mail addresses by fledgling Chinese democracy Internet discussion groups to Web postings by Falun Gong and Christian underground groups—had suddenly mushroomed in China, suggesting that Cisco was not the only one capable of looking deeply into the packets.

Yet Cisco's firewall was far from foolproof. New sites on forbidden topics cropped up daily, and with the proliferation of ISPs that just wanted more subscribers surfing, the lag time between updating the government's list of banned sites and implementation could still be erratic. So Chinese security organs also needed to control the search engines through which new sites can be found.

The business press had painted a picture of a thriving, home-grown Chinese market for portals and search engines—mirroring such companies as AOL, Google and Excite—with names like Sohu and Sina fighting for the top spots, and Chinese Yahoo!, the American outrider, trailing in fifth place. A top Yahoo! representative spoke to me in July 2001 on the condition that I would not use his name or give identifying details other than that he had recently left the company. He admitted that Yahoo! was actually the most popular portal in China by a mile. Yahoo! played a clever game: for every major survey they split Yahoo! into several regional sites so they would not appear to be number one. Management chose to fudge the hit rate, because "We were viewed as extremely aggressive. We were seen as too foreign."

Chinese xenophobia led many other American companies to play similar games, but Yahoo! was particularly eager to please. All Chinese chat rooms or discussion groups had a "big mama," a supervisor for a team of censors who wiped out politically incorrect comments in real time. Yahoo! handled things differently. If in the midst of a discussion you typed, "We should have nationwide multiparty elections in China!!" no one else would react to your comment. It appeared on your screen, but only you and Yahoo!'s big mama actually witnessed your thought crime. After intercepting it and preventing its transmission, Mother Yahoo! then solicitously generated a friendly e-mail suggesting that you cool your rhetoric—censorship with a New Age nod to self-esteem.

The former Yahoo! rep also admitted that the search phrase "Taiwan independence" on Chinese Yahoo! would yield no results, because Yahoo! had disabled searches for select keywords, such as

"Falun Gong" and "China democracy." (Search for VIP Reference, the prominent Chinese dissident site, and you would get a single hit, a Chinese government site ripping it to shreds.) How did Yahoo! come up with these policies? The rep explained, "It was a precautionary measure. The State Information Bureau was in charge of watching and making sure that we complied. The game is to make sure that they don't complain." By this logic, when Yahoo! rejected an attempt by Voice of America to buy ad space, it was just helping the Internet function smoothly. The former Yahoo! rep defended such censorship: "It's fundamental to respect local management.... We are not a content creator, just a medium, a selective medium."

But it was a critical medium. The Chinese government used it to wage political campaigns against Taiwan, Tibet and America. And of course, the great promise of the Internet in China was that it was supposed to be unfettered, not selective. The Yahoo! rep was blasé in the face of this outcome: "You adjust. The crackdowns come in waves; it's just the issue *du jour*. It's normal."

But what is "normal" in China can be altered under duress. As early as 1999, foreign businessmen were quietly aware of Chinese surveillance's wide net. State Security may acquire practically any routine communication it likes, but can it collate all that information, or make any meaning of it? Probably not, we thought. So paychecks were signed, business plans were churned out, venture capitalists went in search of charismatic dot.coms in Beijing's Silicon Alley, all with confidence that serious financial transactions could be encrypted. But that confidence began to erode as warning signs appeared—a government smear campaign against Microsoft's supposed ability to "see" into Chinese transactions (and share the data with the CIA), PLA ambitions of China using an alternate operating system ("Red Flag" Linux) instead of Windows. It all started that summer.

By October 1999, the State Encryption Management Commission, an obscure government entity (which had not even bothered to come up with a translatable English name when it first appeared) was floating a new directive for foreign companies. Give us your source codes, the keys to encryption. Register your computers and provide a photocopy of the passport of every employee using encryption (i.e. practically all popular business software). Laptops would be repaired (and presumably downloaded for State Security perusal) exclusively in government-approved shops. Employee movements within companies, from screen to screen, would be tracked. Palm Pilots and mobile phones would be declared at the border along with infectious diseases.

Western corporations assumed that these directives were a perverse byproduct of some sort of internal Chinese power play. It was whispered hopefully that the State Encryption Management Commission would, soon enough, simply recede back into the darkness. But in January 2000, the commission declared an ultimatum to all of the Western companies operating in China: register with us by the 31st of the month—the first step in compliance—or face confiscation and prosecution.

A controlled panic set in. Three groups began to work on the issue: the U.S.-China Business Council, the American Chamber of Commerce and the E-Commerce China Forum (a Beijing-based lobbying group of Western technology companies). The U.S.-China Business Council had the sturdiest Chinese ministry connections and began its usual strategic approach of wheedling and gentle threats. But given the apparent determination of the Chinese government to settle the encryption issue permanently, no one really knew how to proceed. Even the U.S. embassy seemed to be at a loss. At the weekly assembly of the American Chamber of Commerce, the embassy commercial section promised the eventual arrival of the cavalry: Commerce Secretary William Daley would visit Beijing in a month or two. He would speak to the leadership and put things right. In the meantime, the embassy's representatives explained, we were expected to engage in a holding action: bring up the new encryption regulations with our Chinese business associates—in karaoke bars, saunas, wherever—and ask them to relate our concerns, respectfully of course, to the Chinese leadership.

As a good corporate citizen, I went to a Chinese-American acquaintance whom I had worked with in the television industry, the husband of my old boss, Wei. A kind of crypto-Princeling, he had an office decorated with pictures of himself standing side by side with prominent figures such as Zhu Rongji and Li Peng. This sort of office decoration was common in Beijing, but I knew that my Princeling acquaintance was no poseur. Jiang Zemin had considered his father important enough to stop by his New Jersey home for tea during his state visit to the United States. By the Chinese rules of the road, the son had inherited a direct line to the leadership, if not to Jiang Zemin himself. In addition, Wei's husband was a true believer in the Internet—everything was possible for China if it would only hew to the New Economy.

But he wasn't the type that would go to a karaoke bar or a sauna. So after a bit of small talk about the latest Chinese Internet user figures, an effort to set him at ease, I put it to him very bluntly: if the State Encryption Management Commission stuck to its position, American businesses and possibly a great chunk of Western investment would pull out. Permanent Normal Trade Relations for China could be in the balance. Why would the Chinese leadership risk it all? His expression morphed into what he might have imagined was a kind of distant, mysterious smile. He was clearly enjoying the moment. He said he would make some inquiries and get back to me.

I wasn't being overly dramatic; the Chinese leadership *was* risking everything. Following a strategy session with some industry representatives at the Regency Hotel, I suggested that the legal counsel of Microsoft, Fengming Liu, have a cup of coffee with me. He was a man in a difficult position: After a former China Microsoft VP (Chinese) had written a best-selling tell-all book where she accused the corporation of engaging in anti-Chinese office politics and imperialist plans for China, the firm had become a favorite pile-on target of the Chinese press. So I wondered if Liu, a Chinese-American, had been picked for his job in part because of his background. This was a common *politic* practice in racist Beijing because it tended to smooth negotiations with the Chinese. Yet instead of being a token figure, Liu was perhaps the most competent of all the businessmen that I became acquainted with in Beijing. In the strategy meetings, he would assess the mood in the room for at least an hour, and only then present Microsoft's position, with a quiet, casual logic that soothed his listeners yet unmistakably laid down Microsoft's objectives.

When we were alone at the bar, I sensed that underneath all Liu's usual reserve, Microsoft's legal counsel was seething. After the waiter left, he put it to me frankly: "Give up our source code? We understand what's going on. This mass of regulations is aimed at us. And Microsoft is not going to put up with it." Liu was glaring now, his eyes seeming to bulge against his wire-frame glasses. If the State Encryption Management Commission did not step back, Microsoft would pull out of China: no Microsoft 2000 launch, nothing. Forever.

It was a calculated leak of some import. Microsoft dominated China, and without its products, Chinese commerce would take a hit. It would be an overwhelming vote of no-confidence and other firms might leave too.

A few days later, I took a cab to the offices of an influential representative of the Japanese community, a Hungarian-American named Tibor Baranski who had made his way into the Japanese corporate hierarchy. His conference room overlooked a busy intersection of Chang'an Jie, Beijing's central thoroughfare. As the golden, contaminated Beijing light streamed in and Chinese shoppers swarmed like flies below us, we consumed several pots of high-octane Japanese tea and a pack of noncounterfeit Kents. In four hours, we had the outlines of an agreement. Contingent on Japanese government approval (without which no Japanese business seems to make any move at all), representatives from the Japanese business community would attend the American meetings on the encryption dilemma.

My crypto-Princeling acquaintance called me a week later. When I arrived at his office, he gave me a dour look, sat back in his swivel chair, and proclaimed that he had gone to someone quite high up and received an explicit answer to my question. "Pop-up windows," he said, quietly nodding his head. I thought I had misheard him, or perhaps that his nodding was a signal that we were now entering the Twilight Zone.

"Pop-up windows?" I repeated stupidly.

"Yes, pop-up windows," he said gravely. He explained: The leadership believed that American encryption software, such as Windows, was actually a kind of enemy agent installed on the Chinese mainland. Sure, Microsoft encryption protected financial transactions, but it was really there to immobilize Chinese computers using pop-up windows. "When the PLA enters the Taiwan

Straits [a delicate way of saying 'when China decides to invade Taiwan'], Chinese computers will receive a U.S. satellite signal. A pop-up window will appear asking for a pass-code known only to Americans. All the computers in China will be disabled."

What classic mirror-imaging, I thought. It's what they would like to do to us, if they had the power; so they assume that since we have the power, we'll do it to them. I couldn't resist arguing that these were X Files fantasies. "As usual, you just don't understand China," my Princeling acquaintance said, shaking his head dismissively and effectively ending the conversation.

But after a few days, it became clear that the international business community of Beijing was not going to wait for the cavalry. As Chinese customs seized encrypted DVDs (coded to prevent counterfeiting) in southern China from a top Japanese firm, chambers of commerce from America, Europe and, most notably, Japan got together with the representatives of IBM, Microsoft, Motorola, NTT Docomo, *et al.* At the top of the China Resources building, packed into the American Chamber of Commerce conference room, we nervously hashed out a consensus communiqué that would receive the chambers' seals and then be sent to all the relevant ministries.

The tension was off the charts: what if the Chinese leadership perceived our actions as a return to the days of gunboat diplomacy? Japanese, Americans and European foreign devils uniting to keep China weak? But we were too far along in the process and the peer pressure was too intense to back down, even if Liu had to keep pushing and we had to go over the same language again and again. The only relief was that the conference room had a sweeping view of the Beijing embassy district. Later, when we took a cigarette break, one participant—only half in jest—recounted expecting a PLA helicopter to appear at the window and commence firing *à la Godfather III.*

What appeared instead, a few days later, was a State Encryption Management Agency clarification (actually engineered by the relatively more relaxed Ministry of Information Industry) defining encryption in narrower terms: the laws would stay on the books, but software containing encryption was okay as long as it wasn't the "core function"—i.e. the sole purpose of the software.

Companies didn't have to register. Mobile technologies and laptops could travel freely; and when they broke down, they could
be repaired outside government shops. Microsoft 2000 could roll
out on schedule. And foreign businessmen could go back to building the New China.

Events had revealed an intriguing possibility. When Chinese
authorities ordered Microsoft to surrender its software's underlying source codes as the price of doing business, Microsoft chose
to fight, spearheading an unprecedented Beijing-based coalition
of American, Japanese and European chambers of commerce. Faced
with being left behind technologically, the Chinese authorities
kept the convoluted laws on the books, but reinterpreted them in
a way that effectively dropped all their demands. Imagine: on-the-
ground multinational industry coalitions and chambers of commerce, seemingly uncoupled from their embassies, successfully
lobbying the Chinese government. But in fact, this kind of behavior was exceedingly rare. We may have had the power, but we also
had a strange unwillingness to use it.

Theoretically, China's desire to be part of the Internet should have
given the capitalists who wired it considerable leverage. Instead,
the leverage all seems to have remained with the government, as
Western companies fell all over themselves bidding for its favor.
AOL Time Warner, Netscape Communications and Sun Microsystems all helped disseminate government propaganda by backing
the China Internet Corporation, an arm of the state-run Xinhua
news agency. Not to be outdone, Sparkice, a Canadian Internet company, splashily announced that it would serve up only state-
sanctioned news on its Web site. A leaked memo on how to handle
press inquiries revealed that AOL was quietly weighing the pros and
cons of informing on dissidents if the Public Security Bureau were
to request such a service; the right decision would clearly speed Chinese approval for AOL to offer Internet services and perhaps get a
foothold in the Chinese television market. AOL went on to sign an
unexpected landmark deal with a Chinese station, CETV, in October 2001. (They also provided for Chinese programming to air on

AOL cable systems, thereby fulfilling a longstanding dream of Chinese state television executives.)

Nortel Networks, one of Canada's largest corporations, aggressively went after the surveillance market in China. Back in the 1980s, the FBI had tried to get potential communication partners to cooperate with "Operation Root Canal," essentially a common standard to intercept telephone communications, and was turned down by literally every American phone company. Nortel cooperated—first with the FBI, and then in the nineties, transferring FBI technology to Chinese State Security through their Guangdong Nortel joint venture.

Since April 2001, surveillance technology had been an IT growth market in China. That was the month when the Ministry of Public Security decreed the construction of the "Gold Shield Project," a nationwide digital network designed to strengthen central police control and to increase the efficiency of retrieving records on every citizen in China. The Chinese authorities had signaled their interest in using the Internet as a comprehensive surveillance system and North American companies appeared to be eager to sell. Cisco and other companies such as Motorola and Siemens had already shown interest. Motorola would eventually become one of the big winners with their sale of Tetra, a state-of-the-art encrypted communications system, to the Beijing police. But originally, Nortel was the most active in trying to persuade the Chinese to upgrade their entire firewall system using personalized tracking filters for Web content that could operate seamlessly even with high-speed Internet technology such as broadband.

Nortel spun its optical network in Shanghai as a "Personal Internet Strategy"—suggesting individual choice and a world of empowerment. But the authorities paid $10 million for it because it allowed them to match users' IP addresses to their demographic profiles, and possibly their political profiles as well. Nortel also promoted a digital surveillance network that it claimed could incorporate and analyze not only video surveillance from remote cameras, but face, speech and individual voice recognition. The information would be cross-referenced with ID cards containing microchips. No more need for unpleasant scenes with police stopping people in train stations to ask for their papers; the IDs could be read through silent proximity devices (and the first ones have already arrived in Beijing). Nortel successfully sold packet-switching equipment to China Telecom, and Nortel high-end integrated video surveillance components were put to use on Tiananmen Square and other urban spaces. According to the Chinese press, such spy technology allowed the Shanghai Public Security Bureau to apprehend a suspect at the Shanghai Railway Station through a match-up of surveillance cameras with online photos and other data—just a hair's breadth away from integrated facial recognition.

Smaller American companies and smaller nations, with more cost-effective methods, could smell the blood as Chinese public security officials and IT Goliaths such as Motorola, Philips, DuPont and Siemens crowded into Chinese Internet security trade shows. Companies such as Netfront (a California-licensed network-security products supplier with most of its sales seemingly in China) and RSA Security (the notorious crypto-research company that pioneered the sale of encryption products to China) became de facto partners of the Chinese state. Free download programs (that also put tracking devices in the computer memory) produced by "spyware" companies like Radiate began to appear on Chinese government-sponsored Web sites.

In the wake of 9/11 and with the growth of unconventional warfare (including computer virus attacks), some of the routine byplay between Beijing and its entrepreneurial suitors has taken on new significance. In one particularly flagrant case in 2001, Network Associates (better known as the producers of McAfee Virus-Scan), Symantec (Norton AntiVirus) and Trend Micro of Tokyo gained entry to the Chinese market by donating three hundred live computer viruses to the Public Security Bureau. Taken together, McAfee, Norton and Trend Micro constituted 74 percent of the antiviral market and the lion's share of the human knowledge base of computer viruses. Like human pathogens, computer viruses can be difficult to stop, so companies usually house their viruses much the same way as the Centers for Disease Control and Prevention does: in isolation, available only to a handful of authorized global researchers (in this case, the Computer Antivirus Researchers Organization).

By way of explanation, the antiviral companies claimed that the Public Security Bureau wanted a way to test their software before they released it on the Chinese market. Naturally, the PSB needed some viruses to put the antiviral software through its paces. Yet there is no evidence that the PSB even went through the motions of performing any consumer tests, nor any explanation of why the PSB needed three hundred viruses to play around with. (Nor had McAfee, Symantec and Trend Micro fallen for this ploy in any other country.) The corporations pointed out that up to 90 percent of the viruses they delivered could be found by dedicated Chinese researchers on the Internet. Perhaps, but what about the other 10 percent?

The relatively benign explanation is that the Chinese were simply trying to exploit a little Western technology and research to give Chinese Internet security companies a leg up in the market. Perhaps McAfee, Norton and Trend Micro were so desperate for licenses that they agreed to make themselves technically vulnerable to the Chinese competition (and they would hardly be the first foreign companies to play such a shortsighted game). But along the way, they made the e-world vulnerable to a Chinese attack. The U.S. embassy had quietly monitored the picture.exe virus, which worms into a user's computer and then quietly sabotages the widely available encryption software Pretty Good Privacy by sending the personal encryption keys to China. The notorious Code Red worm, which some thought originated in China, appears to have been little more than an untargeted amateur nuisance. But in July 1999, two Canadian Falun Gong Web sites found that their service was rapidly being degraded by assaults from Chinese hackers (commonly referred to as denial-of-service attacks). They rerouted to a friendly Falun Gong site in the United States, and after a few days, the U.S. site began to experience similar problems. A crosscheck between the source Internet protocol address (IP) and an Asia-Pacific Internet registry organization revealed the hacker's street address, #14 East Chang'an Street, Beijing—the location of the Ministry of Public Security.

These are not isolated incidents, and the increasingly sophisticated attacks on Chinese dissident organizations may be just a testing ground. Annual Chinese military exercises against Taiwan begin with an "information warfare" phase that simulates an attack on Taiwanese communications, using specialty units from different regions. For example, the Shanghai Information Warfare unit would be responsible for an assault on Taiwan's wireless telecom networks and double-encryption passwords.

America is viewed as a special case. Chinese military analysts of unconventional warfare are alarmed by American military strength, particularly the use of precision-guided munitions in the Gulf War, Kosovo and Afghanistan. But they are thrilled by the apparent vulnerability of American society. The Chinese believe that U.S. over-reliance on the Internet is our Achilles' heel. Chinese preemption—a first strike of coordinated virus attacks to debilitate U.S. communication and financial systems during a crisis—has become a tenet of People's Liberation Army doctrine. As a recent Chinese military journal article put it, the highest objective of psychological operations is to "defeat the enemy without fighting." These cryptic words, which echo the guerrilla warfare sentiments of Mao (or even the interminably quoted strategist Sun Tzu), are being backed up with a specialized PLA "Net Force" of young computer engineers who are trained to develop points of attack on the U.S. Internet. Chinese society is trained, in turn, to accept this strategy as normal, even heroic. For example, in the wake of the U.S. bombing of the Chinese embassy, Chinese hackers were lauded as patriots in the official Chinese press, and my giggling Chinese co-workers called up the defaced White House Web site on my office computer. (I diplomatically agreed that the Jolly Roger fluttering in a cyber-breeze above the portrait of President Clinton displayed a characteristic Chinese panache.)

Chinese senior colonels Qiao Liang and Wang Xiangsui are authors of a book entitled *Unrestricted Warfare,* a kind of PLA bible for Chinese hawks and nationalist hacktivists, where they espouse the use of "new-concept weapons." In the book and other forums, the colonels explicitly advocate a debilitating and untraceable virus invasion of the United States, and a "rumor war" that would cause the collapse of the U.S. stock market. The underlying theme is to use the instruments of a free society, such as the press and the market, against that society itself.

A sophisticated exploratory visit from the offspring of a Norton or McAfee sample virus in the near future is quite possible, yet Michael Robinson believes that the Chinese know there are limitations to what the PLA calls an "electronic Pearl Harbor" attack. The Pacific Fleet in 1941 was not backed up, while most of America's information systems are. So again: what will the PSB do with the other 10 percent of the virus samples, the thirty or so that can't be found on the Web? The Chinese need an attack that evolves. Sustained, rapid-punch attacks on the Internet could severely damage the American economy, infrastructure and morale, but you must begin with a full hand of different virus types, and you must deal them out carefully, over time, to keep the players— Homeland Defense, U.S. business, media and the public—continuously off balance, particularly if financial information is surreptitiously altered before the smoke clears. A well-conceived attack on U.S. infrastructure, such as telecommunications, financial systems and power grids, could work. In real life, networks are constantly breaking. If everything breaks at once, the U.S. economy could be swiftly run into the ground.

Although Americans tend to look at Internet attacks as unlikely because they invoke a kind of mutual assured destruction—just plain bad for business in both countries—consider the Chinese view. The Chinese obsession with substituting "Red Flag" Linux for Microsoft Windows as the prevailing operating system in China is a clue; the PLA is looking for a free hand in potential Internet warfare with other nations, while still permitting internal Chinese state business to continue without interruption. Cisco's "firewall boxes" (and upgrades from Nortel) not only prevented Chinese citizens from accessing critical parts of the outside world, they also were the first phase in the creation of what I think of as GreatWall version 1.0—a self-enclosed Internet that can shut down China's access to the outside world on command.

Why did American corporations, which have labored hard to present positive global images, provide censorship and surveillance technologies to what is rapidly becoming the world's greatest Big

Brother Internet? The short answer is, of course, the money. Building China's Internet meant making lots of it for some of the big
players such as Cisco, Ericsson, Motorola, Nokia and Nortel. One
of my responsibilities was to help manage affairs for the E-
Commerce China Forum, a tech-industry-based alliance of Western companies. In our meetings we discussed how to break down
the trade barriers and the unnecessary regulations of the Chinese
IT marketplace, but we rarely touched on the ethics of censorship
and surveillance. If the subject came up (usually from an oblique
angle, such as how to deal with conflicting regulations), it was dismissed as simply part of the price of doing business in China. Getting in the market was the prime directive; but three critical
assumptions about the Chinese Internet that attained wide currency within the Western boardroom culture of Beijing justified
going along with Chinese government objectives.

First, *it's temporary.* At present, access is contingent on giving the Chinese leadership what they want. Eventually, market
expansion and WTO rules will level the playing field.

Second, *it's a critical market.* While U.S. Internet growth slows,
China's Internet population doubles every six months.

Third, *it's the wild, wild East.* Who will know what we're doing
over here?

The Internet gold rush was exciting—so exciting that even
a few from the traditionally canny Chinese peasant class jumped
in to try their luck. I remember making my way across a desolate
intersection on a bitterly cold night, with winter winds that felt
like they were whipping in directly from the Mongolian plain,
and then going into a warm and bright reception at the Beijing
Hilton for an American-backed startup information-technology
investment firm. I glanced at the brochure—something about creating a synergy between investment and ideas—and surveyed the
scene. The ballroom was crammed with the best and the bright-
est of China's Internet scene, feverishly exchanging cards. I recognized about a third of the players; if I started at the other side,
I could smoothly network my way around the room and then propose a cigarette break with a potential client. A lavishly catered
buffet had been placed in the twelve o'clock position. Perfect. As
I started off toward it, a Chinese teenager suddenly began tugging

on my sleeve. I turned and peered down at him; judging from his hand-me-down shiny jacket, his diminutive size and his gaunt eyes, he was clearly from the provinces. "Are you ... a ... venture ... capitalist?" he asked in halting English, but still managing to convey raw ambition and excitement. I was impressed with his chutzpah, but I won't forget the unsettling feeling of that moment. It reminded me of the stories of New York City shoeshine boys in the late 1920s playing the stock market. I smiled, said no, pointed out a few likely prospects in the crowd, and resolved to lose some weight.

That was how the scene looked up close: corpulent and a little queasy. Perhaps the whole thing was just an enormous cash cow for China Telecom, I muttered to anyone who would listen. One day, a top-ranking member of the American business community simply had enough of my skepticism and took me aside. As we stood in a dimly lit stairwell of Fuhua Dasha, huffing on our counterfeit Marlboros, he laid down the gospel: "Ethan, we are talking about the future of e-commerce, the biggest business innovation of our time ... in China, the biggest market in the world," he said, his voice echoing in the stairwell—*"and that gives me a hard-on! And I want it to give you a hard-on too!!"*

It must have been an effect of the Viagra Economy, but his statement seemed inspirational at the time. He was right. All the major Western corporate representatives in China were being given their marching orders: Develop an e-commerce business plan. Do it now. It was suddenly politic for the reps, many of whom barely understood how to operate their own Palm Pilots and Blackberries, to talk about proactive business-to-business and business-to-consumer e-commerce synergies. And for those of us who worked as consultants, it was time to cash in on their confusion, at least in the short term. Why? Because the reality of the Chinese infrastructure was far removed; no real online payment system existed because there were few credit cards (carried by a small percentage of wealthy Chinese citizens, and most e-payment systems would not even accept payment online from a Chinese address because of a history of collection difficulties). No reliable delivery system existed because package deliveries were controlled by a state-run monopoly. Before state-run factories had Internet-enabled

computers, they falsified their inventories; after receiving net-
worked computers from their Western partners, they continued
to do so. In the vast majority of cases, the online systems did not
bring a quantum increase in efficiency. Instead, many Western
corporations seemed to have settled for the appearance of con-
nectivity and accountability, just another annoyance to their Chinese partners, but good enough for a visiting American CEO, who
was unlikely to give a rat's ass about the details.

Yet while most Western companies were hemorrhaging in
other arenas of the Chinese economy—simultaneously overex-
tended and stymied, imitated and undersold—the new company
was big money for some. Nortel was racking up $100 million in
sales. China was becoming Motorola's second-biggest market in
the world. (Motorola became the top foreign firm in China in
2001, supplanting Shanghai Volkswagen.) The others had hyper-
bolic projections floating around that it would be the second-
biggest market in the world for them too, in eighteen months or
so. John Chambers, Cisco's CEO, was quoted in media reports in
2001 predicting that China would surpass the U.K. as Cisco's second-largest market in as little as three years.

Yes, there were Chinese regulatory ministries with Dark Lords
such as Wu Jichan. In the Internet, however, the pace of innovation, particularly Western innovation, outstripped the regulatory
framework again and again. Peter Lovelock slyly summarized the
situation in the autumn of 2000: "What you can and can't do is
black and white; what you are allowed to do is real gray."

U.S. government oversight of this corporate activity was not
even an issue; as Michael Robinson puts it, for the first four years
of the Net era, those with paranoid visions of China's government
were never quite able to square their suspicions with the rapid
expansion of the Chinese Internet. In congressional testimony as
early as 1994, Lyn Edinger, chairman of the American Chamber
of Commerce, Hong Kong, stated that "The people of China ...
increasingly enjoy access to the nemesis of authoritarianism—the
flow of information." As part of the effort to win Normal Trade
Relations status (then called Most Favored Nation status) for China
during the nineties, business pointed to the Internet to argue that
unfettered commerce was the surest way to change China. Many

in the Western business community believed—and, if pressed, could make a strong case in Washington—that for once, we had outsmarted them. I recall a Western business colleague, in the spring of 2000, adding his favorite rhetorical flourish to his commands: " ... faster than the speed of the Internet!" It seemed to encapsulate all of the reigning beliefs in our technological and financial pace, the changes in Chinese culture, and the inability of the Chinese government to control any of it.

American IT experts pointed to evidence that the Chinese Internet was far from closed; in an effort to get Chinese users on the Web—and fast—the Chinese government had set up a China-wide Internet access service that anyone could use simply by dialing the numbers 169 on the telephone. Local phone charges applied and that was it. Michael Robinson originally identified the 169 network as "the canary in the gold mine. They are not serious about security, they just don't want to look like fools." Most Chinese home computer users didn't have to go through a traceable subscription-based ISP, as users must in America. Chinese ISPs were happy to sell prepaid Internet cards (covered with colorful Chinese advertisements for the latest TV series) on the streets of Beijing, just like prepaid phone cards. Although it was widely rumored in Beijing that over thirty thousand State Security employees were monitoring the Internet in that city alone, the monitoring was laughed at. It was said the bureaucrats liked monitoring pornography so much that they had amassed an impressive backlog. State Security was lax, corrupt, full of holes; even the Voice of America homepage was getting Chinese hits. Associations could flourish among the patrons of the cybercafés, using anonymous monikers.

Western journalists followed Chinese whiz kids into apartments in dark Beijing alleys; their precocious comments were raptly recorded as they demonstrated that they could surf through the firewall and beyond. Ah, to be young, Chinese and *weiku* (a sino-version of the phrase "way cool"), young American reporters cooed as they announced a "new cultural revolution" of young urban Chinese sophisticates, impervious to ideologies of any stripe, concentrating instead on techno music, fashion, and a kind of yeah-but-we-got-each-other sensibility. The optimism went beyond youth culture.

Human rights advocates saw a reporting and organizing tool. Over-seas dissidents saw a platform. Many Chinese intellectuals felt that they were glimpsing the future—the Internet as a populist river lead-ing China inexorably into the ocean of the global community.

Then, in October 2000, the Chinese government began con-struction of a cyber version of the Three Gorges Dam. The State Council ordered Internet service providers to hold all Chinese user data—phone numbers, time, surfing history—for at least sixty days, thus making the stealthy prepaid ISP card vulnerable to a phone trace, or to simply linking up a name with a phone num-ber. In November, commercial news sites were banned. In Decem-ber, the National People's Congress decreed all unauthorized online political activity to be illegal. January 2001 saw the criminaliza-tion of Internet transfer of "state secret information," such as reports of human rights violations. February brought "Internet Police 110," software blocking "cults, sex, and violence" while monitoring users' attempts to access such sites. By March, the sur-veillance started to work; thousands of chat room messages on Sina, Sohu and Netease as well as e-mails on the controversy sur-rounding the schoolhouse bombing in Jiangxi disappeared. Around the same time, Chinese authorities announced that a "black box" to collect all information flowing across the Internet was nearly completed. In April, arrests of democracy activists using the Web and a nationwide crackdown on cybercafés reached critical mass. Surviving cafés had to install internal monitoring software and hire personnel to read over people's shoulders. (In Chongqing, the PSB and a local software company even came up with their own filtering system; for a sum of approximately $50, cafés and businesses were required by law to buy "protection.") E-mail to Tibet now took three days to get through, if it did at all, and Falun Gong e-mail was eradicated.

"Better to kill a thousand in error than to let one slip through," said Zhu Rongji back in 1996. Now, in the spring of 2001, the Chinese Internet would slow to a crawl on certain dates, such as May 22 (the anniversary of Falun Gong's demonstration at Zhongnanhai) and June 4 (the anniversary of the Tiananmen crackdown), a result of surveillance and dynamic route filtering (denying certain computers access based on suspicious patterns).

If this was GreatWall version 2.0, by the summer of 2001, the new economy had already begun its retraction. Thousands of entrepreneurial schemes and business plans—along with notions about joining the global community, fomented by young Chinese idealists—quietly went under the knife.

In October, when President George W. Bush flew to Shanghai for the Asia-Pacific Economic Cooperation summit, he was entering an Internet police state. To deflect criticism of China, but perhaps also as a demonstration of power, blocks on Western news Web sites were temporarily lifted by Chinese authorities. The minute Bush was airborne again, the blocks were back in place. During Bush's visit to China in February 2002, any attempt to discuss loosening Chinese Internet controls was undoubtedly brushed aside with the rhetoric of our own struggle against terrorism (what, you're against surveillance?).

There were urgent reasons for the Chinese Internet crackdown, but fighting terrorism wasn't one of them. Instead, look to the slow-motion crisis of a leadership transition; the release of the Tiananmen Papers; the emergence of a cyber Falun Gong; and a stirring on the streets of Beijing—if not for genuine democracy, then at least for greater freedom of expression to accompany people's modern and affluent aspirations. The Chinese Internet had expressed those international cravings: the pretend online payment systems that travel agencies advertised (which actually involved young boys bicycling around Beijing purchasing and delivering airline tickets), the imitation Western Web sites, the chat rooms flooded with sarcastic and witty remarks. The Chinese state needed to channel those urges back, if not into loyalty to the Party, then at least into a kind of crude, insular Chinese pride. Then again, there may have been a more elaborate game afoot. Chairman Mao knew the utility of briefly loosening controls to create a dragnet. His successors had promoted a "Hundred Flowers" period of relative Internet freedom to expose anyone who disagreed with the legitimacy of their rule and, of course, to attract massive Western investment and American technologies of surveillance, encryption, firewalls and viruses.

The American business community downplayed the crackdown, rationalizing that U.S. corporations, libraries and universities had also installed filters that prevent employees from accessing porn or gambling. The underlying assumption, which conformed with the Chinese government's line, is that the Chinese people acquiesced to Web restrictions and monitoring—even in their homes—because they understood the larger need for social stability. Yet a close reading of Chinese surveys indicated that at least a third of Chinese surfers had used technical means (proxy servers) in an attempt to surf anonymously out of the firewall.

The Chinese Internet crackdown did not have to contain comprehensive warnings and penalties. The vagueness of the regulations and the randomness of arrests created internal restraint on homepages, in chat rooms, even in *weiku* sites. (On the incentive side, the example of the "netrepreneurs" suggested that if you kept saying the right thing, you might even get rich.) Peter Lovelock explained: "We are *all* self-censoring. Every two weeks we take my column in front of a censoring committee. We are all terrified that the goon squad will come marching through the door." Lovelock is usually the court jester of the Beijing Internet scene, but he dropped all his mockery and his pretense of ironic detachment when he told me, "The Internet will be the thing that catapults China into superpower status." Lovelock is right: we funded, built, and pushed into China what we thought was a Trojan Horse, but we forgot to build the hatch.

■

Consider a Chinese user in search of an unblocked news article or a democracy site. Perhaps he's looking for something on the Taiwanese elections, or perhaps it's VIP Reference, or a BBC article on the Chinese leadership. He won't expect to get through, and if he does, it will be cause for some anxiety, for the site may be a tripwire—not for spam, but for State Security. Everything he does on the Web might conceivably be used against him. Pornography? Very selectively enforced, but potentially a two-year sentence. Politics? Far more serious: the government is not very threatened by a little mouthing off in a chat room, but if it looks like an attempt to organize other likeminded surfers—permanent loss of career, family and freedom. The middle-school teacher who typed the phrase "overthrow the Communist Party" on a Web site forum was lucky enough to receive only the two-year sentence for pornography in a local penal institution.

These depressing trends were masked by the noise of the grow-baby-grow Internet economy in China and by Western analysts who depended on the continued growth of that economy.* While thousands of cybercafés are closed by police, thousands more pop up across the country, they pointed out. Yet cybercafés were no longer safe havens. Jiang Yonghong, a thirty-four-year-old engineer from Chengdu, had been detained in a labor camp from December 1999 to September 2000. Shortly after his release, Jiang was arrested while viewing a banned Falun Gong Web site in an Internet café in January 2001. He was sentenced to labor camp again in June, but according to the Falun Dafa (Falun Gong) information center, before he made it to the camp he was beaten to death in the detention center.

A friend of mine, Shai Oster, a former editor of *Asiaweek,* went to a small cybercafé in a distant province. Intending simply to catch up on his e-mail, he signed in using his obscure Chinese moniker. After a few minutes, the owners told him to leave. Not only had they picked up that he was a journalist but, eerily, they addressed him by his English name.

---

*I have seen a surprising number of China-based American journalists and businessmen smile knowingly and reassure their ignorant stateside friends that the individual Chinese user can still get through the firewall. They are correct in that there are some brave Net-dissidents out there. Think of the Falun Gong activist who plays cat-and-mouse with the authorities to reach other practitioners. He must have extensive tools: firewall programs that identify tracking PSB computers, several Internet accounts, two or three telephone lines, and possibly more than one hard drive to mask his online identity. The underground Christian movement in China works hard to maintain an Internet lifeline with the larger Christian world. Its isolation is not total, as evidenced by certain online English-Chinese lessons that have been known to use passages from the Bible that the Chinese Christians specifically request. But these are the outliers of the system. Other individuals, mostly in universities, have the know-how and patience to gain access to illegal content, although they may not be doing much with it. As Jack Goldsmith from the University of Chicago put it, "regulation is about raising the cost of getting information." For the vast majority of users, the cost in terms of equipment, persistence and potential consequences has simply grown way too high.

Shortly after arriving in Beijing in 1998, working from my office in a Chinese TV studio, I went online anonymously through a local server and opened my e-mail (in a browser-based Hotmail account, which in theory should be difficult to monitor). A Stateside buddy had pasted a bit of news text into an e-mail for me. The article didn't particularly interest me—just some routine execution of a drug lord in a remote province—but it seemed peculiar that the words "China," "unrest," "labor" and "Xinjiang" were in queer half-tone double brackets, as if they had been picked out by a filter. When I asked my friend about the bracketing, he had no clue as to what I was talking about. At the time, I assumed that what I was seeing was a glitch—the remnants of a keyword search program in Chinese State Security's central computer that the electronic janitor neglected to clean up. Or, I wondered, had my inbox actually been selected for examination by a Chinese security agency? (Computer engineers who work for the PSB have confirmed that both methods are used regularly.) What I didn't realize then is that the capability to search inside my e-mail, using either method, probably came from a Western company operating in China. Looking back over the incident, I now realize that it was unlikely that my curiously bracketed e-mail was an electronic screw-up. Rather, it was an intentional warning and any savvy Chinese user would have sensed it instantly.

It worked. I wasn't a dissident, but going online in Beijing became a tense, frustrating experience. I began to notice other problems in my Web-based e-mail, such as messages in my inbox that I was certain I hadn't seen before, which Hotmail clearly indicated had previously been opened. So I followed the lead of my Chinese friends: when I composed certain e-mail, my first and last sentence would be on some innocuous subject like the weather or films. In the body of the text, I was careful to avoid using political hot-button words, and if I had to write about Falun Gong or the Chinese leadership, I would spell identifying words backwards or put in unnecessary spaces like a spammer. I cleaned my cache obsessively so it would be hard to pick up a pattern in my surfing history. I kept several e-mail accounts with false identities for different functions. And I paid for a more expensive dial-up Internet service, Jitong, said to be lax about surveillance.

Before the crackdown in 2001, one could escape and surf anonymously by employing a *proxy server*—using a Web address to link up to another computer that would act as an intermediary between you and Web sites, hiding the Web footprints, evading the filters, and circumventing the government controls. (I used proxy servers regularly to access U.S. news and Asian papers such as the *South China Morning Post.*) Not surprisingly, the most common search words in China were not words like "Britney" and "hooters," but "free" and "proxy." Fully 10 percent of Chinese users, representing about two million people, actually confessed to using proxies regularly in a survey done in 2000. (25 percent admitted to using proxies at least on occasion and another 5 percent, in a highly unusual response, simply refused to answer the question.) So an educated guess at the real number of proxy users is probably around 30 or 40 percent. In what Michael Robinson calls "the first sign of cleverness" by the Chinese government, a proxy pollution campaign began in spring 2001 when the authorities either developed or imported a system that sniffs the networks for proxy signatures. Previously, it took State Security two months to find a proxy server; now it seemed that security officers were shutting them down almost in real time. A user, frantically typing in proxy addresses until he finds one that isn't blocked, effectively provides the government with a tidy blacklist. The word on the street was that the government had actually created fake proxies as a sting—a way to lure errant surfers in for further surveillance. Even if you didn't believe the government was that clever, many subscribed to a simple rule of thumb: if you got ten failures before you found a cloak, that might be enough to stimulate Public Security Bureau interest in your Web activities. It didn't take many of these paranoid-but-tedious sessions before many of my Chinese friends simply gave up climbing over the firewall.

Few Western journalists remarked on the proxy crackdown, focusing instead on the explosive IT economy, the sistas-are-doing-it-for-themselves rhetoric of the Chinese netrepreneurs, and Chinese government attempts to make the Internet a "service," essentially the use of lower-level bureaucratic homepages to create a fresh new appearance of state accountability. Yet the forced abandonment of anonymous surfing and access to the forbidden

Web was a seismic change in the character of the Chinese Internet—and even the character of U.S.-Chinese relations. It had a
palpable effect on the way many Chinese users would perceive
world events such as the EP-3 "spy plane" crisis. When Chinese
state journalist-shills proclaimed that the lead pilot Wang Wei was
a hero, and that the American EP-3 had willfully banked into the
Chinese fighter, knocking him off his flight path and into the
South China Sea, few Chinese users were able to see the widely
available U.S. Department of Defense seeing-is-believing Web
footage of the Chinese pilot nudging up to the EP-3 and giving
the U.S. crew an obscene gesture.

Because we were an American company, our broadband Internet access was relatively unblocked, and when I went to my office
late one Saturday afternoon during the crisis, I found a Chinese
colleague, alone in the office, downloading and printing out every
U.S. report he could find on the subject. When I asked him about
the printouts, he sheepishly admitted that they were his, and consoled me with the comment that the American crew would probably be released soon; then he abruptly launched into a tirade
about Taiwan being a possession of the mainland, as if to cover
his tracks. Only a tiny fraction of Chinese workers have this kind
of access in their workplace, however. Some of the early Chinese
reactions to the attack on the World Trade Center can be traced
to this lack of access; without the comprehensive footage from
CNN, the story was more abstract, making it easier for Chinese
people, particularly students, to adopt a kind of callous irony, if
not outright glee.

Perhaps American journalists didn't notice because, for a
small fee, expat users could drive the Cadillac of secure surfing: a
Web-based proxy browser, such as Anonymizer. Most of these programs use secure socket layer, a high level of encryption. In the
United States, Anonymizer and programs such as Hiddensurf prevent private companies from sending cookies or gathering information on a user. In China, they prevent government agencies
from examining the user's surfing history while effectively evading State Security's sniffer programs because there is no signature.
But they can be activated only by payment online. Even if Chinese users could understand the English on the Web-based proxy

sites, credit cards were scarce; and just for good measure, Anonymizer was finally blocked as well.

Late in the summer of 2001, I spent a day at the University of Oregon, sitting in the office of physicist Stephen Hsu, watching him diagram the Chinese firewall and its weaknesses on a blackboard. He was a credible instructor; nine months earlier, the company Hsu co-founded, SafeWeb, had been hired by the Central Intelligence Agency's public/private investment fund, In-Q-Tel, to create a secure Internet communication system. Still, for Hsu, whose Taiwanese parents fled from mainland China, the corporate side of SafeWeb was secondary; his eyes lit up when he talked about creating a secure communication for the Chinese Web user, specifically through his proxy server system called Triangle Boy.

Hsu explained that the triangle refers to the Chinese user, a fleet of servers outside the firewall, and a mothership that the servers report to but the Chinese government cannot find. It wasn't hard for the average surfer to use; tens of thousands of Chinese users had connected with the Triangle Boy system and five of the top twenty global Triangle Boy searches were for Chinese-language sites. Every day, Chinese users who had made an initial contact would receive e-mails listing new addresses of Triangle Boy servers, allowing the Chinese users to anonymously visit Web sites that they would otherwise be unable to reach. It could even allow Chinese users to build their own Web sites and user groups, the antecedents of a political movement. Hsu explained that with enough funding for a bank of servers, Triangle Boy would be practically unbeatable. Any attack, especially on the mothership, would require vast resources.

Hsu was optimistic because Voice of America (VOA) had just begun nominal funding of Triangle Boy at $10,000 per month. The VOA officials had come to SafeWeb out of frustration; not only had VOA's Web site been a high-profile target of Chinese blocking, but VOA was attempting to send daily news via e-mail to some 800,000 addresses in China, with little sign that they were getting through. Hsu estimated that supplying one million Chinese users with Triangle Boy (approximately 600 million page views a month) would require $1 million annually—just a dollar per user. Budgeted at $300 million a year, VOA, at least on paper, had the means.

I left the campus impressed with Hsu and feeling a sense of elation: American ingenuity could beat the firewall. Perhaps the message could get through after all; it just needed a push. Yet as I corresponded with Michael Robinson, it became clear that Triangle Boy was still theoretically vulnerable to spoof sites, authorization problems, or a Code Red–style worm attacking the servers. In addition, the publicity surrounding Triangle Boy had already reached China, igniting what Michael referred to as "Murdoch syndrome."

In 1994, Rupert Murdoch declared that satellite TV was an "unambiguous threat to totalitarian regimes everywhere." The Chinese government listened carefully to Murdoch's words, Michael explained. Then they promptly seized control of cable television, tore down rogue satellite dishes across the country and blacklisted Murdoch's Star TV. If Michael could foresee the lines of attack on Triangle Boy, the Chinese Web authorities were likely to be testing them out already, I reflected.

From Voice of America's standpoint, the more lethal problem was that SafeWeb had a high burn rate (like so many other startup IT companies). As Hsu pushed for the big money, VOA engineers began to view Triangle Boy as a potential New Economy boondoggle. So instead of funding it, they worked out a compromise that pleased no one. Hsu's daily Triangle Boy addresses were delivered in VOA's push e-mails—the same ones being blocked, and the first place that a Chinese government agent would look. Chinese State Security quickly snuffed out the proxy rebellion (and Triangle Boy rapidly became inoperable in China).

Given VOA's mistrust of a corporate entity such as SafeWeb, the next wave belonged to the hacktivists, the loose coalition of North American programmers dedicated to keeping the doors of the global Internet wide open. Hacktivists like to do things the government won't or can't do, such as distributing the Tiananmen Papers to China using an anonymous network like Freenet, and the challenge of the Chinese Internet had captured the hacktivist imagination. Consequently, as SafeWeb faded, government officials from the State Department, VOA and the House of

Representatives Policy Committee started meeting quietly with the authors of systems designed to defeat firewalls—systems such as Peekabooty, Pseudoproxy and Socket2me.

A few of these programmers considered themselves to be aligned with Hacktivismo, a young hacker group formerly called the Cult of the Dead Cow. There was a distinctly antigovernment quality to the group's pronouncements, but I wondered if they might follow the traditional aging pattern; several formerly notorious hackers had recently gone legit and were advising corporations on how to protect their networks against their old hacker friends. I spent some time with Hacktivismo's leader, Oxblood Ruffain, talking about what it would take to get the hacker idealists to work cooperatively with the U.S. government on a common cause. Clearly, it would not be easy. Hackers can be an ornery bunch. They aren't fools, nor are they anarchists. They are outright romantics. They have a voracious appetite for power, but they are petrified of being seen by their peers as working with the stodgy U.S. government.

Perhaps, I thought, Washington already had what it needed in Paul Baranowski, the lead developer of Peekabooty. Operating outside the Hacktivismo system, unencumbered with a company or a burn rate, Paul was simply a young programmer with a disarming smile who lived in Toronto and wore a lot of black. As if he were a young gunslinger who just rode into town, he told me, "I've never met anyone who's a better coder than me," and he left it at that. The code he offered is identified as a peer-to-peer system. Unlike a system that uses massive amounts of servers such as Triangle Boy, Peekabooty depends on the kindness of strangers; the system builds organically, from computer to computer, each user introducing fresh users into the network. Even if one of them turns out to be a PSB agent, the system is layered in such a way that, like a revolutionary cadre system, the agent can bust only a small percentage of the network. By its nature, a peer-to-peer system builds trust, possibly insurrection. But it can also fizzle or take years to gain critical mass. VOA would not commit, and in the spring of 2002 Baranowski rode back into the Toronto sunset.

On May 30, 2002, Cisco Systems and the U.S. Securities and Exchange Commission received a proposed shareholder resolution (essentially, a method shareholders use to change corporate policy) from a woman named Ann Lau. A human rights activist from Hong Kong who now lives in Southern California, Lau serves as a networking agent in the dissident community. A shareholder resolution is a page out of the environmentalist playbook; in theory, if a company is publicly embarrassed, it may take remedial action.

Lau knew firsthand how pivotal the Internet was for dissident communication. She also sensed a wave of activism. In the spring of 2002, the China Internet issue had gone from smoke to cyber-fire on the American Web. Slashdot ("News for nerds") held angry discussions on the American companies' role in building the Chinese firewall. The issue briefly hit number five on the "Blogdex," a counter of personal Web-log references, while translations of critical articles started appearing in Chinese, French, German, Spanish and Vietnamese. A few Stanford students began talking about divestment—literally removing Cisco from Stanford's Industrial Partners Program, while convincing the university to cancel its $70 million order of Cisco voice-over-IP equipment.

In a one-page memo, Lau attacked the morality of Cisco's China operations, proposing that the company produce a special annual report for Cisco shareholders, providing detailed information of all Cisco products that are presently sold to state-owned entities in countries, like China, that employ national firewalls or monitor Internet traffic.

Seven weeks later, Cisco's lawyers responded with an eighteen-page document (employing narrow margins). The lawyers rejected the shareholder's proposal as unfeasible and inflammatory. The shareholder's accusations were false and dangerously misleading. It was impossible to keep shareholders informed about what products it was selling on a global scale because client confidentiality would be damaged. In addition, U.S. security agencies were monitoring terrorist activity in the United States; did the proposed shareholder resolution mean that Cisco Systems would have to report on any Cisco products that U.S. law enforcement and national security agencies are currently using? Although the

Securities and Exchange Commission permitted Lau's resolution to go through, the shareholders predictably voted it down by a wide margin.

Yet Lau would be back next year, and what Cisco was trying to deny was common knowledge among industry insiders in Beijing. Cisco's conflict of interest—being forced to consider American democratic ideals while placating Chinese demands—partially explain why the company's lawyers were tied up for weeks refuting a one-pager from one angry shareholder. But the larger story was that Cisco was responding to the political climate in Washington in the spring and summer of 2002.

Congressional committees, such as the Congressional Executive Commission on China, were beginning to explore the Chinese Internet issue. Think tanks from across the spectrum—the American Enterprise Institute, the Carnegie Endowment for International Peace, the Project for the New American Century and RAND—were supplying research and witnesses. The National Endowment for Democracy, stung by charges that they had been working too closely with the Chinese government and ignoring Chinese dissidents' requests for funding, played catch-up, announcing their own hearings. A faction in the State Department launched a discreet investigation while the U.S.-China Security Review Commission, a bipartisan committee that reports on the national security implications of U.S.-China trade, privately questioned Cisco and Nortel Networks on their China operations for their report to Congress.

In late summer of 2002, the House Policy Committee, the voice of the Congressional Republican majority, came out with a report dramatically entitled "Tear Down This Firewall." The committee advocated massive government intervention to free the global Internet, with special emphasis on China. This was a prelude to introducing the "Global Internet Freedom Act" in October (sponsored by Representatives Cox and Lantos in the House, and Senators Wyden and Kyl in the Senate). The bill's purpose was to develop and deploy technologies to defeat Internet jamming and censorship, with a request for $50 million to establish an office of global Internet freedom in the International Broadcasting Bureau, the umbrella organization for VOA. It looked as though another assault on the fortress was imminent, and the prominence of the

Chinese Internet in two major reports, both invoking national security, and a major congressional bill suggested to me that preliminary export controls or, more likely, a corporate code of conduct for American companies operating in China could be waiting in the wings.

I was wrong. The U.S.-China Security Review Commission's report to Congress had explored the Chinese Internet problem in unprecedented detail, explicitly fingering AOL Time Warner and Yahoo! in complying with the demands of the Chinese authorities. Yet the report let Cisco, Nortel and other companies off with a nonspecific reference to assisting "the Chinese Government in sensitive areas such as remote surveillance, online censorship, and virus acquisition." Based on interviews with commission staffers, it was clear that they had gone to the corporations' public affairs departments (and received the predictable denials) but they lacked the resources—or perhaps a clear enough mandate—to actually begin to investigate the charges against Cisco or Nortel by making calls to Internet experts in Beijing.

The House Policy Committee's report urged private cooperation: "The federal government should enlist the help of the private sector in this effort.... [M]any current technologies used commercially for securing business transactions and providing virtual meeting space can be used to promote democracy and freedom." Fair enough, but where was the "or else"? There was no discussion in the report, or in the ensuing bill, of sanctions for the transfer of American firewall technologies, surveillance and antiproxy systems to China. As for the $50 million earmarked for the new Office of Global Internet Freedom, within less than a year it was quietly whittled down to $8 million, and the Internet freedom bill was put on the back burner.

There were still pockets of resistance—individuals at VOA, at State, and in the House Policy Committee who worked to pursue the Internet issue. One of them, an influential government official, spoke to me during the summer of 2002, telling me in confidence, "This is more than a PR problem for U.S. Internet companies. This is potentially the downfall of corporate appeasement to the PRC."

But he was wrong. It was just the beginning.

I was in the gift shop of Beijing's Kempinski Hotel in 2001 when I found an old Chinese curio. The Chinese leadership transition was beginning, and the *Asian Wall Street Journal* had an intriguing cover headline on the subject. I handed some *renminbi* to the attractive Chinese attendant and turned to page four to read the article. But where was it? I looked up, mentioned that my paper was missing a page, and turned to pick up another. She smiled stiffly, embarrassed. "They are all like that," she said.

Labor and scissors were still cheap commodities in China, but the newspaper that I was holding gave me a subtle thrill, at least as a nostalgia item. It conjured up the censorship of old Communist China—crude, stupidly doctrinaire, oblivious to the setting: a top hotel in Beijing's business district. It felt like a moment of historical continuity at a time when every China lobbyist was saying that China was becoming more sophisticated.

Well, the China lobbyists were correct about that; government censorship was becoming far more sophisticated in the new wired China. The inevitable, final stage of content control required international technology, sophisticated PR, and collaboration by ISPs, search portals, practically every business involved in the China Internet. To secure this level of cooperation, China had to have something to offer. It did: by 2002, China's Internet population appeared to have overtaken Japan's. A Merrill Lynch industry report on Cisco's Chinese partners remarked: "With U.S. demand slowing down, the vibrant Chinese Market has become increasingly important.... Carriers are rushing to get 'WTO-ready,' i.e., upgrading their network infrastructure in order to fence-off potential competition after the opening up of the telecom sector." In other words, for companies responding to American Internet saturation and the anticipated enforcement of WTO, China beckoned as the emerging market for American IT investment.

Yet given the growing Western press attention to China's Big Brother Internet, any consultant would have said that both the Western companies and the Chinese government needed to inoculate—that is, work out consistent talking points and a damage control strategy. Ironically, only the Chinese leadership seems to have created such a plan. If the firewall was GreatWall 1.0 and the crackdown was GreatWall 2.0, GreatWall 3.0 was not to block the *Asian Wall Street Journal* Web site, or page four; ideally the offending article should *never exist* on the Chinese Web.

The Chinese authorities introduced three new components to placate the West and to provide cover for their Western technology corporate partners: the appearance of openness, voluntary complicity and, most critically, artificial intelligence.

The first component, the appearance of openness, was discovered while Jiang Zemin was being interviewed by *New York Times* senior editors in August 2001. Asked why the *New York Times* Web site was blocked in China, an embarrassed Jiang feigned ignorance. A few weeks later, the *Times* Web site was no longer blocked. When the *Washington Post* approached Jiang, they received a thumbs-up as well. But CNN and other instant news sites remained blocked, and the Chinese Internet policy simply looked irrational. After several test runs of the press reaction to lifting the blocks on Western news sites, open U.S. news sites became the norm in the spring of 2002. The reaction, at least by local expats, was rapturous. According to one friend-of-China, the Internet was now "as open as a courtesan's thighs."

Yet strange days followed: for two weeks, Internet access to all foreign and overseas sites became painfully slow—it took ten minutes for a *Wall Street Journal* page to load—while the domestic side was as fast as one could want. News sites such as the BBC would be blocked for long periods, seemingly as a kind of punishment for reporting news that the Chinese leadership didn't approve of. In all the excitement, the expats had forgotten several factors: As Peter Lovelock had pointed out, the Chinese authorities had never really cared about the U.S. news Web sites per se. But Chinese democracy, Falun Gong, separatist movements, Chinese labor rights—these were the real forbidden fruit. And these blocks were not only preserved but strengthened. As for the lifting of the blocks on Western news sites, it was conditional; access could be blocked again at any time, or just slowed to the point of being unusable.

Concurrent with the lifting of the blocks on U.S. news Web sites, a shill for the Ministry of Information Industry, the Internet Society of China, rolled out a "voluntary" pledge of corporate responsibility for the industry, emphasizing "self-discipline," "trust-worthiness" and a commitment not to post information that might "jeopardize state security and disrupt social stability"—well-understood code words for preservation of the Communist Party's leading role. Everyone got it. Don't block the entire CNN Web site, but anything potentially offensive to Beijing should mysteriously experience technical trouble. The "self-discipline" pact debuted in March 2002. By July, three hundred Chinese firms had signed the pledge, as did Yahoo!

While Human Rights Watch (a nonprofit watchdog group) savaged Yahoo!'s decision, the *Wall Street Journal* editors defended it, suggesting that Jerry Yang, the company's founder, would have the last laugh. "Merely by bringing honest news about the rest of the world to China, Yahoo! becomes a check on the Xinhua news agency."*

The *Wall Street Journal's* editorial indicated that Beijing had thrown exactly the right bone: the lifting of sanctions on American news sites, combined with voluntary compliance for the censoring that Yahoo! was already engaged in. In short, the Chinese leadership had pulled off a massive public relations coup.

The third component of GreatWall 3.0—the use of artificial intelligence—had been in the works for several years.

As a consultant, I tended to meet most expat businessmen who crossed my path. One well-dressed American used to descend from the China World Tower 2 at the same afternoon hour to get

---

*It was an argument that could have been made back in the nineties, but now it seemed strangely out of step, requiring a kind of willful ignorance. The *Wall Street Journal's* sister publication, the *Asian Wall Street Journal,* was literally getting cut to pieces. Yahoo! was already censoring their search functions; under the pledge, they were likely to be even more restrictive. Acting as a check on the Xinhua news agency was a nice idea. But by signing on to the pledge, Yahoo!—the premier search engine of China and the symbol of the American new economy in Chinese eyes—was perceived as legitimizing Xinhua and the permanent role of censorship in China. The wider context was becoming increasingly difficult to ignore. A tragic Beijing Internet café fire in June 2002 was used by state authorities as a pretext to shut down at least 90,000 Internet cafés nationwide, about half of the cybercafés in China. State Security had perfected the system to hunt down proxies in real time. Arrests for Internet crimes were on the upswing; one man was sentenced to eleven years in prison simply for downloading political content.

a cup of coffee at a quiet little Starbucks outlet on the ground floor. Over a couple of weeks, we developed a nodding acquaintance, and eventually struck up a conversation. He turned out be a pleasant guy, with a sort of fifty-yard stare. Perhaps it was the hordes of Chinese women he dated, or his tough working-class upbringing in a town near Boston, but in the process of reinventing himself as an entrepreneur in Beijing he had also become an unapologetic defender of the Chinese state. He was working hard to hawk a software product called iCognito, developed by Israeli engineers. He called it "artificial content recognition," and he explained that the program surfs along just ahead of you, learning as it censors. All in real time.

iCognito, a so-called neural net program, was specifically built to filter "gambling, shopping, job search, pornography, stock quotes, or other non-business material." As it searches for forbidden sites, it uses over a hundred variables. For example, if a neural net is looking for pornography, it will look for keywords, but it will also use composite measures of the colors on a Web page and look for skin tones. Over time, it learns that there are many different colors of human skin as it cross-references the variables of forbidden sites, and it can become increasingly accurate or, depending on the network settings, just more ruthless. It's particularly good with political sites.

When I asked my new American friend whether he thought such a program would be good for the development of Chinese society, he made a dismissive gesture and said that until the Chinese had money in their pockets, issues like censorship didn't really matter. He told me that selling the product was looking very promising; China Telecom was interested. But, he smiled, the first question from the Chinese buyers was not "Will it make my workers more productive?" but, invariably, "Can it stop Falun Gong?"

The answer is that it can, and iCognito, or a neural net program like it, solved a major problem for the Chinese authorities. Yahoo! has an active presence in China and thus it was easy to control with threats and peer pressure. But what about Google, a company with no representation in China but, because of its nifty caching capacity, able to store virtually any site for a Chinese user to access? Since 2001, Google's search functions had been discovered by increasingly larger segments of the Chinese population. Following the capitulation of Yahoo!, Chinese authorities demonstrated that they hadn't really sworn off blocking access to American Web sites; they blocked Google (and for good measure, AltaVista) in the beginning of September 2002.

The Chinese authorities, however, made the mistake of blocking Google during a U.S. news lull, and the press picked it up, creating new image problems for Beijing. What happened next exposed the guts of the Chinese censorship operation; in a clumsy move, Chinese surfers typing in Google's address found themselves redirected to precensored Chinese search engines. The main effect was to underscore how poor the Chinese search engines were in comparison with Google. Complaints followed, but then the Chinese authorities hit it just right. Google was reopened, but this time, if you used Google to search for Jiang Zemin you would receive the message "no entries found." If you searched for Falun Gong, not only would no entries be found, but your Web access would be shut down for an hour. When the time was up, if you tried to search for Falun Gong again, you would be locked out for two hours or longer—and so on.

Had Google gone along with this plan? Or had the Chinese done it themselves? Or were Western firewall companies playing along, smoothing out the installation of technology to block page four? It wasn't clear who was responsible, but it was clear that a neural net—a program similar to, if not based on, iCognito—was in force and resident all along the Cisco watchtowers. As though conditioning a rat over time not to press a certain lever, the Chinese authorities were teaching extinction behavior to the masses.

In late October 2002, I was back in Beijing to look around and see old friends, after returning more or less permanently to America. I stopped by the U.S.-China Business Council to see Pat Powers, who headed up the China office. We went out for a drink at Frank's Place, a venerable expat bar. I genuinely liked Pat, and he had gone out of his way to look after my interests a couple of times, so it was a friendly scene until I brought up the Internet issue. I made my arguments: American corporations were taking a terrible risk.

The Chinese policy of "voluntary" hair-trigger censorship could backfire. The Communist Party is an unreliable partner: What if Chinese police end the next worker riots using guns and Motorola location-tracing technology? What if Chinese officials actually force everyone to carry a national ID card, developed by Xerox or Nortel or Sun Microsystems, and then use it to round up Christian groups? American IT companies could begin to exercise damage control by avoiding the Chinese Internet pledge and the national ID contract, and they could take credit for showing restraint.

Pat listened, but he wasn't in the mood to discuss my points. His boss, Bob Kapp, ran the U.S.-China Business Council in Washington and had seen some of my writings on the Internet issue. Kapp was "very disturbed" by my views, Pat said, giving me an admonishing stare. I had the distinct feeling that the burden of proof was on me, not the corporations that Pat represented—at least if I expected to have any further viability within the American community.

It went better with Chris Murck, the head of AmCham, in part because we were much closer. Chris was not only a friend but a mentor, and I had a high degree of respect for his intellect and experience. As we had lunch at the China World Hotel, I made the case that American companies in China could guard their U.S. flank by spearheading a collective industry statement expressing concern—something along the lines of "Chinese Internet surveillance and censorship policies have placed American IT companies in a difficult position." At present, the business community's annual policy statement, the AmCham White Paper, didn't even allude to the problem. I argued that the American business community has the integrity to be self-policing, but it has to recognize the problem, even if only by a footnote in the white paper. There would be safety in numbers—no corporation had to tacitly admit guilt or bear the brunt of the Chinese leadership's anger. True, spiteful Chinese ministers might briefly favor European and Japanese IT competitors. But the American presence in any given Chinese market sector is traditionally one of the only guarantees of long-term legal redress, and thus, long-term profitability—even under the WTO regime. And the Chinese know this.

Murck was unusually quiet. He finally responded that it would be out of character for AmCham to take what was essentially a political position in the white paper; there was no precedent for such an action. I sensed that even if he agreed with me (and I suspect that he did), he had made a calculation: the initiative that I was describing would garner little support from AmCham's corporate membership. Our meeting was polite, friendly, and ultimately futile.

In early December, I split a plate of noodles with a senior manager of Nortel's wireless account marketing, Mr. Enoch Chao. Nortel was pushing its "blue tooth" wireless application technology, and Chao explained how a Nortel hand-held could provide an "end-to-end solution" with its "integrated and interoperable capability" to access virtual private networks. Without any prompting on my side, Chao launched into what seemed to be a standard sales patter on how these capabilities were particularly useful for State Security and law enforcement—that is, to dig remotely through a suspect's fingerprints, mug shot, personal history and so on. When I suggested to him that there might be some ethical questions about State Security using Nortel's products for arrests, torture and threats, he looked at me as if I were naïve and responded, "You can use everything for evil. To some extent, it's already happened."

Following the meeting with Chao, I flew down to Shanghai to attend the latest trade show, innocuously titled the "China Information Infrastructure Expo." It was officially blessed by Li Runsen, who heads up the Science and Technology Commission for the PSB—suggesting that China's security apparatus would account for the majority of the customers.

Entering the convention center, the first thing I saw was the word "Cisco." The company's booth dwarfed the others, and the handout indicated that Cisco had also scored the top billing for its Chinese-language presentation, "The CISCO Network Solution for the 'Gold Shield Project.'" It was an interesting series of slides: First it identified the Chinese public security agencies' problems: insufficient police forces; a large undocumented migrant labor population; social instability as a result of WTO; and "high-tech criminals" (an umbrella term which includes Internet dissident activity). Then it touted Cisco's "low-cost" solutions: "Combining voice video and data into one accessible resource," and the ability to integrate judicial networks, border security and "vertical police networks" ("individual departments dealing with secret/confidential business, phonetics, and video frequency").

The Cisco booth entrance was ringed by video screens showing burly cops from Seal Beach, California, pulling over and frisking American citizens, and whipping out Cisco mobile handsets that linked directly to databases containing surveillance footage from stores, waiting rooms and other public places. These images were accented by sound bites from John Chambers, Cisco's broadly smiling CEO. Chambers enjoys a kind of celebrity status in China, as does Microsoft's Bill Gates; but the juxtaposition of a slick Chinese presentation of America as an efficient police state (with no pesky legal impediments or search warrants required to access confidential databases or private surveillance) and Chambers' optimistic New Economy spiel struck me as a revolutionary PR approach.

The other screens were devoted to crisp, high-quality surveillance of the booth, which was divided into specific areas of Chinese security interest: "the IP Telephone Solution for Police Routine Community Surveillance," "the Executive Mobile Solution for Traffic, Patrol, and Criminal Case Police," and "the Video Surveillance Solution for Preventative Control and the Increase of Social Stability." In case you missed the point of all this, Cisco's Chinese brochure featured a prominent schematic depicting an American State Trooper (pot belly, shades and all) connecting remotely to nationwide databases and the Internet.

As Cisco's cameras recorded our conversation, Zhou Li, a systems engineer from Cisco's Shanghai Branch, gave me an enthusiastic sales pitch for Cisco's "policenet" technology, which had just been launched in China. He explained that Cisco's diagram of the policeman linked back to information nodes was technically accurate, but it didn't capture the full scope of what Cisco had accomplished. We weren't just talking about accessing a suspect's driving record here, he pointed out; Cisco provided a secure connection to provincial security databases, allowing for thorough cross-checking and movement tracing. A Chinese policeman or

PSB agent using Cisco equipment could remotely access the suspect's *danwei* or work unit, thereby accessing reports on the individual's political behavior and family history. Even fingerprints, photographs and other imaging information would be available with a tap on the screen. (This wasn't just a sales pitch: according to Chinese sources, Cisco has built a structure for a national PSB database, with real-time updating and mobile-ready capabilities, and as of June 2003 it was already resident in every province of China except Sichuan.) As I questioned Zhou further, the Cisco salesman confirmed that the Chinese police could even check remotely whether the suspect had built or contributed to a Web site in the last three months, access the suspect's surfing history and read his e-mail. It was just a question of bandwidth.

Another Cisco brochure caught my eye. This one touted Cisco's new mobile router, with a schematic layout of vehicles demonstrating the router's potential uses: in a car (traffic control), a train (to make them run on time), an ambulance (emergency and police response) and a main battle tank (presumably to help China win its wars). The Chinese caption next to the tank stated that this was the same technology used by the U.S. Department of Defense, NATO and the United Kingdom. Prices for the 3200 ranged from about $5,000 to $10,000. The Cisco salesman pointed out that the 3200 Series Mobile Access Router was specifically designed to be sturdy enough to be installed in a tank.

At the Sun Microsystems booth, Ms. Angela Ying urged me to press my fingers to a screen. She explained forthrightly that Sun was working with a Chinese partner, Golden Finger (you can't make this stuff up), to implement a fingerprint recognition system and a national facial recognition system ("Facecatch"). They intended to embed these data in a national ID card. For Chinese State Security, it would be a "total solution," Ying claimed. Sun provides the hardware, the server and the computing power. Sony provides the surveillance cameras. Golden Finger acts as the interface with State Security.

Nortel was present at the trade show too, in what appeared to be a somewhat diminished capacity. Inside their booth, a senior engineer assured me that his company was still cutting edge. For example, provided that the aggregate server had sufficient bandwidth, Nortel had developed a "100% packet capture system." These Internet surveillance capabilities were specifically designed "to catch Falun Gong." After the engineer blurted this out, a local Chinese reporter started snapping pictures of us standing together (I was the only American at the trade show, so my presence at any booth could be interpreted as a kind of product endorsement). The Nortel senior engineer decided that Falun Gong could be seen as "a sensitive issue," and quietly asked me to keep his name confidential.

Leaving the show, brochures in hand, I realized that Cisco's defense against Ann Lau's shareholder's proposal was correct. Creating a special firewall box that could be used to censor the Chinese Web may have been the "original sin," a significant cornerstone in constructing the Big Brother Internet, but it was not illegal per se. Yet the products that Cisco (and Sun Microsystems) were now selling to China appeared to be directly flouting the Foreign Relations Authorization Act (fiscal years 1990 and 1991), which suspended "The issuance of any license ... for the export to the People's Republic of China of any crime control or detection instruments or equipment" until the president chooses to try to reverse the suspension. No president has tried to remove these laws, yet they are eroding. When President Bush visited Shanghai in 2002, certain exemptions on bomb-sniffing technologies were temporarily lifted because of the legitimate fear of a terrorist attack. According to a confidential U.S. government source, some major American corporations are already lobbying to use that exemption as a precedent to override the entire policy.

China is the largest rapidly expanding market for IT on earth, so it's extremely tempting to play the Chinese game, particularly for companies such as Cisco and Nortel, which have experienced severe market corrections at home. These companies have depended on the perception that Internet technologies, new and relatively undefined, are a gray area. But they're not; they're a black market where state-of-the-art equipment is sold to an unabashed police state. Cisco is no longer simply assisting the censorship of the Chinese Web; they are assisting the roundup of

Chinese dissidents. And Internet dissidents are the fastest-growing group of political prisoners in China.*

∎

Is China's Internet beyond redemption? Is it destined to be a tool of surveillance and repression, managed by the Chinese government and serviced by a few cynical Western partners?

Michael Robinson, the father of the Chinese Internet, recalls taking a group of Chinese officials on their first tour of the U.S. Internet. The question they kept asking was, "Who's in charge?" The fact that anyone can be a player on the Internet is inherently a subversive idea to the Chinese government. Simultaneously, as Peter Lovelock points out, "The Internet is creating expectations and desire. The government can't stop that. Nothing can." They are both right; a free Internet would be a way to levy a Web-based democracy tax on the Chinese government. Yet unless the administration makes Internet freedom in China a top priority (and at the moment it is a laughably low priority), the signs do not look good.

As Robinson notes, "In the Chinese Internet's infancy, the first three sites that the government blocked were two antigovernment sites—and one Maoist site. What threatens them? ... The heartland." Ultimately, it won't be the intellectuals who are the key to bringing democracy to China. Rural communities and workers in rustbelt cities are slowly getting online (and if Falun Gong is a portent, it may not be pretty). Peasants are less than 5 percent of the Chinese market now, but like it or not, irate overtaxed peasants with Internet-enabled cell phones ten years from now are America's target market. But those who dream

---

*Microsoft was not represented at the trade show. But the corporation that had led an industry-wide revolt against the Chinese government on the issue of encryption, had since made a stunning about-face, first agreeing to share its long-protected source codes with Chinese government entities, and then, according to a Xinhua release in July 2003, contracting with the PSB to build an Internet security technology laboratory with almost four hundred employees. At an initial investment of $10 million, the lab will furnish China's finest with new policing equipment and imaging technology.

of democracy in China are operating with diminishing points of entry, for the American business presence in China is deeply, perhaps fatally, compromised as an agent of liberalizing change.

The Internet is still the strongest force for democracy available to the Chinese people. But it remains a mere potentiality, yet another American dream, unless we first grapple with the question: Who lost China's Internet? Well, we did. And until we—in Michael's words—"lay down the communication network for revolution," his progeny may not forgive us.

7.
Roaring Across
the Horizon

The bomber cruising down the runway was deafening. Peering through the scrub trees of a Chinese air force base outside Beijing in early August 1999, I saw what I now believe was an FBC-1, usually called a "Flying Leopard" or, more colorfully, "Great Wall of the Air." As I studied the aircraft from a hundred yards away while also trying to appear as if I were simply having a quiet smoke, it occurred to me that I was perhaps the first American to see the plane operating at close range.

While its engines were made by Rolls Royce, the Flying Leopard was touted in the Chinese press as the first supersonic fighter-bomber with nuclear capability entirely conceived and built from scratch in China. With a range of over 1,000 miles, it is claimed to have the capacity to transport multiple air-to-air and air-to-sea missiles, up to five tons of ordnance. I would catch a glimpse of a Flying Leopard again a few months later, on October 1, 1999, in a majestic flyover of half a million people at Tiananmen—the highlight of the gala event marking the fiftieth anniversary of Communist rule that was televised throughout the world.

I was at a Chinese air force base not to spy, but as a favor to a fellow Chinese producer. A film shoot was taking place about two hundred yards away from the runway, outside a large and somewhat anachronistic Soviet-style terminal with enormous white columns. The extras were appropriately dressed in period style, women in over-the-knee skirts and braided pigtails, men in carefully ironed Mao suits and Red Army uniforms.

173

This major historical film was being shot by one of China's most acclaimed "Fifth Generation" directors, Chen Guoxing. Although my role was unclear, I was told he needed a white face or two. Foreigners are always in demand, especially for Chinese historical docudramas. If the picture is about the Japanese occupation of China, you might get by using Chinese men—plumper and shorter than the average Japanese, of course—with a little sinister makeup and prosthetic buck teeth. But for a picture about the Opium Wars, you would need plenty of white expats in British army gear to burn down the Summer Palace, bayonet screaming peasant women, and arrogantly water their horses next to the Temple of Heaven. Similar requirements held for the Korean War, with just a change of uniform, really. In the endless rounds of gift-giving that pervade professional television production in China, I had already appeared in several foreigner guises on Chinese national TV: as a solemn smokers'-rights advocate (with a southern drawl); as a New York Jewish producer promoting film investment; and most improbably as a sentimental American fan moistly reminiscing about China's favorite American chick-flick, *Ghost.*

Now, on the set, I was haltingly told to play an American physics professor, a Marxist, a fellow traveler of the Chinese Communist Party from the early 1960s, accompanying another American-Chinese physics professor through an airport, somehow involved in the Chinese development of military technology. At least I wasn't playing an evil foreigner by Chinese standards, I thought. And my lines were simple enough: "Where are they taking us?!" And, "That looks like a Russian plane!" Since I knew that the action took place in the early sixties, I brought along my thick black drugstore glasses. Appropriately, these gave me the appearance of a useful idiot. The other foreign extra, a breathtaking red-head from a top Russian diplomatic family, seemed to think the whole shoot was a lark. On the drive to the air force base, she had whispered to me her belief that the Chinese people were nothing more than animals. (I'd heard the same claim about the Russians; so much for the bear-and-dragon scenario.)

The shoot took all afternoon. It would have been over quickly, but it was interrupted every hour by a vast armada of planes flying overhead in formation, like some sort of newsreel from World War II, practicing for October 1, darkening the sky.

Roaring Across the Horizon has been accurately described as a propaganda film with art-house characteristics. It was screened in Beijing on National Day (my Chinese producer friends gave it a thumbs-up) and it went national in Chinese theaters the next year, winning the 2000 Golden Rooster for Best Chinese Feature Film, and the same at the Changchun Film Festival. It even made the film festival rounds in the United States, with mild critical acclaim from American independent film critics.

The film also has buddy-movie characteristics, as it is centered around two main characters: Doctor Lu and Commander Feng. Lu's character is based loosely on the real-life Qian Xuesen, an MIT and CalTech professor who worked closely with U.S. ballistic missile experts until the early 1950s, but then fell under suspicion of spying for China. Circumstantial evidence suggests that Qian had something to hide, but definitive proof is unlikely to surface because his case was poorly handled; in a shortsighted political deal, Qian was sent back to his native China, where he promptly became the father of the Chinese nuclear program — both in name and in reality — as well as a dedicated cheerleader for the Chinese state (and its crackdown on the Tiananmen movement, Falun Gong and so on). Commander Feng is loosely based on the real-life Marshal Nie Rhongzhen, who, as a protégé of Premier Zhou Enlai, served as the chief of weapons research for the People's Liberation Army.

No Chinese film director would be given access to such important individuals, let alone any historical documentation surrounding the making of the Chinese bomb, so instead the director based the characters of Lu and Feng on Robert Oppenheimer and Leslie Grove, the scientific and military leaders of the Manhattan Project, about whom he could read in American books.

The film portrays the heroic construction of the Chinese atomic bomb. Its first historical revision serving current Chinese objectives is that the bomb was not developed against the Soviet Union (a far more menacing threat to the PRC than the U.S. was in the 1960s) but against the American hegemon.

And what a hegemon we are! Near the end of the film, there's a quiet moment on the testing ground. Doctor Lu listens as Commander Feng justifies what is about to transpire by picking at an old Chinese scab, the Korean War: "We were bullied because of our backward weapons. I will never forget our soldiers burning from head to toe by napalm bombs. Struggling, they could do nothing but cry for their mothers." The usual tears of righteous anger follow, then the commander pulls himself together and continues, "America should be the 'land of the beautiful.' It should not be the way it is now. Bullying you no matter what you do. Forcing you to shout out: No! Fuck you!"

Doctor Lu's gaze shifts to the horizon. Gently, maternally, he says to the commander, "Feng, your atomic bomb has arrived." Cut to shot of the Chinese gadget, a countdown, a blinding flash, a yellow mushroom cloud, followed by endless slow-motion footage of ecstatic Chinese soldiers jumping up and down to "Fanfare for the Common Man" (like a Nike ad).

As propaganda for the masses, the first point made by *Roaring Across the Horizon* is straightforward enough: China has the bomb. The Communist Party made it for you. Be proud. It was a point that created continuity between the Marxists of the Old China and the Big Brother capitalists of the New China. Yet there was a new virulence to that claim. It could be seen in the parades of Long March and Dongfeng missiles on the fiftieth anniversary celebration of October 1, the government-sanctioned press gleefully modeling the effect of electromagnetic pulse on Taipei, the announcement that China had mastered neutron technology, the open talk of deploying multiple independent reentry vehicles (MIRV) warheads in the long-range missiles targeted at Los Angeles, and the leaked testing of the Julang-2, a submarine-launched ballistic missile comparable to the U.S. Trident D-5 SLBM. Somebody up there did not want the Chinese people to view these devices as weapons of last resort, but as working assets. Films like *Roaring Across the Horizon* were made to prepare the Chinese people for a war—a war that also demands infrastructure, state-sponsored capitalism and Western technology.

The second point of *Roaring Across the Horizon* is that the Chinese did it by themselves. When the atomic research team portrayed in the film cannot get computers or adding machines shipped into China, the final calculations are done by a stable of attractive young girls with nerd glasses furiously manipulating abacuses. And then there's the movie's final narration: "While China was contained and blackmailed by America, China relied on her own strength to develop advanced defense technology, including the hydrogen bomb, the nuclear bomb, and . . . the technology necessary to miniaturize nuclear devices." Note to members of Congress: if you think the Cox Report didn't draw blood across the Pacific, consider that this kind of film does not happen simply because an art director suddenly has a fit of patriotism. When I interviewed the director, Chen Guoxing, he smilingly admitted that the film was entirely state-funded—and that the "miniaturization" line was provided by the Chinese equivalent of the State Department.

Such films are made to order by the top, yet these points— we have the bomb and we did it ourselves—are, to repeat, for public consumption. The Chinese leaders watched the end of the Cold War just as we did. They may want a rough parity of nuclear terror, but they have no immediate intention of getting into an expensive counterforce pissing match with an economy six or seven times stronger than their own. The second point—that they did it themselves—is a lie (which even the movie itself subtly acknowledges by placing an American-trained scientist at the helm of the bomb project). But it's an important, ambitious one, a stand-in for the indigenous research-and-development capability that the Chinese would like to have down the road, a holding pen for national pride until a land-based army like the PLA gets what it really wants: the military capability to neutralize the American presence and win wars in Asia, starting with an invasion of Taiwan.

While we can't divine what exactly is in the collective mind of the Chinese political and military leadership, we can look at their actions for clues. I received some of these clues after meeting repeatedly with a source from inside the U.S. embassy's military structure. He agreed to discuss Chinese military objectives and the U.S. government's attempts to control technology transfer, provided that the interviews were done on a strictly confidential basis—no physical descriptions, no speech mannerisms, no clue as to rank. I won't speculate on why he agreed to speak with me.

The interviews with Black, as I'll call him, confirmed something I had already observed: That the most important Chinese military initiatives are often hidden in plain sight. There has been a pronounced tendency in America, both in the press and in the Washington political establishment, to focus on stolen U.S. military secrets, particularly those found in strategic weapons programs, and the even more exciting world of Chinese spies: John Huang's mysterious phone calls to the Lippo Group; Johnny Chung's Christmas tree check for the Democratic Party; Princeling Wang Jun's presidential coffee klatch while a Cosco ship prepares to unload a container of PLA AK-47s in Long Beach; Wen Ho Lee's cryptic downloads from Los Alamos; and most recently, Katrina Leung's sex-pionage and doublecross of the hapless FBI. All worthy of investigation, all bearing some significance for American security, and all good copy. Yet the striking thing about the New China is the degree to which the prudent and ruthless center still holds. And as Black suggested to me, what if the Chinese leadership could get what it needed without using such colorful and newsworthy characters? Our focus on spies and Princelings is, in part, our own form of mirror-imaging, the transposition of American individualism and interest-group politics on the Chinese state structure.

The other problem is that we are viewing events through a rearview mirror. The premise is that the Chinese will follow our own path of development, or at least a familiar one. But the Chinese are reinventing the process of weapons development—and objects in the mirror may be closer than they appear. A quick glance confirms that the familiar Chinese nuclear program is moving along at its expected pace, while apparently peripheral forces, such as the Chinese mastery of advanced communication technologies, shoot by our blind spot unnoticed.

This blind spot, as Black noted, serves the Chinese leadership. The U.S. invasions of Afghanistan and Iraq—which the PLA has studied closely—suggest that a critical element of success is the presence of fourth-generation warfare communication technologies. And this blind spot also serves the Western corporations that are transferring such technologies to China.

China hands have pointed out that the current Chinese military has had no practical combat experience since Vietnam, is dominated by a leaden bureaucracy, and has more pressing needs than seriously planning for a major offensive war—such as simply feeding the largest army in the world. These beliefs have some validity. Although by Chinese standards, troop strength is rapidly being reduced, the Chinese army can be fairly compared to a state-owned enterprise, with all the inefficiency that entails. If one were to model a set-piece Red versus Blue battle, the U.S. military would triumph in most categories very quickly. But that is not how the Chinese intend to fight.

Black's rundown of the trajectory of Chinese military development over the last decade suggests, even given its relatively scarce resources, a far more creative PLA increasingly capable of posing an effective challenge to U.S. forces, particularly in the Taiwan scenario.

From 1990 to 1993, the PLA's goal was simply to establish and acquire the building blocks of a general industrial base: advanced manufacturing techniques, automotive production lines, and computing power, particularly big mainframes. The Japanese were the ascendant foreign investors. American corporations also were interested in the opening of the China market, but were still inhibited by the fallout from Tiananmen.

By 1993 to 1996, the PLA began responding to Desert Storm. The Chinese emphasis shifted to controlling the information sphere: semiconductor manufacturing, attracting information-revolution investment, and avionics. American companies became the dominant players and investors, and the main target of systematic reverse-engineering by companies such as Huawei. Under pressure to modernize military command, control, communications and intelligence, the Chinese began to diversify dramatically their sources of technology. Based on French, Russian and Israeli technology (usually offered with free training), military command centers full of sophisticated electronic equipment began to emerge.

In 1996, the Chinese threatened Taiwan with a series of missile tests; the United States responded by placing a carrier battle group near the Taiwan Strait (and had AWACs flying all over China). The Chinese backed down, but the incident (whose lessons would be brought home with the U.S. military's performance in Kosovo) had created a new sense of urgency in the efforts at modernization. From 1997 to 1998, Chinese graduate students flooded U.S. science programs, while the PLA focused on launching a full-blown effort to find ways to blind and neutralize U.S. AWACs. The Chinese government approved large investments in optical tracking solutions (to find U.S. satellites) and huge ground laser programs (to kill them), along with the development of micro-satellite prototypes that could identify enemy assets, or pop-up and maneuver to destroy U.S. satellites, or simply explode in proximity—technologies that came from the United States, Russia, Israel and even Brazil.

From 1999 to 2003, the first results were in. "By 2002," Black explained to me, "they could actually build this stuff." The first micro-satellites were in production. Using a Soviet knock-off as a prototype, the Chinese began to experiment with MIRVing their ballistic missiles, potentially increasing the Chinese deliverable warhead count as much as tenfold. Even more promising was the accelerated development of conventional ballistic missiles, particularly land-attack cruise missiles. Other deficiencies were narrowing: combined-forces training was still a scripted affair, but PLA military communications, using U.S. technology (passed through the Ministry of Information Industry to the Ministry of State Security), were improving, particularly in the area of internal security and surveillance, which conveniently doubles for battle-tracking—the critical element for a Taiwan Strait operation.

"The planned time is 2008 to 2010," Black says. "That's when the weapons systems converge." He calculates that by the end of the decade, the Chinese will have a critical mass of Su-27 and Su-30 multipurpose fighters, Kilo subs and Sovremenny-class destroyers. In addition, he says there is "incontrovertible evidence" that the Chinese will have a new SLBM, MIRVed, with a 300–500 yard Circular Error Probable (CEP) with about 100 deliverable nuclear warheads.

Put in broad terms, the preferred Chinese strategy for invading Taiwan is to deter the United States from preventing the war, first through nuclear escalation, then through the threat to blind American satellites, and finally by putting American aircraft carriers at risk should they try a replay of 1996. In the Chinese view, it's our turn to back off and, like any good bluff, it helps to have the capabilities to carry out these threats convincingly. Finally, the PLA must establish air superiority over Taiwanese forces, followed by an invasion using combined air, sea and ground assets.

"You won't lose L.A. to save Taiwan" may have been a slip by a PLA rep at a California cocktail party; but it's a common trope at most cocktail parties in Beijing. The Chinese have a newcomer's tendency to forget how long the United States has been playing the game of escalation dominance, and one senses that the PLA views nuclear brinkmanship as its least demanding requirement. This view has a degree of plausibility, as Black points out: "Their truck missiles use low-frequency communications and they have to assume that we can find them. So if they are reading our stuff, then they know we will take out the land-based missiles. But they will have the SLBM and that's when they will move." The U.S. vulnerability is in its forward positioning: "You can't use SDI [the Strategic Defense Initiative] to protect Guam and Hawaii." Perhaps for this reason, according to Black, the Chinese are not unduly concerned about Star Wars, which they believe in any case will take ten years to actually deploy. "But on the tactical level they are furious because we could throw up a net [against Chinese conventional ballistic missiles] around Taiwan in eighteen months. There are no attempts to get our SDI—instead they will use antisatellite capabilities to blind the system. Antisatellite is *real*. They can reduce us to the military equivalent of two cans and a string."

The Chinese are currently developing AWAC killers, based on Soviet warheads that have the capability to seek distinctive signals. They have developed impressive missile ranges, and conventional electromagnetic pulse weapons for tactical blinding. Black predicts that the PLA will soon have the capability to electronically black out any U.S. commander, isolating him from the overall Strait conflict. "What they are developing is the capability to force the U.S. to *stand off*."

Finally, Chinese exercises use unconventional tactics: "Howitzers on the deck of a ship—and other goofy shit—but it makes it hard for us to model. The carrier problem is still an open question. We will kill the Sovremenny destroyer—that takes the first shot. Yet they think that all *they* need is one shot." Black shakes his head at this classic case of wishful military strategy and crisis instability: "*They will stumble into this war.*"

Chinese defense spending is estimated at less than one-third of U.S. defense spending, and China also lacks a robust avionics industry. The Chinese have learned a lesson from the Soviets: don't try to outspend the United States. Yet given a limited budget, how can they hope to establish air superiority? It is estimated that a cruise missile in China costs 20 to 30 percent less to produce than in the U.S., and Chinese defense analysts assume that it will cost the U.S. about nine times more to defend against a Chinese missile than it costs China to build one. The PLA currently has over 450 conventional ballistic missiles and it is deploying about 75 every year—over 900 conventional ballistic missiles by the end of the decade, and enough for a comprehensive first strike on Taiwan's airfields, command and control, and other military assets. Even on the cheap, the PLA believes that it could attain air superiority over Taiwan in 45 minutes. According to Black, "The PLA believes that they could get Taiwan to cave in four to six days."*

But the Chinese ballistic missile strategy, as overwhelming as it appears, may be the weakest link in the chain of the entire Taiwan strategy. As my source pointed out, "Four hundred missiles and counting, but they fire and that's it. So what? The Taiwanese lived through a terrible earthquake. Psychological impact won't bring you air superiority. The PLA *really* doesn't understand."

Ultimately the PLA will have to go beyond the terracotta missile force and threaten credibly to invade Taiwan, and here's where the term "fourth-generation warfare" comes in. Like a lot of strategic terminology, it's vague and ill defined. But the Chinese under-

---

*This view—that the soft, mercantile Taiwanese will sue for peace shortly after the first shot is fired—has been drummed into Chinese society. It's also shared by a surprising number of American expats. One of the creepier long-term elements of living in China is encountering this contempt for the strength of Taiwan's democracy—similar to Adolf Hitler's dismissal of Great Britain in the 1930s as "a nation of shopkeepers."

stand the basics; they know that the Soviet tactic of massing forces is bankrupt. So drop your density and go for mobility in small but effective units, with coordinated attacks and firepower (which means acquiring assets like naval inland cables, streaming videos, fiber-optics to increase information security, and complex encryption algorithms). "They believe everything they read. Even Tom Clancy," Black added with a smile. "We have real-time battlefield imaging, and they don't yet, but they really want it. They understand the power."

█

It's hard not to add a codicil to this scenario: this is in part our creation. What we regard as dual-use technology changes over time. The internal combustion engine is essential for mechanized warfare. A quieter propeller in a submarine is dependent on composite material. Commercial radar satellite data can also build a cruise missile's path to target. China has received all of these technologies from the United States, regardless of how we have defined China over time. In broad terms, we considered China an *ally* during the 1980s, allowing both selected lethal weaponry and dual-use technology into China without too many complications. Belatedly, we began to consider China a *proliferator* during the 1990s, cutting back on the sale and transfer of the most sensitive technologies. Still, there were also major lapses and business end runs: Loral was stopped before the Chinese got military satellites, but did make Chinese rockets more reliable; the Shenyang-Boeing factory was making civil aviation parts for the Su-27 until it was given a cease-and-desist order; Sun Microsystems moved heaven and earth to sell supercomputers to China, and when it did, Legend, China's top computer manufacturer, gave them directly to the PLA. The Chinese have a list of assets that have, so far, been denied: custom chip-making and algorithms (chips are hard to reverse-engineer because they zero themselves out), stealth technologies and military application software among them.

American Telecom and high-tech industry executives in Beijing commonly assume that the Chinese are not our potential enemies, and short of selling a missile guidance system, they believe there is no great harm to American interests occurring in the course of "normal" business. Besides, the technical attributes of Chinese information systems have to be essentially equivalent to the U.S. standard or business communication will be a global mess. There are at least two experts from this world who diverge from this prevailing wisdom, and each of them also agreed to speak with me, but only with the same confidentiality as Black. I'll give them similar names: White (consultant to several major IT multinationals) and Gray (technology and Internet analyst).

White sees an ongoing revolution in military technology that is dependent on the Internet revolution: "The biggest threat to the U.S. would be a Chinese commitment to information superiority." China, he points out, can easily produce one million engineers a year, and all the fundamental capabilities are in place. Encryption is the "functional equivalent of the space race," and the Chinese have gone from 0 to 256 bit encryption in five years. He points to a widespread hubris among American technology companies, the belief that the pace of our innovation is so fast that there's no commercial way for the Chinese to reproduce a microprocessor. (While it's slow by American standards, the Chinese recently created their first microprocessor, the Godson chip—also called "the dragon chip"—and they claim it cost only $1.3 million to develop. Curiously, Intel's contribution to PRC universities last year came out to the same amount.) "When it comes to the Internet, there is a very thin line between military and civilian use," White says. "The U.S. Army is using laptops right off of the shelf.... So where is China's money best invested? Steel? Or on info-war capability? ... How many moon shots and Manhattan Projects can the Chinese government afford? Only a few, but they can do it."

White goes through the methods. One way to acquire cutting-edge technologies is to purchase from a country such as Israel. Gilat sells cable systems with high encryption, advanced algorithms, software, chips, voice scrambler and so-called "addressable encryption" to the Chinese. Canada is another weak link, particularly through Princeling connections in Vancouver. Another way is to improvise; supercomputers are desirable, but you can also do massive parallel computing—basically a hangar full of linked computers, the kind of thing that's cheap in China.

The Ministry of Information Industry has built spying into the public process, particularly by using smaller firms under the radar of the U.S. security apparatus, which Black confirmed: "There is a huge dedicated effort to purchase technology. The target changes all the time, but it's government-led and very controlled. The number of [Chinese] delegations going back to the U.S. is expanding. Delegations are largely sponsored by U.S. corporations on fast-track visas. . . . The companies over here [in Beijing] fall all over themselves to improve their image. The U.S. corporations, the hosts, are not going to sell them anything—but they grant access. Once the Chinese have made the contacts, then they send in a cut-out company to get the technology."

In November 2002, a story appeared that a Securities and Exchange Commission aide, Mylene Chan, a young Chinese woman from the mainland, had been forced to leave the SEC. Chan had access to CTRs, or confidential-treatment requests (company-written secret reports to the SEC containing proprietary and sensitive information). Among the companies that Chan handled were various defense and intelligence contractors. It was reported that she had actually sent CTRs to China. The SEC never reported the case to the FBI, in what looked suspiciously like a cover-up.

The story was met with hoots of derision by some of my journalist friends in Beijing, largely because it was reported by Bill Gertz of the *Washington Times* (considered to be out to get China) and possibly because it contained the word "espionage," which they regarded as archaic. But I wondered, if the CTRs contained information on both the classified projects the company was working on and its financial health, wouldn't those be things that the Ministry of State Security would want to know? In one of my meetings with Black, he quickly confirmed the story and added that it fit the profile exactly. In the time of the sub-10,000 Dow, the Chinese were looking for wounded animals, small high-tech companies with advanced military software that were failing, which then could be approached by a company that didn't appear to have links to the Chinese military.

Gray confirmed what Black said and added that it wasn't just small companies: "China prefers vendors that can help China. Nortel and Lucent are *failing*. China is their savior. China would prefer them alive." The most valuable dual-use technology transfer takes place in China, directly and through reverse-engineering, and never sees press coverage. Especially in a competitive industry environment, Chinese ministries have high leverage. But it goes both ways, according to Gray: "You get more red carpet as the head of a technology company than you do as the head of a medium-sized country." In return, China's lack of transparency, the fact that it has no equivalent to the SEC, helps these companies not only to drum up investment and raise stocks by playing on Wall Street's China illusions, but also to transfer technology. White asked, "What's there to stop them? There are no controls. Don't sell? In a market sucking wind like this? The only question becomes: how do we sell the order? If Loral can do it—with its close U.S. government connections—what's to stop anyone else from doing it?"

We have already seen that Motorola's allotment for bribes was approximately $60 million a year in 1995, about 3 percent of budget. There is growing evidence that since then, Chinese government demands have not slackened, but they have come under tighter state control. And American companies are meeting the challenge, not so much by bribing officials as by building an indigenous research and development capability for China.

For example, Xinhua, the official Chinese news agency, reported in 2003 that "Motorola Software Group has poured 10 million U.S. dollars into expanding its software center in Nanjing." But that's only one of the eighteen centers that Motorola has reportedly set up on the mainland. An additional seven plants are said to be under construction. These are not small operations; Motorola's plant in Suzhou has seventy senior semiconductor professionals. In the middle of the SARS crisis, Motorola (apparently embarrassed by the news coverage of its temporary shutdown of Beijing company headquarters) announced plans to spend another $90 million on its R&D plant in Beijing, with $500 million more to come over the next five years. Motorola also planned to increase its total China investment to $10 billion, with up to five thousand researchers and engineers by 2006.

Yet the numbers tell only so much. Observer and industry accounts of Motorola's R&D plants claim that they are top-of-the-line facilities, fully equivalent to Motorola's R&D plants in the United States. The only difference appears to be that in some cases, they are specializing in R&D that hews to Chinese military objectives. While many other American corporate R&D pledges are still at the PR stage, Motorola's plants are engaged in advanced research for the Ministry of Science and Technologies "863" project: fourth-generation wireless technology using a speed of ten megabits per second, mobile technologies with both commercial and defense applications, semiconductors, and biotech—all dual-use technologies. While many of the managers are Chinese-American, motivated to return to the old country by prestige, ideology and money, at least 80 percent of the staff are native Chinese. Company sources have confirmed repeatedly that there is no attempt to do background checks on the Chinese engineers.

"Great training grounds for these guys," Black said, speaking of the labs. "It's like a bribe, a scripted bribe. We have no access whatsoever." I asked him who gets in. Party members? PLA moles? Are there any safeguards on their proprietary knowledge? "None. All the technology goes straight out."

Motorola is only one of many American corporations to move its research and development centers to China. Initially, White explained, this was seen as a kind of corporate philanthropy device to further government relations: yes, we pledge $750 million in research and development investment, we just haven't found a location yet. But somewhere along the line, in the last two or three years, it went from being a PR stunt to something that was expected of all companies who aspired to a piece of China's market share. IBM's main research lab is located by Beijing's Qinghua University. Intel's lab is close by. Honeywell has set up a research lab in Tianjin. Microsoft has invested $130 million in regional research and development centers in Suzhou, Shanghai and Beijing, while giving the Chinese government "controlled access" to its source code. General Electric's R&D center in Shanghai is said to be its third-largest in the world. Lucent already has four R&D facilities and has pledged $50 million to further strengthen its research commitment to China. Alcatel is developing the first high-capacity Chinese telecommunications satellite for the China Academy of Space Technology and is setting up a "world-class" R&D center with a team of 3,500 engineers. (Alcatel's slogan: "Based in China, Targeting the World.")

I asked Black why corporations would choose to go down this road. He said that American companies (and other foreign companies) in China are raising the ante because their rate of transfer has outrun their rate of innovation. Building state-of-the-art research and development facilities is an attempt not only to buy the Chinese government's goodwill but, however temporarily, to renew Chinese dependency. It may even seem like a good investment for the corporation because Chinese engineers come relatively cheap. But in China, adherence to industry confidentiality is considered laughable, and while Motorola might claim that the same things happen in Silicon Valley, California has no competitive equivalent to the Ministry of State Security.

Even back in the early nineties, when corporate contacts were at a historic low because of the Tiananmen massacre, the Chinese leadership sensed American corporate pliability. By 1993 the Chinese leadership had signed off on a strategy of using close business ties and trade to influence the U.S. government and Congress's attitudes toward unimpeded technology transfer to China, the so-called strategy of 'handling trade by the means of trade'" (a policy that would eventually be used with Taiwan as well). Trying to capitalize on the new policy, American PR consultants who wanted to lobby for the Chinese unabashedly listed such objectives as "Advance China's policies on regional security issues" in their pitches.

As we have seen, on the American side, the offensive would center on the adoption of Permanent Normal Trade Relations (PNTR, previously called Normal Trade Relations, and prior to that, Most Favored Nation Status). The debate over adopting PNTR in 2000 was framed around whether U.S. businesses could reap the trade benefits of China's entry into the WTO in exchange for dropping the annual debate over trading relations with China. Yet the adoption of PNTR was also simply a ratification of how the fight over Normal Trade Relations had played out year after year, like an extended trench war.

A key anti-PNTR player, the AFL-CIO, keeps extensive files on the debate. Three large boxes devoted to the year 1994 contain congressional hearings, news clippings, and propaganda on both sides. The China business lobby was beginning to use the arguments that I've outlined throughout this book—China is changing; American business is the vanguard of change; U.S.-China trade is a win-win; and who are we to talk about human rights anyway? Eventually these arguments became standardized for congressional consumption, differing little from year to year. The anti-PNTR side—union leftists and political conservatives—were always trying for breakthroughs. One year it was Chinese prison labor exports, another year it was the Loral scandal or Chinese AK-47s being sold to American street gangs. Yet they were never able to muster the votes to overturn MFN, and by 2000, the year of the critical PNTR vote, the files barely fill a box, as if both sides had lost interest. If you ask a few of the veteran union activists why they lost this war, they will roll their eyes and say, "Bob Kapp."

In 1994, the U.S.-China Business Council hired Bob Kapp, a respected China academic, as president, and the China lobby had found its bard:

> Since the day after Tiananmen, I have carried with me a photograph that everyone here would instantly recognize. It shows a young man in a white shirt and dark pants facing a column of tanks. None of us should or will forget that scene. But none of us should inadvertently help to restage it.... The economic advancement of China, linked part and parcel to China's immense engagement with the world economy, is the best hope we have of witnessing the evolution of a more humane and tolerant Chinese domestic political environment.

Brilliant, intense, and audaciously willing to trash the sentimental logic of the anti-China position (even to the point of co-opting the Tiananmen massacre in rhetorical support of Normal Trade Relations), Kapp organized the U.S. Chamber of Commerce, the Clinton administration, academics, think tanks, NGOs and business leaders into a unified force. In what was labeled an "industry grassroots initiative" to influence the China MFN congressional outcome in 1996, every major company with a China presence—Boeing, Rockwell, Motorola, GE, TRW, GM, Ford, Eastman Chemical, Nike and others—was assigned a state's worth of congressmen to lobby. Kissinger and Scowcroft, the political heavies, were wheeled out to make a final pitch for their life's work, the opening of China. (Given Kissinger's remarkably profitable consulting company, Kissinger Associates, he was also pitching his livelihood.) Even the ambassador to China, James Sasser, urged American CEOs to lobby Congress on MFN: "Nothing makes an impression on a member of Congress like a visit or a phone call from a CEO from the member's district or state." In the well-organized "doorknock" campaign for Permanent Normal Trade Relations, Beijing AmCham representatives had talking points prepared for the possibility of an embarrassing crackdown on Falun Gong (what about how Janet Reno treated the Branch Davidians?), and to help ensure that Beijing would host the 2008 Olympic Games, the business leaders quietly promoted the notion that it would buy peace in the Taiwan Strait at least for eight years. They even sent communiqués from Washington back to the Chinese leadership, urging it to refrain temporarily from any threatening moves against Taiwan until after Congress's vote. By 2000, in the final days, the Business Roundtable, a key PNTR supporter, clearly had money to burn. Phone cards with a ten-minute value bearing the legend "The Right Call: YES on PNTR" were handed out on the street corners of Washington.

Yet at the end of the day, Kapp won because he could offer an optimistic picture of the future: a reformed China and a wealthier United States.* Without explicitly stating it, he also played to a widespread American assumption that China's problem was still communism. Every step away from Chinese communism and toward a Chinese free market thus became evidence that the business strategy was working. The anti-PNTR side seemed to offer only grim options, like isolationism (as Kapp characterized it) or perhaps just that young man in a white shirt and dark pants facing a column of tanks.

---

*Another key to Kapp's success was that he did not ignore opposition, no matter how insignificant. I wrote a short critique of American business involvement in China for the *Asian Wall Street Journal* in 2001. By several accounts, "fuming," Kapp tried to pressure various top managers in my D.C. home office to fire me. The on-the-waterfront message I received from Kapp's Beijing rep: I was "biting

Bob Kapp's free-market world was much in evidence throughout my time in Beijing and it still is. But I could also sense a growing, bellicose Chinese nationalism. To make sure that I was not imagining this, I visited a top Chinese public opinion expert whom I had come to know pretty well over my time in Beijing. He was happy to see me, and using some confidential polls, he confirmed that there was a significant uptick in pro-Chinese nationalist attitudes among all young Chinese (18 to 32 years of age), particularly in the urban and coastal areas. He saw this as a natural outgrowth of all the recent points of light: China entering the WTO, China winning the Beijing Olympics, China's GNP growth, China receiving floods of new foreign investment, and China starting a high-profile space program. Yet all this national self-esteem hadn't softened Chinese attitudes about international relations, especially where it came to Taiwan. The Taiwanese were thought of as "typically narrow-minded, grudge-holding, old-time landlord slave-drivers." But even that didn't matter because the mainland was "no longer a poor relative." Taipei, Taiwan's capital city, was now "rather shabby looking" compared with Shanghai. The first million-dollar Bentley had just been sold in the mainland. A stronger, more prosperous China would ensure that it was just a question of time before the PRC would take the errant province back into the fold, by any means necessary. Warming to the subject, the expert explained that England had set a goal to attract Chinese students to its universities, and that Germany was now bidding for Chinese tourists. "We are finally winning the Opium War!" he shouted exuberantly.

I also looked up Wang, the student who had led the demonstrations against the American embassy in 1999. Now a professional, he was eager to run through the nationalist checklist: Taiwan will be returned to the mainland, nationalism means dignity and

---

the hand that feeds me." Ultimately my company stubbornly stood by me (although any further advancement or lateral moves to another regional office were probably shot), but only after a top company rep, a former congressman, had taken Kapp out to breakfast and mollified him. (In turn, I had to fly back to Washington to mollify the unsmiling former congressman.)

self-respect, and we will win the competition with America. "This country has such potential that cannot be controlled. No one can control it," he said. " ... In not a long time, we will catch up, and Americans will have to use a mobile phone made in China with a Chinese trademark, like *Kejian.*" Wang smiled: "Maybe the American consumer will have a problem to spell it. ... At that time there will be conflict."

Profit-oriented Americans had forfeited their right to complain. After all, they were complicit in allowing the Xinjiang Muslims to be labeled "terrorists," Wang noted. "That is interest-driven. ... I think few Americans hold real beliefs. They do not care about the ideas. They only see the numbers. Foreign companies maybe should bring some value, some business belief into this market. But they surrender."

Wang revealed that, using a proxy server, he had managed to download some political content from the Web. Two videos were very important to him. Would I like to see them? The first clip was a gruesome tape of the Tiananmen massacre. He acknowledged that he had not realized how violent the PLA troops had been until he saw it. The second clip was a catfight in the Taiwanese parliament with two female representatives slapping and screaming at each other. While it played, Wang supplied a caustic laugh track.

Wang does not hate America. He hates what he sees as the hypocritical talk of democracy. In fact, it seemed impossible for Wang to say the word without giving a little wince. Wang—and everyone else in China—knows why the world is beating down the Chinese gates: China offers the world a market, entrepreneurial skills, and a vast, cheap export platform. No one really wants to disturb the status quo.

But then the problem becomes: What does a superpower China offer the world? Given Communist China's terrible history—Mao's famine, the Cultural Revolution, Tiananmen, events that the country has still not come to terms with—what ideals, what purpose, what possible beacon of "Chinese characteristics" can they export? One senior government advisor is reported to have said: "We still don't stand for anything. We are not a democracy, we're not communist. We are just big."

This too is Kapp's world: the beginning stages of a state whose legitimacy is built on nationalism without content, expansionism without ideals, and American technology without the restraints of democracy. The Chinese leadership, unaccountable and isolated, offer little reassurance of a cooperative global future; these are leaders who won't answer the hotline when their own embassy is hit, and who collude in the deception when the Hainan military command tells them an Su-27 fighter was attacked by a lumbering EP-3 surveillance plane. China's leaders publicly assert that Taiwan is their major territorial claim, but bringing back Taiwan is likely to be a test case as well, similar to the Germans' claim to Sudetenland. As Black says, "The Chinese leadership cannot expand their influence without removing the American protectorate. The next stop is Guam."

Hindsight is faultless, and we cannot hold someone like Bob Kapp responsible for a social experiment that didn't work out. The China business lobby promised a politically reformed China in exchange for PNTR and it sounded like a reasonable proposition, especially in the early 1990s. Yet now we must reap what we sowed; in the next ten years we will be forced to consider China as a *military competitor.* We will continue to grapple with China's legacy of military proliferation to states like Iran (and possibly even groups like al-Qaeda).* We will also face an army that has absorbed American battlefield communication technology, space technology and a plausible nuclear deterrent—with the indigenous capability to replace, modify and improve on these assets over time.

"We can't stop it." Black's hands are folded on the table now, indicating that our interview is over because there is not much

---

*China has provided air-defense systems to Iran and, in what appears to have been a pass-through from Kiev, a radar detection system to Iraq. U.S. intelligence indicates that China also provided equipment to the Taliban: SA-7 surface-to-air missiles (according to Indian intelligence, they also supplied artillery rockets and anti-aircraft guns), while Chinese companies built Kabul's communication systems. Even so, when the Chinese state verbally committed its intelligence services to assist in the U.S.-led war against terrorism, career State Department operatives hailed it as yet another step along the road to China's becoming a more trusted world citizen, and China was given approval to label Xinjiang Muslim separatists as "terrorists." The main effect of Chinese antiterrorist activity seems to have been a rise in the Muslim execution rate.

more to say. The hotel coffee shop where we have had our final talk is emptying out, we are on our third cup, and unlike our first meeting, there are no well-dressed Chinese men listening intently to our conversation. Black toys with a few final details. Exceptions? Maybe encryption. On the commercial side, it's stealing outright. But they have high-end encryption developed in public research institutions. 128 bit, so we go to 1028 bit. The bottom line is we need to break their encryption. Can we limit the tech transfer to something we can break? No, we can't limit it, he admits.

It's a floodgate: "The intelligence agencies are swamped. The problem set is too big and too dark. The solution, too expensive."

What Black is telling me is that the export restrictions, the press investigations into Loral, Boeing and Motorola, the congressional committees and commissions, even the administration's slap-down of Norinco—these only scratch the surface, giving us an illusion of control.

█

Rewind to the air force base. After they broke down the set of *Roaring Across the Horizon,* I caught a ride to Beijing in the back of the mobile food truck with a man who made significant intellectual contributions to the film. He was supremely intelligent and likable, with an engaging personality. He was also a writer of state propaganda, and a good one. After a bit of sparring over the embassy bombing—it always comes up, but it was really his way of testing whether he was talking to a serious person or another submissive expat—he relaxed and spoke freely. With vats of bean curd sloshing around at our feet as the truck rushed past the canyons of the pyramid-skyscrapers that make up west Beijing, he told me there was a great problem in China now. While the corrupt sons and daughters of the leadership demanded ever more resources for their enterprises, the state was reaching into the ordinary people's assets to pay the bills. There was no safety, no chance of advancement for the peasant and the ordinary worker, just unemployment and financial insecurity. It was over. The system had failed. The only options were immediate and complete reform or a Maoist revolution.

"Maoist revolution?" I asked, staring out at the shifting high-way lanes as we picked up speed: "What do you mean?"

"Maoist revolution means violent revolution," he said. "There is no other option."

What's odd is, he was daring to say the things that expat businessmen—in some nameless fear of appearing anti-Chinese—simply don't say. Not in the embassy, not in the office, not in a drunken expat bar. Probably off-limits in the home office too.

Perhaps I should have argued—for evolution, or for Chinese economic advancement, or for not restaging a terrible event. But I didn't, because a part of me agreed with him. He was playing a propagandist of the Chinese state; I was playing a Marxist professor. Later, I would play a business consultant. But like it or not, we were roaring toward the same horizon.

8.
Rex and the City

Rex was implicated with my decision to leave China.

As I learned after becoming his confidant, Rex had never held a "real" job—something secure, respectable, with a contract and health benefits. But then, he had been out of college for only a little while, and he had always resisted directly pursuing the legal, medical or business track. He had come this far—the first in his family to go to college (to say nothing of getting a liberal arts degree from a top-ranked one)—so why shouldn't he keep his options open?

But after graduation, Rex quickly realized that he would weary of the bleak post-college dating scene, the empty lawns of the mid-Atlantic suburbs, his working-class family's financial troubles. Rex wanted to be miles away from the "roach coach" (a van that his father drove around every morning, selling breakfast sandwiches to workers). A few phone calls to potential employers established the value of his degree: Liberal arts majors like him with a concentration on East Asian studies ended up at Starbucks, Rex thought grimly—first drinking coffee as they rewrote their résumés, and then after a couple of months, donning an apron. If breaking free from this dismal orbit meant going to China, a culture in which he had grown increasingly interested throughout college, then that's what it meant.

He needed a warm-up. That would be Taiwan, the place where many aspiring China hands begin. He flew over, studied Chinese, taught English, and lived in a concrete apartment with a lot of

other language students in the heart of Taichung, in Taiwan's heartland. Rex quickly observed that the secret of success there was to
get a *pillow dictionary*—a native girl. All the male students who
effortlessly excelled in conversational Chinese were *rice kings*—
they basically ignored the other American and European students
and chased after Taiwanese women. If you could sleep with Taiwanese girls, eat with them, argue with them—well, that was true
immersion, and you were on your way to learning the language
and a lot more besides.

Yet Rex had always been a normal hapless male trying to do
the right thing in the politically correct way, and Taiwanese girls
seemed fairly unapproachable. He managed a fling with a Chinese
neighbor, but he still learned most of his Chinese through the
time-honored method of language exchanges with equally retir-
ing Taiwanese students at the local university.

Taichung got old. Rex flew to Hong Kong, looking for opportunities. There were none. But he received an e-mail from Julie,
an Asian-American girl he had dated in college. She had just arrived
in Beijing. So Rex called her and said: Do me a favor. Go to the
American Chamber of Commerce. Call up the Foreign Commercial Service. Talk to some people on the ground there and feel out
whether or not there are any opportunities.

A few days later, Julie called back. Yeah, she said, it looks like
there are some opportunities for a white guy with no real professional skills.

Rex said: OK, that's me. I'm getting on a train for Beijing.

He was just one of many young American males who had
arrived in Beijing with next to nothing. But it was a seller's market for a young Asian-American girl, a fact that became clear to
Rex as soon as he arrived and tried to get back together with Julie.
The closer he tried to pull her in, the more she seemed to push
him away, even as he was awkwardly trying to adjust to the strange
world of the mainland. Julie started dating a guy from California,
and the rejection was a nightmare.

But all around him, as Rex later told me, he saw possibilities:
relatively high-status expat jobs, flash clubs, and everywhere, Chinese girls—well-dressed, badly dressed, smiling coyly at him, pretending to ignore him, demurely lowering their achingly beautiful

eyes from his gaze. He thought about the American suburbs that he had left behind. How gargantuan the women were, how disgusting. The metabolism of the Chinese female must be much faster. They burned like expensive candles, Rex thought, clean and fine.

On Sanlitun bar street, the meeting place of young, hip Beijing, the establishments pay off the police, import beers that they think foreigners like, and string up copious amounts of colored lights into words like COWBOY, LOVE, NASHVILLE and HIDDEN TREE. Looking down the otherwise dark alley on a bitter winter's night, there was something about all this floating, shimmering kitsch that was laughably merry and alternately sinister. It spoke to Rex, whispering of a new ethos: if you can't beat 'em, join 'em. I'm going to do what I never did during college, Rex said to himself, I'm going to go out with people. I'm going to make a checklist of sexual experiences and tick them off systematically, detachedly, by the numbers. Rex dropped the sincere, respectful persona that he had carried like a heavy suitcase for so long and strode out, traveling light, looking for an odyssey in the New Beijing.

■

Although it isn't commonly recognized outside a relatively small circle of Sinophiles—and I didn't realize it either when I first arrived—China is the epicenter of a new sexual revolution, one that expats can sample as little or as much as they want. Like everything else in China, it's huge. In September 2003, something like nine hundred people, about half of them Japanese businessmen, took part in an extended sexual bacchanal in a Chinese hotel in Zhuhai—unusual only because it was reported in the newspapers. A great part of the attraction to China as a sex destination is that, unlike the Philippines or Thailand, it's a quiet storm, a revolution that will not be televised, and one where foreign men are not shunned but held in great desire, even in a kind of awe, sometimes by many women simultaneously. Unlike Europe or Japan, it's dirt cheap, foreign men have little accountability, and discretion is practically assured. So for a small group of American businessmen and diplomats, in an age of sexual-harassment corporate training sessions and lawsuits, China is an oasis.

There are many reasons to be in love with China. Some are intellectual, because Chinese culture has a quality of idiosyncratic brilliance that is original, puzzling, and second to none. Some are financial, because China has breathtaking economic potential. And some are sensual. Do I mean sexual? Of course, but look at all the other pleasure factors I've mentioned in passing throughout this book: the charm and nobility of the Chinese character (when it is teased out); the musicality of the language; the phenomenally creative cuisine—again, second to none; the singular beauty of a Beijing *hutong;* and the raw energy and earthy humor of a modern state on the rise. Even the riveting intrigue of totalitarianism and its will-to-power aestheticism play a role; power, in fact, is where sex takes its place in the forefront of the sensual attraction to China, exerting a kind of hidden gravitational pull.

Are American males in China just the latest carriers of a conditioned Orientalist despotic fantasy?* Perhaps, but it happens to be a fantasy that can be fully realized at this particular juncture of China's development, in part because it seems to meet a corresponding fantasy on the Chinese side. Start with the basics: traditional values were deeply eroded by Communist ideology, atheism and the Cultural Revolution's animus toward the family. Add money: as one Chinese public opinion specialist put it to me, the sexual revolution in China is tied to the practical revolution of rising incomes. It means jobs, which in turn means extra cash because most young people still live with their parents. It means there are things like cars around for young people to be alone in. It means that young people aspire to live a modern life, rejecting the stranglehold of the Chinese family. It means that there is a proliferation of modern media, women's magazines, illegal pornography. It means that given the ever-present surveillance and crackdown on all other forms of political dissent, by default most young

---

*Some expats in China—"rice kings," as Rex called them—take advantage of this opening. Other expats come to China with their wives or girlfriends and eventually return home with them. Still others have Chinese wives, and Chinese in-laws and half-Chinese children, and sex is nothing more than an important part of love and the creation of a family that is as solid as they come. The latter groups can skip the chapter, but they will have to pat their own backs.

urban Chinese are revolutionaries, as Orwell's Winston Smith might have put it, only from the waist down.

█

After Rex arrived, he became my neighbor, moving into the squalid Chinese apartment directly below mine. Initially, he made little impression on me—just another hungry expat, I thought. He approached me respectfully, as you would an older brother, asking about jobs. I was polite; I told him that I didn't think my PR firm had any openings, but I could give him some useful contacts at other firms around town that might be hiring. Despite Rex's lack of experience, he soon had an interview with one of the American business consulting firms that serviced Beijing's ever-expanding corporate community.

The young man who interviewed him had a ready smile and a personable manner. He was also an American, also excited about Beijing and fun and advancement. His name was Jack and he explained that the job involved a lot of drudge work, a lot of document handling and attention to detail, but he seemed impressed with Rex's easy manner and his East Coast academic background. The managing director, after a brief meeting and a few jokes, signed off. Rex was now an associate with the company—actually a paid intern with the possibility of a full position down the road. But he was in.

After a week or two, Rex surfed into a new Internet dating service named Asia Friend Finder—something he would never have looked at in the States, except perhaps as a joke. But on the site there were thousands upon thousands of advertisements from Beijing women looking for all kinds of relationships. Significantly, three-quarters of the copy had some English thrown in. It was obvious to Rex that Chinese women were looking for foreigners. He responded (as he told me in one of the bull sessions that we both became addicted to) by posting an ad titled *waiguo shuaige*, "handsome foreign guy."

Within a week, Rex had received a deluge of e-mails from Chinese women as far away as Chongqing, two thousand miles from Beijing. He decided on a Beijing-only policy, and of those, to respond only to about one in five e-mails. His first encounter was risk-free—a professional girl who worked at a magazine and claimed to be interested in working on her English. "I hope we might become good friends," her return e-mail said. They met at the Starbucks in Full Link Plaza and began a standard language exchange, just like in Taiwan. But this time, Rex ignored the banal conversation and concentrated on being physically seductive: complex facial signals, aggressive intention movements, and keeping his voice low and leathery. He didn't really think she was very attractive, but hey, it was only a test to see how far it could go. There was a lot of hanging out: the Great Wall on the weekend, and after that it was Ditan Park in northern Beijing. Sitting on a secluded bench, Rex asked, "What do you want to do now?"

She smiled and looked at her feet.

Rex asked, "Do you want to take me home?"

He slept with her a couple of times, but Rex had this feeling that there was someone in the background. There was, but it didn't matter to Rex; it had only been a man-woman-China test and all the working parts were in order.

A few days later, he was approached by a couple on the Internet. The e-mail was tersely worded, as if they were afraid that they were being watched. It said, "There is a Chinese girl interested in having a threesome with a foreigner." It proposed a meeting near the Asian Games Village in the lobby of the Continental Hotel.

Inside the entrance, a Chinese man in his late thirties and an extremely young and voluptuous Chinese girl approached Rex. For some reason, perhaps just because it's what you do in China, they immediately went out to eat. Over eggs and tomatoes and soup, they spoke in circles about the potential liaison. There were a lot of Chinese double-entendres and loud embarrassed laughter, the girl giggling with her hand over her mouth.

No, he had never done anything like it before, Rex admitted when the Chinese man asked. Had they?

"Once, with another Chinese couple," the man said.

The Chinese man was doing all the talking, but none of them seemed to know where exactly it was going. To move it along, Rex asked, "What are we going to do?"

The girl looked at the Chinese man.

The man said, "We were just going to meet. Is that okay?"

"Yeah, that's fine."

"Were you thinking of something different?"

"Yeah, well, sort of."

"Oh. That's okay."

They whispered to each other. Then the Chinese man said, "Why don't you come back to her place?"

Rex began to suspect that the Chinese guy was probably married—perhaps this was his second wife, his mistress—and that's why he insisted they go to her place. She lived in the far north of Beijing, well off the fourth ring road. It was a tiny, state-owned, workgroup-provided apartment in a vast, empty complex. The walls were made of concrete, thinly painted white. Outside of the steel-girded windows, one could see nothing but similar blocks stretching out to the horizon. There was no living room, only a television, a washroom, a little kitchen and a bed with a weak fluorescent light above it. They sat on the hard bed, the young girl between the two men. The Chinese man gently stroked the girl, seemingly trying to get her in the mood. "It's okay, it's okay," he said over and over, as if he were talking to a child.

She would not look at Rex and her shoulders sagged forward as if her stomach hurt. Sitting like that, she looked like a different person from the vivacious girl that Rex had met in the hotel lobby. She was obviously scared—and Rex was feeling increasingly claustrophobic. The Chinese couple asked Rex if he wanted to watch TV.

"Not really," he replied. Then, to fill the silence, he said with resignation, "We can do this some other time. We don't need to do this now."

"I've never been with a foreigner before," the girl said suddenly. "I've only heard things about foreigners. Like—I have heard that you are big. I don't know if I can take it."

Rex felt a pounding in his head; this was happening in *China*, he thought, everything suddenly becoming hyper-real as if he were directing a film with an actor playing himself. He felt an erection spring up under his business slacks.

The girl noticed it and smiled faintly.

The Chinese man said to her, "Look at him, look at him. He's so big." He said earnestly to Rex, "You know, Chinese men are very small. I want to see it." He urged the girl to touch Rex, to rub him on the inside of his leg, to undo his pants. The girl went along. The Chinese man seemed amazed, and he kept babbling, "You see, it is true what they say about foreigners, you see, it is true...."

But the girl had become extremely frightened. Over and over she said, "No way, no way."

The Chinese man repeated to her, "No, no, you'll like it."

"No," she said. "No, I can't do it, I can't.... Have you slept with other Chinese girls before?"

"I've slept with a few."

"Were they able to do it with you?"

"Well ... yeah."

"But you are so big and Chinese women are so small," she said, making a tiny hole with her index finger.

"Why don't you start with your boyfriend? Maybe that will get you in the mood and you will loosen up. I'll just sort of touch you. I won't try anything."

The Chinese man took off her clothes. They went at it while Rex watched, talking to her occasionally. After two minutes, the Chinese man was finished, and he asked Rex, "Do you want to do it?"

"Yes," Rex said.

The man found a Chinese condom for Rex. Initially Rex could not roll it on. Then it broke during sex. The young girl said that it hurt, but she also seemed to enjoy certain moments. When he finished, the Chinese man suddenly looked at his watch and said, "Oh, she has to go. I have to take her to her English lesson."

It was obvious that the man desperately wanted to be alone with the girl, that a wave of embarrassment had come over him, but Rex felt a postcoital sense of fatigue with the Chinese man and his silly conventional worries. Perversely, Rex wanted to dig at them a little. When they got on the subway headed toward Andingmen, Rex asked the girl, "How long have you known your boyfriend?"

"He's not really my boyfriend."

"Well, what do you mean?"

"You know that apartment, and all of my clothes? He pays for it."

Rex nodded and looked away. As he got out at his stop the Chinese man hurriedly said they should meet again sometime. Rex nodded, but didn't bother to look back.

The Chinese man would call Rex back several times. A few weeks later they went over to the girl's apartment again, but this time she kept saying, "No, I don't want to," from behind the locked door. Rex didn't think that was the whole story. They were in a very Chinese area. People would talk about a foreigner like Rex visiting, perhaps for days. It could be a stigma, but worse, the apartment probably wasn't in her name, and the cops could raid the place and kick her out.

The Chinese man was disappointed and obviously thought he had lost face. He kept apologizing to Rex, and as they sat in his Jetta, stuck in traffic, his defenses seemed to drop: he confessed that he had a wife and a four-year-old son. Rex asked about the girl.

"She's from a distant province. I pay for that apartment, give her money for food and clothes, some education. She's basically, you know, my mistress. Her method of reciprocating is to provide me with sex."

"What about your wife? Does your wife know what you are doing?"

"I think she knows. . . ."

"Doesn't that hurt your marriage?"

"It could if it was made public. If everyone questioned her about it," he said pointedly. "But it is kept discreet. I'm still a good father. I love my wife."

"If your wife did this, would you be mad?"

The Chinese man's stare suggested that Rex had just broken a universal rule of casual sexual encounters. Then he looked out the windshield again and seemed to turn philosophical. "You know," he said slowly, "I guess I wouldn't have any reason to be mad if she did this. Because I am doing it."

Rex's interest in the question wasn't purely academic. While the man's behavior was almost traditional—any Chinese man who owned a car and had a good job in the tech sector was likely to have a mistress—Rex had already received countless propositions on Asia Friend Finder from married Chinese women. And he knew the divorce rate was approaching American levels in the big Chinese cities. Anything was possible in the sexual jungle of the New China, he thought, but only an outsider could see the contours of the landscape.

A few weeks later, the Chinese man called Rex again and asked if he could bring two girls over to Rex's apartment. When they arrived—the Chinese man with two stunning girls, one short and one tall—it seemed almost as awkward as their first ménage à trois. Times were tough, Rex explained, and the only furniture he had in his dingy apartment was a full-size bed. There was suspicion, then discussion, then the usual embarrassed laughter, then they all piled onto the bed. The Chinese man finished with the short girl in two minutes, just as before, but Rex had decided to go beyond the checklist. After the tall girl went through the now-familiar shock-and-awe over his foreign body, he really got into it with her and he knew she liked it too because at one point she screamed *shufu sile!* (Literally "comfortable till death!"). The tall girl urged the short girl to do it with Rex too.

When it was over, Rex lay back on the bed, running the high points over in his mind, like a cat licking his chops. But the Chinese man stood up, put his clothes on and said that he wanted to go dancing at a Chinese club called Nightman. He wanted to go *now.* After they climbed into the Jetta, it soon became apparent that the Chinese man had no idea where he was going; he began heading rapidly south of Jianguomen, although the club was in the northeast—Rex had been there before. But the Chinese man refused to turn around.

"No, really, I know where it is," Rex said.

"Fine," the Chinese man said. "You know where it is? You get out and take the girls there."

"What about you?"

"No, no, I want to go home."

Rex took the girls to Nightman. The night wound down and when they got to the taxis, the girls suggested that they go home with Rex. He had to get up at 7:30 for work, so they settled for exchanging numbers. The next morning, the Chinese man called Rex:

"Did you take the girls to the club?"

"Yes, I did."

"Did you dance and drink with them?"

"Yeah."

"You paid for it, right?"

"Yeah, I paid for their drinks and their cabs home."

"You sent them home, right? You sent them home? They didn't go home with you?"

"They went home by themselves."

"Are you sure?"

"Yeah, I'm positive."

The Chinese man was telling Rex that these were *his* women. But Rex knew that underneath the bluster, the Chinese man had lost face: once during the sex, and then by getting lost. Rex was beginning to grasp why he was succeeding with women in China after struggling in the United States. At the end of the day, it wasn't his nationality or his looks; it was the vulnerability of the Chinese male psyche that created the opening. Even the advanced Chinese guys, the ones who thought of themselves as free thinkers, seemed mainly concerned with controlling the situation when they got into the bedroom. Chinese women were not sexually aggressive—not yet—but beyond being uninhibited about pleasing men (or nagging and pestering them, depending on their mood), they were far more open to the possibilities. Like children growing up, the girls of the New China seemed to be perpetually ahead of the boys.

That was the surface impression and—well, Rex didn't have time to think about the Chinese man's e-mails anymore; he was busy processing over fifty Internet responses a month from interested women, and systematically exploring other avenues of seduction beyond the Internet. For the most part, he concentrated on the clubs: the Loft, the Velvet Room, Vic's, Banana, Havana, and Orange. The Den, near Sanlitun, became Rex's personal stomping ground. It was crowded, the dance floor was intimate and, as the name suggested, lit like a basement. Roaming through the Den a couple of nights a week, Rex developed The Look: hungry, bedroomy, intense and somehow good-humored at the same time. There was always a girl who wanted to go out and have fun and just didn't care about much. Rex usually would end up sleeping with her. She would introduce him to her friends and he would wind up sleeping with one of them. Eventually it would come around full circle: if he really liked a girl, he would stay in contact for a couple of months (while he got to know her friends), then sleep with her again. Rex was getting five calls from different girls in a single night, driving his roommate insane with envy. He was getting invitations to the Louis Vuitton opening in China World and hip dissident art shows. He was hanging out with China's World Cup soccer team and going to the Loft's VIP lounge with the biggest art dealers in China. Roll of bills on the table, snorting ecstasy or coke off their fingernails, while they had beautiful girls wiggle their breasts in the guy's faces and they invited other girls to come over and sit on Rex's lap, just because he was a foreigner, just because he was new and interesting.

At the same time, work was demanding. Rex was spending long days looking up Chinese regulations, formatting them, calling up experts for background interpretation and neatly summarizing the regulations in English sound bites for corporate consumption. It was going okay; the managing director had even named Rex to a potential client as one of the company's up-and-coming stars.

One day Jack, his supervisor, approached Rex's cubicle and explained that a former member of the Australian Parliament, a potential client, was in town. He wanted to check out Beijing's liquor scene and see what the Chinese were importing. "He has to be, you know, taken around to the bars for research. But I can't do it tonight," Jack said. "You can handle it. Show this guy a good time. Take him to Maggie's."

Rex had never been to Maggie's, but he knew where it was located and he knew its reputation: a Chinese prostitute bar that serviced foreigners. "No problem," said Rex, smiling back. A secretary booked a Red Flag limo and another company official gave Rex a big wad of cash.

Rex picked up the former MP at the St. Regis Hotel and initially decided to take him to Durty Nellie's, a simulacrum of an Irish pub in the heart of Sanlitun Alley. The Australian would want to know what the expats were drinking, Rex figured. After checking it out, they headed over to Boys Club, Girls Club on the Chinese strip. It was getting on now, so Rex suggested they hit Club Vogue, a large and stylish disco. It made sense: since the club attracted both expats and Chinese, the former MP could see a hybrid liquor establishment. Yet as they stood in the VIP section of Vogue, Jack's command—"Take him to Maggie's"—was ringing in his head. The limo was waiting outside and the cash was in his breast pocket. When the two men walked out of Club Vogue and got into the limo, however, Rex told the driver to go to the St. Regis. Setting up the potential client wasn't on his personal checklist. Rex didn't know why he wanted to keep his two worlds separate, but he did. The Australian turned to Rex and said almost sympathetically, "Look, son, I've had a very interesting night. It doesn't need to get any more interesting," a hint that he had been led to expect much more. Rex pretended to take the statement at face value and dropped the former MP off at the hotel.

The next morning, Jack approached Rex's cubicle, smiled, and asked, "Did you take him to Maggie's?" Rex began a convoluted description of the evening, and Jack looked away, a wave of frustration rippling across his face.

They never got the contract.

█

If Rex was a sexual freelancer, he didn't really know who he was dealing with, for Jack represented the other side of the coin: sex not as an existential maneuver, but sex as commerce. With an easy smile, Jack recalled for me his first days in China:

> I felt freer here than I did in America because there was no Big Brother watching me . . . no peer group, no parents, no career track or reputation. I couldn't have gotten away with it in the States. . . . As a foreigner in this country you are freer than in any other country in the world. The laws do not apply. You're protected. *Unbelievably protected.**

---

*I must have looked a little skeptical when Jack used the term "freer," because he launched into a story: A couple of years ago, there was a club in Beijing called Velvet Underground. Back then, it was cutting edge—stylish, dark, with mauve neon and plenty of plush couches hidden away from the dance floor. "A really jumping place even by American standards" according to Jack, Velvet

Through a Tianjin University study program in 1994, Jack arrived in China at a time when, the joke went, the national bird was the construction crane. He had imagined 1920 Shanghai—sultry, sexy, adventurous. Instead, Tianjin was "an armpit of China, an industrial wasteland." Chinese girls were ugly: tons of makeup, wearing cheap ankle-high nylon stockings rolled halfway down. Jack plunged into his first depression, what another expat referred to as the "heart of China darkness," a feeling of generalized China-disgust, accompanied by a strong dose of Western guilt. The feeling crept up about six weeks in, curiously similar in timing to the reaction of men facing a long prison sentence. But the slump didn't last; by the next year, Jack and his friends had found Chinese housing, skillfully evaded the police, and were jumping on trains to the hinterlands every chance they got. "It was wonderful," Jack gushes. "Jack Kerouac on the road in China." Chinese girls still seemed intellectually vapid, but Jack supposed it was a result of the by-rote education system. They seemed very traditional, very subservient, yet he was beginning to get a taste for them—"like going out with the maid. . . . It was potentially very hot."

---

attracted beautiful people, particularly beautiful Chinese people, to an atmosphere that cried out for beautiful designer pills: Ecstasy and ketamine and lines of cocaine. Around 2 A.M. one night, Jack and nearly two hundred people were jamming to a European DJ who was playing the latest techno and trance. Outside of the club, official Beijing was preoccupied with a major meeting of the National People's Congress. Yet politically symbolic events always bring Public Security Bureau crackdowns on dissent and vice, so perhaps it shouldn't have been a complete surprise when twenty armed policemen suddenly burst into the club. But the raid was unexpectedly harsh; the music went dead as the cops screamed for everyone to shut up and get down on the floor. Within seconds, people were throwing pills all over the place. The police grabbed the Chinese revelers by their necks and forced them down to the ground, and then, passing plastic cups around, ordered everyone to produce urine samples. It was a sight that would remain with Jack—the crème de la crème of China's nouveau riche youth, male and female, pants down, trying to pee into little plastic cups. The police weren't interested in the foreigners; Jack and the other whites simply received a firm gesture toward the exit. The Chinese paid a huge fine or went to jail. Yet as a drug bust, it had an element of comical Chinese inefficiency as well. Jack remembers: "When the police broke in, one of my friends stuffed drugs in the couch." Two weeks later, they went by the club. "The drugs were *still there,* underneath the cushions." Jack laughs: "You cannot believe how happy *he* was."

Settling in Beijing after his Tianjin University program, Jack quickly made his way into a job as a business consultant with an American firm. His boss's biggest client was a major multinational, a top American beverage company. Jack helped to arrange a visit from its vice president and the director of legal and government affairs. At the end of the day the executives wanted to relax, so Jack's boss had arranged for a private room at a swanky cocktail lounge, where he decided to impress the VP with a little Eastern color by inviting along five Mongolian prostitutes.

The night was doubly portentous. Tuya, a prostitute sitting across from Jack, awed him with her beauty. Everything about her seemed to embody the good and the bad equally, alternately, simultaneously, and it played into every instinct he had brought to China. He felt sorry for Tuya, protective and paternalistic, but mostly he just felt deeply aroused. That night they went back to his boss's pad and he slept with her. It was a revelation: "The Mongolian girls were just two hundred times better in bed than the Chinese girls ... free-thinking, free-spirited, taking the initiative, not wanting to be subservient ... which turned out to be a double-edged sword down the line."

Below the Workers' Stadium and partially hidden by trees, there's a red neon sign that glows in the night, like every other bar in Beijing; but as even Rex knew, Maggie's is different. If you go there early in the evening, before the foreign men trickle in, the young prostitutes in little black dresses line up at the bar, looking up theatrically like an honor guard when a foreigner enters. Maggie's owner has major connections to the Chinese government, and because the girls are touted to be Mongolian nationals, Maggie's service to the foreigner community is not supposed to reflect on the Chinese people. No raids by the Beijing police are expected.

Half the bar looks normal—a circular bar, a pool table, a dance floor, some stand-up tables and ashtrays—while the other half is filled with carpeting and low-cut make-out couches. This half is kept dark for privacy, though nobody seems to care much about that; expat alpha males French-kiss girls right at the bar and pick fights that they know will be broken up before the second punch. Liberated white girls—Russians, Americans, the occasional

German or naughty Brit—gyrate on the crowded little dance floor, grooving on the sordidness of it all. It's cinematic, but in a faintly sepia-toned way, as if one had been transported back to the post-World War II world of GIs and the South Pacific and rum and Coca-Cola. Tuya operated out of Maggie's, and as she became Jack's girlfriend, Maggie's became his corrupt version of *Cheers*—where everyone knew his name and everyone was friendly.

Tuya opened important doors for Jack. The night they met, the visiting VP had slept with one of the five prostitutes. While Jack had his doubts about doing it at first, this incident had established a pattern: it was to become a major part of his job to act as a middleman—really a pimp—for visiting business delegations and clients. The clients were older American executives who wanted discreet and inexpensive sex with a local girl but didn't want to go through the bargaining process. One business executive told Jack that he didn't go for the fancy high-priced prostitutes (the kind you had to hire in Europe, to ensure discretion); he enjoyed the "cheap and easy." Jack facilitated and encouraged this kind of sexual behavior, because he understood instinctively that this was one of the key tenets in the Beijing reward system—even if the corporation was losing money in China, even if there was no reason to throw more investment in, simply satisfying the pleasure principle on the cheap would go a long way to protect the regional office's interests.

Yet it also became demanding; whenever executives from home hit town—or even politicians, such as the former mayor of Jack's own city—Jack had to drop whatever he was doing and spend the night setting them up with the girls. Sometimes the hand-holding didn't end when the prostitute had gone back to the five-star hotel with the executive. For example, a VP of a major American multinational called Jack early one morning whining that the girl wanted to leave because she had a *boyfriend*—saying the last word in a low nasal tone as if there couldn't be anything more ridiculous. Couldn't he do something? Jack tried to handle these little bimbo explosions as best he could, perceiving such requests as a kind of loyalty test by the bosses, as important as any other aspect of his job.

One night Jack took some senior executives from another multinational on a wild sex tour. On the car ride home, one of them said to him, "With what you know tonight, you could make a lot of money. *But you'd never live to spend it.*" Jack understood the thinly veiled threat, but he laughed right along with them.

Jack was beginning to rise rapidly in the AmCham committee structure and the clients were impressed. His double life became increasingly integrated; he invited Tuya and three of her prostitute friends to live in his spacious apartment, and the girls performed sexual tricks for just about anybody he brought over; he actually asked his boss for a raise during a bacchanal in the apartment and he got it. Success came at a cost—supporting Tuya's family came out to close to $20,000 a year. But thinking back and savoring the times, Jack reflects: "I've managed to have these experiences with the cosmetic appearance of being a straight-up guy—getting away with these things, doing these things with impunity.... God, it was *wonderful*. I wouldn't trade it for the world."

In Rex's world, on the other hand, there were moments of panic when he wondered if he was spiraling downward into a sexual point of no return. But in reality, it was his sexual stock that was rising while his professional stock went into a ditch. Perhaps because of the Maggie's incident, perhaps not, Jack suddenly found endless problems with his work and began referring to him as an idiot behind his back. Soon Rex was being shunted around the company. A new supervisor watched him vigilantly for errors, while he was constantly being upstaged by another intern, a North American girl with a permanently sunny expression. The clients loved her. It was left to Rex to do the menial labor, setting up the screen for PowerPoint presentations.

Even as Rex felt increasingly impotent at work, his sex life began to intersect more tightly with power and money. One night, a U.S. Commercial Service officer invited him over to his apartment to have drinks with a Chinese girl, Nan. The girl was extraordinarily cute, intelligent and charming. After a while Rex excused himself and went out clubbing on his own, only to run into Nan later that night at a club filled with prostitutes. They danced, made out, and then went back to her place in Lee Gardens apartments near Wangfujing, the central shopping district of Beijing. The opulence of her apartment stunned Rex; he couldn't afford a share at Lee Gardens and she had a roomy two-bedroom. Then he stopped thinking about it and just had sex with her—over and over until the first light. When he ran into the Commercial Service officer the next day, he thanked him for introducing him to Nan. The officer laughed: he had slept with Nan just before she left for the clubs. He explained that she might seem like a trophy girl, but she was actually from the countryside of Changchun. And she belonged to a British water company executive who gave her $5,000 a month simply to wait for him in Lee Gardens.

A few nights later, the Commercial Service officer introduced Rex to four Chinese girls who hung out at the Den. Dressed to kill, they spent three or four hundred dollars on drinks, and then one of the girls, Chen Li, drove Rex back to her place at the end of the night. She lived in a government compound located in the *hutongs* of Chaoyangmennei, so Rex had to hit the floorboards as an armed guard waved her Volkswagen Santana through the gate. Her parents—government officials—lived next door, so he had to sneak into her apartment as well. Even though Rex had never been to the room of a high-class Chinese prostitute, he assumed it would look something like this: a huge black lacquer table surrounded by cubic chairs on an immaculate hardwood floor; Hong Kong style red crushed-velvet couch with leopard throw pillows; a state-of-the-art entertainment system. Every room featured massive, dreamy portraits of Chen Li, even above the toilet (this one was in black and white and was clearly supposed to resemble Rodin's *The Thinker*). It's almost tasteful, Rex thought as he peed. Her bedroom was done up in plush white carpeting and oyster pearl-painted wood, ever-so distressed, which offset the leopard-print comforter, the rose silk sheets, and an elaborate nightstand with a drawer of condoms. (Trojans thoughtfully provided for the foreigners.) There was also a huge walk-in closet and a huge mirrored wall, which she insisted they face when they had sexual intercourse so she could see everything.

The next morning, she told him she was a *People's Daily* marketing manager, which meant that she was making approximately 4,000 RMB, about $500 a month. Rex later learned from her friends that she was the mistress of a *dakuan,* a Chinese millionaire. In fact, all the Den girls had *dakuans.* They passed Rex around, always paying the bills, always looking after his needs. There was a whirl of calls, dancing and sex, all leading to Mimi.

She was the little sister of the bunch, twenty years old, with perfect Gucci boots and perfect doll-like features that hid a mean-spirited, childish personality. Her brother was a Beijing policeman, but she lived in Hong Kong with an organized crime boss, a leader of a triad. After a few drinks one night, she invited Rex back to the Kunlun Hotel, an opulent palace favored by Japanese businessmen across from the Great Wall Sheraton. It was her first time with a foreigner, and Rex found himself feeling coolly mature, treating her gently but firmly, telling her what to do next, upping the ante with every move.

It was okay, another mark on the checklist. A few weeks later, Rex borrowed the foreign Commercial Service officer's mobile phone to chat with Mimi in Hong Kong. The triad boss retrieved the phone number from her phone a day or two later and the Commercial Service officer received an explicit death threat. Rex lay low, avoiding the Den girls for a few weeks until one of them showed him a Hong Kong magazine with Mimi and the triad boss on the cover, with a torn heart between them. A brush with money, a brush with organized crime: it's time to get out of the vortex, Rex decided.

His career intervened; he had left the consulting company, and now the only places that were ready to hire him were New Economy companies that hadn't managed to burn all their capital quite yet, and poorly managed consulting firms that paid only on commission. After extensive interviews, one of them hired Rex; but as he arrived for his first day of work, the offices had already been locked up, never to reopen. He was racked with health problems—giardia, nausea, even malaria at one point. Without health insurance, he went to Chinese doctors who prescribed foul-tasting and ultimately useless herbal remedies. He took on a commission job at an investment consulting firm, but it barely paid enough for him to buy a cheap Chinese knock-off of a designer suit.

If Rex's professional life had become the portrait of Dorian Gray, socially he was still respected and envied. He felt curiously compelled to finish what he had started. There were submissive girls, aggressive girls, and a successful Chinese businesswoman who was trying to persuade him to attend her S&M parties. (She even had metal poles installed in her apartment like Bada Bing!) To lure him in, she put the word out and set up a meeting for him at Henry J. Bean's with a foreigner and a Chinese girl looking for a two-on-one experience.

At Bean's, the foreigner turned out to be a specialized construction engineer, with a kid in Beijing and a wife in the States about to sue for divorce. Around thirty-five, he had a villa by the airport and a friend's apartment in town that he employed for sexual encounters. He introduced Rex to Lily, a bright-eyed Chinese IT engineer for a foreign joint venture. It was straightforward: They took a cab to the apartment and she took off her clothes, then theirs. Under the ever-present fluorescent light, they went through various sexual positions, Lily repeating phrases from pornographic videos as if she had studied them in a language lab. Rex had wanted this, but now that it was here, he felt inhibited, as if the whole situation was vaguely ridiculous. Lily sent an e-mail to Rex a few days later: "I hope we can meet together." Rex thought: I can't get into this. I have got to fight the darkness.

A few weeks later, a prominent American expat named Freddy called Rex and asked if he wanted to attend an orgy. He claimed to have one every couple of months or so. Rex said he had never done anything like that. Freddy said, "Well, you got to try it."

When Rex arrived, sitting around a living room there were four men—two Chinese and two white—surrounded by ten Chinese girls. Rex was shocked by the eagerness of the girls, the blatant curiosity. They all looked much the same, like sisters.

Freddy put on a Japanese porno video showing a girl being tortured on a pool table with cue sticks. Eventually they turned it off, but only after a couple of the Chinese girls had freaked out and left. Then Freddy went off to the bedroom with one of the girls, leaving everyone else in the living room tapping their feet. Then the Taiwanese guy went to the bedroom with one of the girls. Now they could hear moaning coming from the bedroom. Rex got up and went to take a look. A girl came in, started kissing him, and that was it.

It went on for hours, Rex doing it with three girls, stopping only when Freddy passed out fresh condoms and Viagra like a host handing out candy. Then everyone was exhausted, clothes were back on, and Rex went home. Well, I did it, he thought.

Rex is back in America, where he and I have reconnected. When he's in the mood to talk, what emerges is that he doesn't consider his experience unique. He came of age in Beijing, that's all, and Beijing was a great place—and an awful place—to do so.

Yet Rex remembers mainly feeling extremely lonely the entire time he was in China. "I was getting over so easily," he explained. "I never took the time to get to know anyone." He admits that with a few exceptions, "the white women are right. Chinese women are a bit unsubstantial." He tells a story about a friend of his who became very close with a Chinese girl from the provinces, close enough that he actually took a trip to meet her parents. The mother, a quintessential no-bullshit peasant woman, was unimpressed by his respectful praise of her daughter. She stated that he shouldn't think twice about disciplining her: "My daughter is like a small child. That's the way you should treat her."

Why, then, the attraction to—even the fetish of—Chinese women? "There's a basic insecurity to the white men in Beijing," Rex says, gesturing to himself at the same time. "A lot of them are not very attractive. A lot of them are not very nice. Or perhaps shallow. They leverage their money, their background, and their ability to offer greater opportunity. They take advantage of the fact that Chinese women Occidentalize them. And in return, American men are—quite literally—seduced by China."

Rex points to a Xinhua report from July 2002 that the owners, bouncers and callgirls of Sanlitun Bar Street have set up a new branch of the Communist Party. The Party was already letting capitalists in, but the inclusion of sex workers who specifically cater to foreigners raises a question: Why does the Chinese government allow foreigners such freedom? The Chinese conceive of Americans as barbarians—oversexed, easily corrupted fools. Seduction softens them up. Sex is good for business, Rex says, and good for China.

As I reconstructed it through our conversations—both in Beijing and later, in a less frenetic way, in the United States—I couldn't help thinking that if Rex, from a professional standpoint, had been treated as the runt of the litter in Beijing, perhaps it was a sort of grace. Rex's story was both exciting and cautionary. For me it would always be the road not taken.

When I first joined my wife in China, we planned to be there only a year. We stayed on, in great measure, because we had a nice life. Not because we were wealthy; between my part-time salary and her academic grants, we technically just edged into middle-class America. Yet by the latter half of 2000, living in our small-but-cool penthouse apartment in the old section of Beijing, we had a driver on call and a maid, and we went out to dinner every night, pretty much wherever we wanted. If we'd had children, we would have had our pick of full-time nannies, all for a pittance by American standards.

We made many friends—although few so symbolic of the New China as Rex—and we organized get-togethers: barbecues, wild martini parties, fundraisers, country club outings for interesting self-selected expats and Chinese artists. My wife's face is forever young, although in truth, we were both creeping into middle age. Yet expat life, by necessity, opens your mind, allows you to reinvent yourself, and "acting your age" becomes pretty elastic too. Not long after arriving in China, on a party dare, I successfully chugged a Frisbee full of beer (and I didn't even get sick until I was on the way home). Almost every week, we would go out dancing—serious, sweaty dancing—to hardcore music at clubs, parties, even the occasional rave at the Great Wall. There was a full calendar of adult events, so my tuxedo received far more use in Beijing than it had in New York: the British Ball, the Irish Ball, the Correspondents' Dinner, rugby matches in the fall, Yale Club lectures, Capital Club banquets, American Club fundraisers and, if you were lucky enough to be invited, you could wear whatever you wanted to Mitch's Sunday night movies.

All this activity didn't have a bad effect on our marriage; if anything, it was a kind of a stimulant. And that's why, in spite of the fact that I had become a China critic over the course of my time in Beijing, when my wife said it was time to go after two years, I argued against it. Besides, I was writing for major publications, I was building a reputation, I was vice chair of an AmCham committee, I was lunching with the embassy chief of staff and the occasional visiting congressman. There were so many career possibilities and all I had to do was network, it seemed, and let it all happen, as if I were on a great ship headed to some glamorous destination.

As for my wife, she complained about staying, but she certainly seemed busy enough, so I figured her research and writing were coming along—until one night in early October. Maybe it was the full moon (an old Irish belief), but I just couldn't sleep. I went downstairs to surf the Web on my wife's computer. Idly going through her favorite sites, I was struck by the sophistication of the work she had done for a dot.com project. The site was amazingly complex, intellectual and graphics-rich. So was the Beijing Ultimate Frisbee site (which she webmastered). Suspicious now, I clicked back to her desktop and looked through her extensive research folders. She hadn't accessed a single one in over a month.

It wasn't as if I had discovered reams of paper with *all work and no play makes Jack a dull boy* typed on them, but I had a creepy feeling. I suppose it was the guilt of looking through her stuff that made me expect her to appear malevolently at the door, like Jack Nicholson in *The Shining*.

But she wasn't isolated in Beijing—far from it. She had essentially completed the fieldwork portion of her research, and now there were so many distractions, social imperatives, projects to be worked on. What she needed was a *Shining*-like setting, a big empty place in the mountains, where she could write in isolation. Fortunately we had an old family home in the southern mountains of Vermont, and although there might be a few ghosts in it, at least they were family.

The next night, we went out to dinner and talked about it. For once, my analysis was right. Underneath all the activities, socializing and dot.com work, my wife was miserable. She was hanging out in Beijing for me, but her real work was beginning to drift. As we made plans for her to go to Vermont, at least for a time, I could see the tension leave her eyes and that was enough for me. I would join her at Christmas, and a couple of months after that, I said, I would close up shop. A few weeks later I found myself at the airport, kissing her goodbye.

Following my return from the airport, I was seized by a sudden urge to pack my things as well. I did so in part, pretending that I was on my way to Washington, New York, or the open American highway, rather than facing a sort of Beijing prison term with a fine view of Oriental squalor. Looking around for some lost treasures, I entered our loft. Before my wife left, she arranged for her things to be shipped home, but the movers hadn't come yet, so all her books and academic materials were carefully packed in oversize boxes, neatly labeled in a kind of code and spaced evenly in rows. In the darkness, it reminded me of an Egyptian tomb. The loneliness was overwhelming, almost terrifying.

There had been other moments of deep longing for home. When the Yale Whiffenpoofs, a high-profile glee club, were passing through Beijing the previous summer, my Yalie wife and I took them to lunch at our favorite Peking duck restaurant deep within the southern *hutongs*. It was a dreadfully hot August day and the light in the courtyard was vintage Beijing, yellow and poisonous. When the boys had finished their duck, one diminutive Whiffenpoof walked out into the light of the courtyard. Standing in front of the peasant Chinese waiters and cooks, he began an incongruous solo:

> *Down by the salley gardens my love and I did meet;*
> *She passed the salley gardens with little snow-white feet.*
> *She bid me take love easy, as the leaves grow on the tree;*
> *But I, being young and foolish, with her would not agree.*

And I could feel my throat catch as his tenor, clear and perfect, seemed to embody all of Western civilization, and in particular the lush green hills of my Vermont home.

This time, being in China without my companion, my wife, my best friend—it was worse now, searing in its intensity. Yet the thought of returning to the real playing field—Washington and New York—where I would be just one more white guy with some indefinable business and experience in China (interesting but distant and irrelevant) was more terrifying still. America seemed like a cavernous club, full of potential adventures, but utterly mysterious and controlled by the big moguls of politics, business and entertainment. It was a table at which I had no reservation. At the airport I had reassured my wife that it would be only a couple of months, but in truth, I had no intention of leaving Beijing.

Perhaps as a consequence, in the summer of 2001 I entered my personal Chinese heart of darkness. Beijing began appearing to me as a series of pyramids and walls, sinister and blockheaded, a one-eyed idol built on a furnace fired by yesterday's chopsticks. The *hutongs,* at least, seemed relatively placid, disturbed only by the sound of pensioners arguing in gnarly Beijing accents and toddlers peeing on my bicycle. I fell asleep in the fetid afternoon heat and dreamed of my wife, only to be awakened by the melody of a Beijing garbage truck making its evening pass to the Drum Tower.

One summer night I was invited to a dinner party out by Peking University. I was drinking heavily, and when it was over, about 3 A.M. or so, a Chinese girl that I knew from work and an older Chinese woman, a friend of hers, gave me a lift back to Ju'er Hutong. They came up to my place for a final drink just as the first light was breaking over the Beijing sky. We sat on the porch with our martinis for a while, and after the girl had fallen asleep in her chair, the older woman began talking about how much she liked foreign men and how she wanted to have sex with me. I had done nothing to start this, so at first I just felt flattered. Eventually we started seriously making out. But in the middle, after the clothes came off, I began to feel guilty. A second before, I had been urging her to wake up her friend so we could have a ménage à trois; now I was explaining that I had never been unfaithful to my wife. The woman was incredulous, but she put her clothes back on and left.

I didn't have a sexual history to bounce the experience off, not in Beijing anyway. I used to compose absurdist responses to personal ads on my office computer sometimes, but I had no intention of sending them. I had joked around with a Chinese intern at my office, but I ignored her love letter. At parties, I had flirted with cute Chinese women, but I went home alone. But now, although I could attempt to write it off as some sort of drunken spring-break interlude, I had crossed a Rubicon of near-infidelity— and the world looked different.

A few weeks later, I was at a pool party at a Chinese health club when some American girls, friends of mine, asked if they could throw a naked martini party at my place tonight, just our gang. Sure, I said. Perhaps they were serious. Or perhaps they were only serious about the martinis. But the gang came over—three girls, about six guys, from all walks of government and the American business community—and I wanted it to happen and I still remember how slippery and cold the floor was, smeared with all that gin and ice. How far did it go? Not very: one girl simply left, and after a while, the remaining two girls went into an adjoining study, left the door open and began to make out, while I watched. Then I walked around offering people injections of testosterone (legal for a medical condition I had, but illegal for them). It seemed comical at the time. The guys were hungry, so I pulled thick, gristly Chinese steaks out of the fridge and we naked Americans—as white as fish bellies—grilled them on the balcony. Then the dawn broke and I got paranoid about the Chinese air force installation that had a clear view of the porch.

So nothing really happened, no one got hurt, and the girls were lovely to look at, and nobody touched me . . . but I suddenly saw how it *could* happen. Here in Beijing, I could be a thinking man's Rex, the *man,* the one who throws the orgies every couple of months—better than Freddy's, really stylish ones that included a few top professionals from the expat business community. Maybe Jack could help slip in a sophisticated call girl from Maggie's just to keep things moving in the right direction. I could supplement the down time with Chinese girls, divorced women, what have you. Maybe I could finally mine a piece of the Gold Mountain, that idea that Terry and I had talked about on Thanksgiving years ago. I could grow old as a grand expat, the Henry Miller of Beijing. Oh, and I could continue to write my anti-China screeds—maybe—well, perhaps I could work on my legitimacy, get a few powerful friends in the Chinese government . . . maybe invite them to one of the orgies. . . . Looking down into the abyss, I could see it all so clearly.

A month later, my driver was taking me to the airport. Expat China often feels like a great ocean liner where the passengers have become preternaturally close over a long voyage—partying, gambling great sums of other people's money, and occasionally puking over the rails. So when a fellow passenger prepares to disembark, people make a fuss. Parties are thrown and sentimental toasts are made. My departure was no exception. A friendly U.S. embassy couple threw a nice little reception with government-sponsored catering. At my final, final farewell party, one that I held on my porch for a few special friends, such as Rex and Chris and Freda Murck, there was a kind of closure when Wang, the Peking University student who had led the demonstrations on the U.S. embassy, showed up. He gave me the impression that simply because we all worked in China, we had been on the same side all along.

He was wrong, but as the car neared the airport expressway, I didn't care about Wang's nationalism or Laurence Brahm's books or Motorola or Cisco or Maggie's; as I watched the city go by, it felt like a beloved childhood home. Every building, every corner had some association, some aroma, some unsolved mystery. I loved Beijing, and with the Olympics coming in 2008, I knew I would never see it again like this.

At the airport curb, I gave my driver a gentle hand-clasp— most Chinese people aren't comfortable with hugs—and twenty hours later, I was back in the green hills of Vermont with my wife on a lovely August night.

I knew there would be difficulties, beginning with what I had done and almost done in China, then with money and what to do next. Down the road, there might even be a baby to worry about. But for tonight, we were down by the salley gardens, and it was enough.

Acknowledgments

I had no plans to write a book before I left for China. The thought crossed my mind while I was in Beijing, but it was only after I had returned to the States that I began to consider the idea seriously. Therefore, I have divided my acknowledgments into pre-China, in-China and post-China parts. People who made important contributions to the book in the first two stages were not aware that they were doing so.

For the pre-China phase, I am particularly grateful to Randolph Quon. Initially, Randolph was a useful source on the Princelings and Chinese finance. Over time, he became my China guru and also a close friend. Without his intellectual guidance and encouragement, I would not have gone to Beijing. Other individuals who encouraged my interest in China and helped to develop some of the themes in this book include Paul Weyrich, Dr. June Teufel Dreyer, Roger Robinson, Frank Gaffney and Danny Schechter. In the months before my departure, Mimi James and Terry Halsey invited me to stay at their home in New York City, Globalvision provided office space, and Daniel McDonald of the Potomac Foundation gave me seed money.

During the in-China phase, without the friendship, irreverence and openness of my American and Chinese colleagues (and the businessmen that I worked with on a daily basis), every day would have been Visiting Day, and I would have little to tell. Some of these individuals are named, such as Michael Furst and Chris Murck. Others I have taken some trouble not to name. You know

225

who you are, and a few of you may be upset or offended by this book. In one or two cases, that may be my fault; while I have an excellent memory for dialogue, it's not dead-on perfect, and any inaccuracies or contextual misinterpretations are mine.

I am also indebted to the management of my public affairs company, both in Asia and in America, for giving me a platform and sticking by me. Within the U.S. embassy, I especially thank the military attachés who helped me, and on the commercial side, I am grateful to Thomas Lee Boam and Stephen Anderson for their insights. Within the Beijing journalistic community, particular thanks go to several reporters (some of whom are no longer in Beijing), including John Pomfret, Henry Chu, Michael Sheridan, Shai Oster, Noah Smith, Andrew Batson, Chris Billing, Edward Young, Simon Cartledge, Andre Mrevlje, and especially Jasper Becker. Several Beijingers also had a special influence on the flavor of this book: Kim Barnet, Dan Brody, Tang Di, Alice Fu, Po-Wen Huang, Francesca de Lago, Harry Miller, Freda Murck, Todd Stellfox and Russell Young. Within the Internet community, I would like to acknowledge my gratitude for Michael Robinson's willingness to go on the record, even when he did not agree with some of my conclusions, as well as his patience in explaining the more technical aspects of the Chinese firewall. Peter Lovelock not only gave brilliant analysis in an entertaining form, but consistently supplied new leads and sources. I also thank the *Weekly Standard* for encouraging me to investigate the Internet topic and covering initial research expenses, and Richard Starr for his skillful editing.

In the post-China phase, I wish to thank my father, David Gutmann, who convinced me to pursue a book contract. A generous research grant from the Earhart Foundation allowed me to fill in the critical gaps by enabling me to return to China for several months, during which I had the opportunity to do extensive interviews. I gratefully acknowledge David Kennedy and the entire staff at Earhart, especially Ingrid A. Merikoski and Cheryl D. Gorski. Thanks also to Dan McMichael for steering me in Earhart's direction, and an extra special thanks to Dick Allen, who mentored the book from the beginning.

Among the many background sources for this book, I am grateful to Jiang Xueqin, James Mulvenon, Arthur Waldron, Ying

Ma, David Welker, Mark Bayuk, Stephen Hsu, Kenneth Berman, Alan Tonelson and Ann Lau. Dan Southerland, Peter Lovelock and Rebecca MacKinnon were kind enough to read the manuscript in its final stages and offer useful commentary. I would like to express my gratitude to Jeffrey Fiedler and the staff at AFL-CIO Food & Allied Services Trade for providing access to their files. Thanks also to Gary Schmitt and the Project for the New American Century for their continued support.

Peter Collier, my editor, nurtured this book. He maintained a close interest in the manuscript and helped to strengthen the themes immeasurably. I am a longwinded and prickly writer, and he handled the first couple of drafts and the necessary bloodletting with the skill and patient bedside manner of a star surgeon. Carol Staswick's intelligent editing also plays a large role in the final product. I am profoundly grateful.

My wife's contribution goes beyond the routine acknowledgment format. In addition to her proofreading and editing—and she is second to none in those areas—she took me to China and back. She never asked me to tone down a single word, even though she knew that her access as a China scholar could be adversely affected by what I wrote. And finally, she supported my writing in the final push—as did Ethan Zachary's grandmother, Joanna— when the parental emergency abruptly superseded the creative process. For all these reasons, and for others too deep for me to express, this book is hers.

Notes

Preface

p. x: The phrase "trans-Pacific Tammany Hall" was originally coined by Randolph Quon (to the best of my knowledge).

pp. xi–xiii: My brief summary of American post-Mao perceptions of China was influenced by James Mann, *About Face: A History of America's Curious Relationship with China, from Nixon to Clinton* (Alfred A. Knopf, 1999). Mann's earlier work, *Beijing Jeep: A Case Study of Western Business in China* (Westview Press, 1997)—an account of American Motors' high-profile joint venture in Beijing during the 1980s—is also an excellent book.

p. xiii: The song about the streets of Beijing is an adulteration of Ralph McTell's "Streets of London," Reprise, 1974.

pp. xvi–xvii: Some of my points about Chinese nationalism were originally published in an opinion piece: Ethan Gutmann, "Big Bush, Little Bush," *Asian Wall Street Journal*, 28 February 2001.

p. xvii: A good introduction to the issue of technology transfer and Chinese military objectives can be found in Richard Bernstein and Ross H. Munro, *The Coming Conflict with China* (Alfred A. Knopf, 1997). The most comprehensive work on losing money in the New China is Joe Studwell, *The China Dream: The Quest for the Last Great Untapped Market on Earth* (Atlantic Monthly Press, 2002).

Chapter 1. The Happening
My personal account of the events of May 8, 1999, was previously published in an abbreviated version: Ethan Gutmann, "A Tale of New China," *Weekly Standard,* 24 May 1999.

"Wang" is, by necessity, a pseudonym. I interviewed him on November 18, 2002. It should be noted that Wang's cynical view of the student organizers of the Tiananmen Square movement was not just a rationalization for inaction but had some basis in reality. On the student protesters' undemocratic decision-making, see Andrew J. Nathan and Perry Link, eds., *The Tiananmen Papers* (PublicAffairs, 2001). On the Tiananmen organizers' current occupations, see Ian Buruma, *Bad Elements: Chinese Rebels from Los Angeles to Beijing* (Random House, 2001).

p. 12: Ford and IBM's messages of regret over the embassy bombing are from the *PLA News,* 12 May 1999; Motorola's comments are from the *Beijing Evening News,* 9 May 1999; see also *Beijing Morning Post,* 12 May 1999. All are found in Sinopolis.com—Special Edition Newsletter, <http://www.sinopolis.com.cn>, 12 May 1999.

p. 13: The comments of Michael Furst are a composite from various personal conversations from 1999 to 2002. Furst was also helpful in filling in the gaps about the AmCham doorknock, and about how American businesses handled the Chinese reaction to the embassy bombing.

pp. 13–14: Regarding Ezra Vogel's statements, see Philip Cunningham, "Probe Shows Bombing No Accident," *Hong Kong Standard,* 14 June 1999. Vogel's repudiation of the *Hong Kong Standard* story appeared as an open letter on the Harvard University Fairbank Center website ("To Whom It May Concern," Ezra F. Vogel, 15 June 1999).

p. 16: Regarding Bob Kapp's reaction to the embassy bombing, see "Testimony of Robert A. Kapp, President, United States-China Business Council: Subcommittee on Trade, House Ways and Means Committee," 8 June 1999. Although I did not attend the AmCham doorknock of 1999, several AmCham members, including Tim Stratford, spoke to me about it during the so-called "spy plane" crisis in 2001.

p. 17: The *People's Daily* statement calling on the nation to accelerate the modernization of PLA weaponry is cited in Willy Lo-Lap Lam, "Self-Destructive Nationalism," *South China Morning Post,* 19 May 1999.

A surprising number of Americans persist in the belief that the U.S. bombing of the embassy in Belgrade was not a mistake, but a conspiracy (often echoing stories that ran in the British press shortly after the incident; see John Sweeney, Jens Holsoe and Ed Vulliamy, "NATO Bombed Chinese Deliberately," *Observer* (London), 17 October 1999; also Martin Kettle, "CIA Was Warned off Target," *Guardian* (London), 25 June 1999. Careful investigative journalism has been done on the topic, and a close reading of it does not suggest a conspiracy; instead, it suggests that the CIA was tasked with that most challenging objective in an open society: trying to prove a series of negatives while attempting to protect its methods and staff. The CIA's detailed, tedious and ultimately embarrassing description of employing a street address to select an aerial target, combined with the absence of cross-checking— or indeed, any form of interagency cooperation—is still by far the most credible explanation for the incident. See DCI Statement on the Belgrade Chinese Embassy Bombing, House Permanent Select Committee on Intelligence Open Hearing, 22 July 1999. See also William M. Arkin, "Infamous Anniversary," and "Bombing Q&A," washingtonpost.com, <http://www.washingtonpost.com/wp-dyn/world/issues/ chinaembassy/>, 17 December 2003.

Chapter 2. MTV for War

"Wei," "Mao" and *Shared Street* are all pseudonyms. For an insightful look at the intellectual development of Chinese television propaganda, see Geremie R. Barme, *In the Red* (Columbia University Press, 1999).

My description of Falun Gong may offend some of its followers, and I sincerely apologize if, even in a minor way, I have caused them any more trouble than they have already endured. This section is largely based on my own experience with a few members of the group; I make no pretense of having a deep understanding of the exercises or spiritual practices involved. Because my observations about Falun Gong appear in a narrative context,

I have simply recorded my feelings about the group at that time (which were decidedly mixed), and even though I have sympathy for the group's plight, I cannot change it. As a reference point for dates, I used Wang Gungwu and Zheng Yongnian, eds., *Religio-Political Significance of Falun Gong* (Singapore University Press, 2000), particularly ch. 4, William T. Liu, "Reform, Legitimacy and Dilemmas: China's Politics and Society." For a general look at Falun Gong, see Danny Schechter, *Falun Gong's Challenge to China: Spiritual Practice or Evil Cult?* (Akashic Books, 2000).

p. 44: The point that State Security's crackdown on Falun Gong may have been used to keep the muscles from atrophying is properly attributed to Peter Batey, the current head of the EU Chamber of Commerce in Beijing.

Chapter 3. Visiting Day

pp. 51–56: The spokesperson training that I refer to is based on a handout entitled "AmCham China Washington D.C. Doorknock 2000 Spokesperson Training." I am not entirely sure which author, authors or PR company created the original presentation. For background on the Codels' political concerns and the Clinton administration's relationship to China, see James Mann, *About Face: A History of America's Curious Relationship with China, from Nixon to Clinton* (Alfred A. Knopf, 1999).

pp. 58–59: I was not in Beijing during Governor Ventura's trip, but the event had good press coverage: Audra Ang, "Flamboyant U.S. Governor Tours Beijing," Associated Press, 11 June 2001; Dane Smith, "From Minnesota to China," *Minneapolis Star Tribune,* 2 June 2002; "Ex-Wrestler Urges Business Leaders to Get to Grips," *South China Morning Post,* 11 June 2002; Patrick Sweeney, "Ventura Begins to Woo China," *Pioneer Press,* 10 June 2002; "Minnesota Gov. Ventura Promotes State in China," China Online, 11 June 2002; Dane Smith, "Seeking a Slice of China's Megamarkets," *Minneapolis Star Tribune,* 12 June 2002. For a typical account of how the Chinese leadership handles foreigners, see Dane Smith, "Ventura Tours Hormel Pork Plant; Meats Seasoned to Chinese Tastes," *Minneapolis Star Tribune,* 11 June 2002.

p. 60: On Congressman Ortiz's visit, see "US Congress Members Call for Enhancing Understanding of China," People's Daily Online, 5 April 2002, <http://fpeng.peopledaily.com.cn/200204/05/eng20020405_93515.shtml>

pp. 60–62: On the SARS epidemic, see John Pomfret, "Epidemic Is a 'Test' for China's Leadership," *Washington Post,* 22 April 2003; "Singapore Quarantines 2,500 over SARS Fears," CNN.com, 21 April 2003, <http://www.cnn.com/2003/HEALTH/04/21/sars>; Catherine Armitage, "SARS Infects Propaganda Machine," *Australian,* 5 May 2003; Erik Eckholm, "Beijing Acts to Calm Public," *New York Times,* 30 April 2003; and Ellen Bork, "Great Wall of Lies," *Weekly Standard,* 5 May 2003.

pp. 62–63: The former embassy officer was interviewed in July 2002.

pp. 65–66: "Jimbo" is a pseudonym.

Chapter 4. El Dorado
On the history of foreigners' involvement in the PRC and the Chinese Communist Party's attitudes, see Anne-Marie Brady, "The Political Meaning of Friendship: Reviewing the Life and Times of Two of China's American Friends," *China Review International,* 1 September 2002; see also Anne-Marie Brady, *Making the Foreign Serve China: Managing Foreigners in the People's Republic* (Rowman & Littlefield, October 2003).

p. 83: The real estate ad is from the Elite Beijing Realty, <http://www.eliterealtychina.com/propertylistdetails_eng.php?property_id=84>, 22 January 2003.

p. 83: On American business promoting the Beijing Olympics, see Glenda Korporaal, "Selling the Golden Rings," *South China Morning Post,* 26 February 2002; and Evelyn Iritani, "Rings around Beijing," *Los Angeles Times,* 21 February 2002.

pp. 83–84: On James Murdoch, see Tunku Varadarajan, "Bad Company: Rupert Murdoch and His Son Genuflect before Chinese Communists," *Wall Street Journal,* 26 March 2001.

p. 86: My assessment of the *South China Morning Post* dismissals is based on an interview with Jasper Becker in November 2003.

p. 92: Regarding Zhu Rongji's proposed use of the American business class to promote Chinese objectives, see Willy Lo-Lap Lam, "China's Business Card Trumps 'Bush's Push,' " CNN, 22 May 2001.

pp. 94–98: Regarding the flap over Peter Batey's chapter, the quotations and the correspondence surrounding the quotations are taken from Peter Batey, "China Opening the Window" (unpublished draft, e-mail correspondence and revisions by permission of the author, November 2000), written for Laurence Brahm, ed., *China's Century: The Awakening of the Next Economic Powerhouse* (John Wiley & Sons [Asia], 2001). Brahm's interview can be found at <http://www.business-in-asia.com/china_century. htm>; see also "Premier Meets Authors of 'China's Century,' " People's Daily Online, 16 March 2001. A close friend (who does not want to be named) coined the phrase "bright, shining lie" to describe Brahm's portrayal of the weather at the PRC's 50th anniversary parade.

Chapter 5. How to Succeed in China without Really Succeeding

pp. 104–5: Counterfeiting figures are from my participation in the Quality Brands Protection Committee (QBPC, formerly the CACC or China Anti-Counterfeiting Coalition). In addition, see Richard Behar, "Beijing's Phony War on Fakes," *Fortune,* 30 October 2000. See also Trish Saywell, "Fakes Cost Real Cash," *Far Eastern Economic Review,* 5 October 2000.

pp. 111–13: On the debate over China's GDP, see Thomas Rawski, "What's Happening to China's GDP Statistics?" 12 September 2001, <http://www.pitt.edu/~tgrawski/papers2001/gdp912f.pdf>, accessed 21 December 2003; "China Economy Growing at a Far Lesser Pace Than Data Indicate—MIT's Thurow," *AFX News Asia,* 19 March 2002; Thomas Rawski, "Beijing's Fuzzy Math," *Wall Street Journal,* 22 April 2002; Arthur Waldron, "China's 'Growth' Is Not What It Seems," Mercury News Service, 25 March 2002; Vanessa Gould, "Economist Doubts GDP Numbers," *South China Morning Post,* 20 March 2002; "Higher Speed, Less Guzzling," *China Daily,* 19 April 2003; Stephen Roach, "China Is Not an Oasis," Global Economic Forum, 3 December 2001, <http://www. morganstanley.com/GEFdata/digests/20011203-mon.html#

anchor0>; "Truth or Consequences: China's GDP Numbers,"
China Economic Quarterly, no. 1 (2003). See also Carsten Holz,
"The Art of Measuring GDP," *South China Morning Post,* 22 Octo-
ber 2002.

The interviews with the former AGC executive (pp. 118–19),
with the high school teacher (pp. 119–20) and with "Buster" (a
pseudonym, pp. 120–25) were all done in December 2002.

Chapter 6. Case Study: Who Lost China's Internet?
An early version of "Who Lost China's Internet?" was published
as an essay in the *Weekly Standard,* 25 February 2002. Portions of
this chapter also appeared as a short article in *Investor's Business
Daily* and an essay in *Red Herring.* Michael Robinson and Peter
Lovelock were both interviewed several times in the late spring
and early summer of 2001. The interview with the former Cisco
engineer took place in July 2001. "Wen" is a pseudonym.

On the early days of the Chinese Internet, see "PRC Internet: Cheaper, More Popular and More Chinese," Report from the
U.S. Embassy, Beijing, October 1988.

p. 131: IBM's role in financing the first Chinese firewall was con-
firmed in an interview with Matthew McGarvey, International
Data Corporation Asia Pacific Internet research senior analyst,
June 2001. The interview with David Zhou, Cisco systems engineer manager, took place in Cisco's Beijing office at the end of
July 2001. On the case of Chi Shouzhu, see "Burundi Leader
Condemns Coup," *Pittsburgh Post-Gazette,* 20 April 2001.
pp. 132–33: The phone interview with the former Yahoo! China
representative took place in July 2001. Yahoo!'s refusal to run a
VOA ad (p. 133) comes from my interview with William Baum,
chief, Chinese Branch, Voice of America, late August 2001.
pp. 138–39: On AOL's consideration of informing on dissidents,
see Steven Mufson and John Pomfret, "You've Got Dissidents?
AOL Weighs China Market—and Rights Issues," *Washington
Post,* 29 August 2001; see also Craig Smith, "AOL Wins Some
China TV Rights," *New York Times,* 23 October 2001.
pp. 139–40: On Nortel's surveillance plans for China, see
Greg Walton, "China's Golden Shield: Corporations and the

Development of Surveillance Technology in the People's Republic of China," International Centre for Human Rights and Democratic Development, <http://www.ichrdd.ca/english/commdoc/publications/globalization/GoldenShieldEng.html>, 2001; also Anh-Thu Phan, "Nortel to Supply Key Mainland Cities," *South China Morning Post,* 26 March 2002; "Railway Arrest Gives Rare Glimpse of Cyber-Police," *South China Morning Post,* 29 October 2001; and Anh-Thu Phan, "Nortel Helping China 'Monitor Its Citizens,'" *South China Morning Post,* 19 October 2001.

p. 140: On the smaller companies and trade shows alluded to, see Judy M. Chen, "IT Multinationals: Willing Partners to Repression in China?" <http://www.hrichina.org/Beijing_IT_Trade_Show-Judy_Chen.html>, 27 November 2000; and Charles Bickers and Susan V. Lawrence, "A Great Firewall: Surge in Networking Creates New Security Needs," *Far Eastern Economic Review,* 4 March 1999.

p. 140: On spyware, see Records 21, 61, 62, 63 and 641, at <http://www.tomcat.com>, 21 March 2002. See also <http://www.chinaglobe.com>, 10 February 2002.

pp. 140–41: On Chinese virus acquisition, see Ted Bridis, "China Exacts Computer-Virus Samples," *Wall Street Journal,* 30 March 2001. On other corporate giveaways, see for example, reference to Motorola's i.250 convergence platform in Ran Nianci and Peter Lovelock, MFC Insight Update, <http://www.mfcinsight.com/products/iframe/article/020405/news.html>, 5 April 2002.

p. 141: On the "Code Red worm," see this postmortem: <http://www.caida.org/analysis/security/code-red/>

p. 141: On Web attacks originating from the PSB, see Michael S. Chase and James C. Mulvenon, *You've Got Dissent! Chinese Dissident Use of the Internet and Beijing's Counter-Strategies* (Washington, D.C.: RAND, 2002), p. 66.

pp. 141–42: On Web attacks on Taiwan, see Craig S. Smith, "Beijing Stages War Games, Mostly for Taiwan," *New York Times,* 11 July 2001. See also Al Santoli (editor), "China Info-War Plans Described; China Submarine Operations Undetected by U.S. Navy," *China Reform Monitor,* no. 389, American Foreign Policy Council, 4 June 2001; and He Dequan, "We Must Act Immediately to Protect Our Information Security," *People's Daily,* 17 October 1999.

pp. 141–43: An interview with James Mulvenon, RAND, Washington, D.C., September 2001, was very useful in supplying a general context of Chinese thinking about information warfare. On the Chinese military journal article mentioned (p. 142), see Al Santoli (editor), "Applying Chinese Ancient Psychological Operations to Modern Warfare 'Under Hi-Tech Conditions,'" *China Reform Monitor,* no. 428, American Foreign Policy Council, 11 February 2002 (excerpted from the Chinese military journal *Beijing Zhongguo Junshi Kexue,* Issue no. 5, 2002, pp. 88–94). On Unrestricted Warfare, see Qiao Liang and Wang Xiangsui, *Unrestricted Warfare* (PLA Literature and Arts Publishing House, 1999); see also Al Santoli (editor), "'Decline of the U.S. as a Superpower,' Claim Authors of Chinese PLA's 'Unrestricted Warfare' Doctrine," *China Reform Monitor,* no. 408, 25 September 2001 (excerpted from an interview with Qiao Liang and Wang Xiangsui in the 13 September 2001 PRC-owned *Ta Kung Pao* newspaper in Hong Kong).

pp. 143–45: Regarding New Economy optimism, for one particularly breathless example (written just before the dot.com bust), see Lawrence Jeffrey, *China's Wired! Your Guide to the Internet in China* (Hong Kong, Asia Law & Practice, 2000). See also David Sheff, *China Dawn: The Story of a Technology and Business Revolution* (Harper Business, 2002).

p. 146: Most of the corporate projections are from the Lovelock interview. Cisco's projection is from Jeffrey Lin, CFA, Merrill Lynch Comment, "Cisco Channel Partners: The Direct Beneficiaries of Cisco's China Growth," 26 February 2001.

pp. 147–48: On *weiku* culture, see Lisa Movius, "To Be Young, Chinese and Weiku," *Slate,* 30 May 2001.

pp. 148–49: On the crackdown, see "Purifying the Net, China-Style," Digital Freedom Network, <http://www.cubdest.org/0106/c0310not.html>, 27 February 2001; Ken Grant and Peter Lovelock, *MFC Insight Update,* 9 February 2001; "Beijing Accused of School Blast Cover-Up," BBC, 9 March 2001; "China Plans to Build Internet Monitoring System," China News Digest, <http://www.cnd.org/Global/01/03/20/010320-3.html>, 20 March 2001; "Freedom of Expression and the Internet in China: A Human Rights Watch Backgrounder," Human Rights Watch,

<http://www.hrw.org/backgrounder/asia/china-bck-0701.htm>, 22 December 2003. The information on the unreliability of e-mail to Tibet is from an interview with Greg Shea, vice chair of the E-Commerce China Forum, July 2001.

p. 150: Regarding the self-censorship system in China, see Perry Link, "The Anaconda in the Chandelier," *New York Review of Books,* 11 April 2002.

pp. 150–51: On a middle school teacher receiving a prison sentence, see Ken Grant and Peter Lovelock, *MFC Insight Update,* 23 March 2001.

p. 151: On Falun Gong activists using the Net, see Craig S. Smith, "A Movement in Hiding," *New York Times,* 5 July 2001. On the case of Jiang Yonghong, see "Police Brutality Claims Four More Falun Gong Lives in China," Falun Dafa Information Center, <http://www.faluninfo.net/DisplayAnArticle.asp?ID=5328>, 20 February 2002.

pp. 151–52: On PSB methods of intercepting e-mail, see Michael S. Chase and James C. Mulvenon, *You've Got Dissent! Chinese Dissident Use of the Internet and Beijing's Counter-Strategies* (Washington, D.C.: RAND, 2002); and Geremie R. Barme and Sang Ye, "The Great Firewall of China," *Wired,* June 1997.

pp. 153–55: On the widespread use of proxy servers, see "The Questionnaire & Responses of Survey on the Internet Usage and Impact in Beijing, Shanghai, Guangzhou, Chengdu and Changsha in 2000," Center for Social Development, Chinese Academy of Social Sciences, 2000.

pp. 155–57: On Triangle Boy and other attempts to overcome the Chinese firewall, Stephen Hsu of SafeWeb and William Baum of VOA were interviewed in August 2001. On potential vulnerabilities of Triangle Boy, see David Martin and Andrew Schulman, "Deanonymizing Users of the SafeWeb Anonymizing Service," <http://www.cs.bu.edu/techreports/pdf/2002-003-deanonymizing-safeweb.pdf>, 11 February 2002.

pp. 158–59: On the Cisco shareholder resolution, see Ann Lau, "Resolution on Government Controls on Internet Worldwide," Communication to Cisco Systems, Inc., delivered on 30 May 2002; Mark Chandler, Vice President, Legal Services and General Counsel, "Re: Proposed Shareholder Resolution," Letter to

Ms. Ann Lau, 15 July 2002 (including "Exhibit B," Statement to the United States China Security Review Commission, Statement of Cisco Systems, Inc., 31 May 2002 and Supplemental Statement of Cisco Systems, Inc., 2 July 2002); Brobeck, Phleger & Harrison LLP, Letter to Securities and Exchange Commission, Office of Chief Counsel, Division of Corporate Finance, "Re: Cisco Systems, Inc., Shareholder Proposal Submitted by Ann Lau, Rule 14a-8 / Securities Exchange Act of 1934," 13 July 2002.

pp. 159–60: On the U.S. political backlash, see U.S.-China Security Review Commission, "Report to Congress of the U.S.-China Security Review Commission: The National Security Implications of the Economic Relationship between the United States and China," July 2002; also House Policy Committee, Policy Statement, "Establishing Global Internet Freedom: Tear Down This Firewall," 19 September 2002.

p. 161: The Merrill Lynch quote is from Jeffrey Lin, "Cisco Channel Partners: The Direct Beneficiaries of Cisco's China Growth," *Merrill Lynch Comment,* 26 February 2001.

p. 162: Regarding the temporary lifting of blocks on Western news sites, see John Ruwitch, "China Unblocks Foreign Media Web Sites," Reuters, 16 May 2002; and Jennifer S. Lee, "U.S. May Help Chinese Evade Net Censorship," *New York Times,* 30 August 2001.

p. 163: On Yahoo! signing the Chinese Internet pledge, see Ken Roth, "Yahoo! Risks Abusing Rights in China," Human Rights Watch, <http://www.hrw.org/press/2002/08/yahoo080902.htm>, 8 August 2002; and "China's Internet Illusion," *Wall Street Journal,* 21 August 2002.

p. 167: I interviewed Cisco salesman Enoch Chao in December 2003.

Chapter 7. Roaring Across the Horizon

p. 177: I interviewed film director Chen Guoxing in the summer of 1999.

pp. 177–86: Black, Gray and White were all interviewed in November and December of 2002.

p. 184: On Intel's contributions to Chinese universities, see Justin Rattner, "Extending Moore's Law," PowerPoint presentation, 29 October 2002, <http://www.intel.com/research/mrl/news/files/

MRFKeynote_Overview.pdf>, 21 December 2003.

p. 185: On Mylene Chan, see Bill Gertz, "SEC Aide Quits after Leak to Chinese," *Washington Times,* 11 November 2002.

pp. 186–88: On R&D centers, see "Transnationals Locate More R&D Centers in China," *People's Daily,* 19 March 2003; "Motorola Vows to Enhance Presence in China," *People's Daily,* 14 November 2001; "Motorola to Sink $100 mln in China Research Centre," Reuters, 7 January 2003; Winston Chai, "Motorola Sinks $90 million in China," CNET News.com, <http://news.com.com/2100-1037_3-1008106.html>, 20 May 2003; "Microsoft and China Announce Government Security Program Agreement," Microsoft PressPass, <http://www.microsoft.com/ presspass/press/2003/feb03/02-28gspchinapr.asp>, 28 February 2003; "Lucent Technologies Strengthens Commitment to R&D in China with Additional Investment," Lucent Press Release, <http://www.lucent.com/press/0603/030604.nsa.html>, 4 June 2003; "Alcatel Opens Research Center in SW China," *People's Daily,* 1 March 2003; "Nortel Networks Invests US$200 Million in R&D in China," *People's Daily,* 17 September 2003; "Welcome to the Alcatel Shanghai Bell Website," <http://www.alcatel-sbell.com.cn/en/aboutus/elepress11.asp>, 21 December 2003.

p. 188: On Beijing's trade strategy, see "PRC Works 'to Avoid Trade War' with U.S." FBIS-CHI-93-091, 13 May 1993.

p. 188: On PR pitches to the Chinese, see "Managing a Public Affairs Program in the United States," Unpublished PowerPoint presentation, Robinson Lerer Sawyer Miller, November 1995.

pp. 188–90: A general outline of the China lobby can be found in Robert Dreyfuss, "The New China Lobby," *American Prospect,* 1 January 1997.

p. 193: The Senior Chinese government advisor quoted can be found in John Pomfret, "In Its Own Neighborhood, China Emerges as a Leader," *Washington Post,* 18 October 2001.

p. 193: On China's connections to terrorism, see Al Santoli (editor), "U.S. Underestimates Range of New Chinese Missile; Sino-Ukrainian Military Sales May Have Led to Iraq," *China Reform Monitor,* no. 477, American Foreign Policy Council, 5 December 2002; Al Santoli (editor), "Chinese Military Provided Training to Taliban/al Qaeda; Beijing Remains World's Number One

Weapons Importer," *China Reform Monitor,* no. 452, 26 June 2002; Al Santoli (editor), "China Constructing Air-Defense System in Iran; Beijing Paid bin Laden for Unexploded U.S. Cruise Missiles," *China Reform Monitor,* no. 410, 22 October 2001; Al Santoli (editor), "India Claims China Provided Weapons to Taliban and Allies; Beijing Fails to Budge on Missile Proliferation to Pakistan," *China Reform Monitor,* no. 409, 15 October 2001; Al Santoli (editor), "China Asks for U.S. Support to Combat Taiwan and Dalai Lama; India: China Has Armed the Taliban and bin Laden Terrorists," *China Reform Monitor,* no. 407, 24 September 2001.

Chapter 8. Rex in the City
I interviewed Rex in August 2002, Jack in December 2002. Rex, Jack, Tuya, Freddy and all of Rex's girlfriends are pseudonyms.

p. 220: "Down by the Salley Gardens" was written by William Butler Yeats.

Index

243